SPACES OF FEELING

SPACES OF FEELING

Affect and Awareness in Modernist Literature

MARTA FIGLEROWICZ

CORNELL UNIVERSITY PRESS
ITHACA AND LONDON

First published 2017 by Cornell University Press

Printed in the United States of America

Library of Congress Cataloging-in-Publication Data

Names: Figlerowicz, Marta, author.
Title: Spaces of feeling : affect and awareness in modernist literature / Marta Figlerowicz.
Description: Ithaca : Cornell University Press, 2017. | Includes bibliographical references and index.
Identifiers: LCCN 2017023144 (print) | LCCN 2017024267 (ebook) | ISBN 9781501714238 (pdf) | ISBN 9781501714245 (ret) | ISBN 9781501714221 (cloth : alk. paper)
Subjects: LCSH: Modernism (Literature) | Literature, Modern—20th Century—History and criticism. | Affect (Psychology) in literature. | Domestic space in literature. | Subjectivity in literature.
Classification: LCC PN56.M54 (ebook) | LCC PN56.M54 .F54 2017 (print) | DDC 809/.9112—dc23
LC record available at https://lccn.loc.gov/2017023144

Cornell University Press strives to use environmentally responsible suppliers and materials to the fullest extent possible in the publishing of its books. Such materials include vegetable-based, low-VOC inks and acid-free papers that are recycled, totally chlorine-free, or partly composed of nonwood fibers. For further information, visit our website at cornellpress.cornell.edu.

For Michael

CONTENTS

ACKNOWLEDGMENTS

I first began to formulate the ideas that became this book at the University of California, Berkeley. *Spaces of Feeling* would never have come into being without the advice and support of my many mentors and colleagues there. Since we first met in 2010, Dorothy Hale has been an adviser and a friend to me of a kind that I could not have dreamt of. Charles Altieri, David Bates, and John R. Searle engaged with early versions of this manuscript in a way that continually forced me to revise and reexamine my views; I often think back to our many conversations with wonder and gratitude. Other Berkeley faculty members and graduate students who generously commented on parts of this project include Elizabeth Abel, Oliver Arnold, Juliana Chow, C. F. S. Creasy, Anne-Lise François, Jordan Greenwald, Suzanne Guerlac, Jennifer Hudin and the Berkeley Social Ontology Group, Martin Jay, Matt Langione, Manya Lempert, David Marno, D. A. Miller, Kent Puckett, Jennifer Pranolo, C. Namwali Serpell, Peter Skafish, Janet Sorensen, and Adeline Tran. For their friendship during my graduate school years and beyond, I thank Sanders Creasy, Gaby Wyatt, Pete Skafish, Ryan Perry, Simon Porzak, Jordan Greenwald, Zak Manfredi, Sarah Johnson and James Marks, Padma Maitland, Christopher Miller, Jennifer Hudin, and Jennifer Pranolo. I am also grateful to the University of California for its generous financial support in the form of a Michele McNellis Fellowship, a Mellon-Berkeley Fellowship, and a Dean's Normative Time Fellowship.

This project came to fruition during my time as a Junior Fellow at the Harvard Society of Fellows and an Assistant Professor of Comparative Literature and English at Yale. At Harvard, I thank Elaine Scarry for both her advice and her friendship; Kelly Katz, Diana Morse, and Yesim Erdman for helping me make the most of my time at the Yellow House and the Green House; Michaela Bronstein, Len Gutkin, Daniel Williams, and the American Literature Colloquium for reading successive drafts of these chapters; Hillary Chute, Noah Feldman, Stephen Osadetz, and Maria Tatar for many productive conversations. I also thank Daniel Williams, Len Gutkin, Scott Kominers, Michaela Bronstein, and Chris Grobe for numberless evenings of discussion and scotch.

At Yale, I thank Dudley Andrew, Marijeta Bozovic, Ben Glazer, Martin Hägglund, Langdon Hammer, Margaret Homans, Amy Hungerford and her graduate student working group, David Quint, Ayesha Ramachandran, Jill Richards, Katie Trumpener, Michael Warner, and Sunny Xiang for engaging with later versions of this book and for supporting me as I revised it during my first years of teaching. I cannot thank enough Heather K. Love and Lee Edelman, without whose intellectual generosity and careful engagement I would never have been able to bring *Spaces of Feeling* to its final form. Ayesha, Giuseppe, Zazie, and Viola, Marijeta and Tim, Jill, Mary Jane, and Dave: you make my time in New Haven a true pleasure.

Cornell University Press shepherded this book to publication with grace and generosity. I thank Peter J. Potter and Mahinder S. Kingra as well as my two anonymous readers, all of whom showed much open-mindedness and patience as the theoretical framing of this project kept changing. I was extraordinarily lucky to have worked with them and their editorial team. This book was published with the assistance of the Frederick W. Hilles Publication Fund of Yale University.

Finally, I thank my family, old and new: my parents Magdalena and Marek, my sister Matylda, my grandmother Maria, and Jackie, Alan, and Matthew. This book is dedicated to my partner, Michael M. Weinstein, who read and edited drafts of it many times over. Michael might never manage to teach me how to cook, but he makes me a better writer, and a better person, daily—and the life we share makes this work worthwhile.

SPACES OF FEELING

INTRODUCTION

In James Baldwin's *Giovanni's Room*, an American tourist named David finds himself talking to another man at a gay bar in Paris. David looks around, and it hits him: everyone in this room knows that he and the other man are flirting. Moreover, everyone knew this long before he himself realized it. "I knew that they were watching, had been watching both of us," David repeats to himself. "They knew that they had witnessed a beginning."[1]

The possibility that someone else might notice my affect before I do is built into its very definition. Unlike their more commonly invoked counterpart, feelings, affects are not immediately or even necessarily conscious. A delay often exists between the moment when an affect begins to inflect a person's mind and body and the moment when she becomes cognizant of its effects, if she ever does. To demonstrate this delay, Brian Massumi famously invokes scientific test subjects strapped into encephalograph machines and timers.[2] This multiply mediated analysis supposedly shows that an intention can form in one's brain before one becomes consciously capable of voicing it.

I would contend that experiences like the one Baldwin attributes to David (whether or not we see them as neurologically inevitable) are at least as formative as the ones pursued by these experiments to how affects shape our daily phenomenology and our understanding of ourselves. Indeed, what else but such experiences might make one conduct empirical trials of affective cognition in the first place? Because we often do not immediately discern our affects, they lay us open to the people around us. The gap between our affective expression and our awareness of it makes us vulnerable to our environments. It also casts doubt on whether we are always the best judges of what we bring forth into them.

The men surrounding David and his lover-to-be Giovanni neither further nor impede their courtship. Despite David's preoccupation with their gazes, they act as if this interaction—which astounds him—were merely commonplace. And yet, David's self-discovery seems to depend quite strictly on this apparently indifferent, just casually curious group. A great part of his shock comes from the way the other people's knowing looks help him articulate something about himself without their even intending or trying to do so. He relies on them to reach this insight about his affects' names and stakes.

Spaces of Feeling examines a series of modernist novels and poems that make such distributed forms of affective awareness central to their depictions of personhood. I engage with these works to illustrate reasons why the dispersed, intersubjective access we have to our affects should figure more prominently in the philosophical and political frameworks we build around affective expression and self-scrutiny. Affects have long been described as subverting our sense of ourselves as coherent subjects because of the delayed conscious access we have to them. I stress that they also undercut our pretense of autonomy in even belatedly interpreting our bodily and mental states. Furthermore, affects give rise to a tension between our dependence on others for our self-awareness, and these others' relative lack of concern about whether or not we can explicate our feelings to ourselves.

The term "affect" was coined by psychoanalysts to describe an "external" view of the analysand's mind and body. Implicit even in its origins is thus the possibility that some parts of our inward selves were not (and maybe could not have been) discernible by our own lights alone. On an abstract level this observation is rather obvious: we did not ourselves invent the language through which we describe our feelings. But a less obvious, and—as Baldwin's depiction of David shows—quite unsettling version of this statement is that the empirical or deictic act of registering something as intimate as our own affective experience cannot always be accomplished without outside help. There are some parts of our felt sense of self that we only remark on through their resonances in the bodies and minds of others. This claim becomes even more troubling if these other people's capacity to notice parts of our minds and bodies does not usually translate into an equally deep investment or even interest in the affects that we find confusing. Indeed, sometimes the people by whose interpretations of our affects we feel unprecedentedly recognized and interpellated might not have intended to have that effect on us at all, even when they are not actively hostile to what our self-expression signifies to them. I integrate these paradoxes into an understanding of our relationships to others that steers away both from illusions of our subjective inscrutability and autonomy, and of the intrinsic broad interest of our inner states. I also argue that charting a course between these two fantasies constitutes one of the more significant and complicated problems in our intersubjective relations.

Early- and mid-twentieth-century Anglophone and French literature stages many episodes like the one I just described, in which an outward environment, or another person, prompts characters and speakers to recognize a gap between their affective effusions and the introspective awareness they have of these affects. These poems and novels depict most of their speakers and characters as strongly wedded to a notion of themselves as capable—if not of fully controlling their minds and bodies—then at least of retroactively observing and interpreting them on their own. The revealed dependence of their insight into themselves on outward, contingent encounters leads to a provocative uncertainty about the extent to which a more autonomous form of affective introspection would be possible for them at all. It also gives rise, in the works I examine, to an appreciation of how unrelated our own quests for affective self-awareness often are to the cares and concerns of those around us. *Spaces of Feeling* examines works by James Baldwin, Marcel Proust, Virginia Woolf, F. Scott Fitzgerald, Wallace Stevens, Sylvia Plath, Ralph Ellison, and John Ashbery. These writers are not typically known for their depictions of affects as insights into our uncontrolled blind spots and inward limitations—and indeed, their work is also rife with moments when affective expression leads to personal empowerment and enriched mutual understanding. Many of them also highlight, and criticize, the hostility with which a community might actively disregard some of its members' affects and the needs that these affects indicate. I show, however, that these authors' better-known preoccupation with what E. M. Forster famously describes as an injunction to "only connect" frequently has an additional, more ironic undertone. These writers also capture moments when a character or speaker awkwardly tries to gather herself back into coherence in the midst of her overwhelming feelings, finding she cannot do so without external help. These episodes do not subvert the value of entering into and contributing to affective exchanges, whether for political or for personal reasons. But they depict characters' and speakers' cognitive reliance on the people around them as vulnerably necessary because of their affects' inarticulateness and unpredictability. They also draw attention to incomplete overlaps between the different senses in which these represented beings are connected to or disconnected from, reliant on or independent of others—and to the misunderstandings that collapsing these various categories of relation or dependence can create.

These characters' and speakers' reflections on their cognitive processes instantiate a long-standing theme of literary representation. However, the authors whom I examine reshape this tradition by redefining self-awareness to include knowledge of our dependence on, and exposure to, contingent surrounding environments and the people within them. Placing their characters and speakers in living rooms, bedrooms, and basements, on thresholds and in front of mirrors, they stage instances when other people seem better able to convey the content and significance of what a speaker or character is feeling than she herself can. The relative enclosure of these domestic settings, along with the promise of intimacy they foster, highlights the limits of these characters' or speakers' control over the ways in which and effects to which their affects become noticeable to others. The stable, knowable sense of one's boundaries suggested by a threshold or a bedroom is unachievable to them even if they self-identify with these limits and enclosures very strongly. Indeed, these well-bounded spatial correlatives for the forms of self-reflection they want to nurture ultimately highlight the great difference that another person's presence makes to their sense of themselves. These enclosed spaces represent the process of naming and interpreting one's affects as one not simply of self-assertion, but of ongoing negotiations and exchanges between the self and its communities—indifferent as these communities often are to the self's affective ruminations.

Someone might remark on my affect before I do, or might discern an aspect of it that eludes me. Out of this simple, even quotidian observation, the writers in *Spaces of Feeling* mount a series of challenges to the interpretative autonomy of our bodies and minds as well as to the strength of ties that bind our introspective efforts to others. We tend to have our intersubjective relations to others all backward; their works ironically suggest: people notice more about our affects than we might imagine but are also much less concerned than we assume about what they see. In psychoanalytic terms, these novels and poems make the so-called unconscious seem fearsome and scandalous not only (the way it is more typically read) as a crisis of rational will, but also—more importantly to them—as a crisis of even very suspicious and self-questioning introspection as a mode of knowledge. Our own efforts might not be able to substitute for the effects of outside input about how we feel: this possibility is both mesmerizing and frightening to the authors I examine here, because it makes even the most immediate kinds of inward self-scrutiny—what contemporary theorists might call autoaffection—seem like inevitably collective, cognitively distributed endeavors, even if only one person's stakes in them are consistently deep. Such a view of affect further suggests that, even though others *are* sometimes actively hostile to the affects we want to explore and affirm in ourselves, our sense of aloneness in our introspective efforts does not always, necessarily, stem from such outward hostility. Its more basic, inalienable cause is simply that we care more about our affects than anybody else could. The alternative model of intersubjectivity projected by their works involves acknowledging both our need for other people's engagement in making sense of our feelings and our inability to control the forms that their help, or the reciprocal insights they derive from us, might take.[3]

As it attempts to reassess our attitudes toward how others figure in our personal affective reflections, *Spaces of Feeling* considers cognitions and representations of affects rather than affects in themselves. I do not focus just on the experience of having affects, as many theorists before me have done, but on the process of becoming aware of them. As my title—spaces of *feeling*—might already suggest, I am less interested in the unconscious rawness of affective experiences than in the means by which they make their way into our or somebody else's consciousness.[4] For these reasons, *Spaces of Feeling* reflects on representations of affective and cognitive experiences attributed to literary characters and speakers, and not on the affects these representations might be attempting to incite or approximate. Rather than focusing on readerly affective responses to these works or on authorial psychology, I analyze these poems' and novels' internal perspectives on affects and their means of conveying these perspectives. The mediated nature of affects depicted in literature has at times made contemporary theory wary of poems and novels as modes of affective inquiry. Indeed, the represented affects I examine exist in the realm of what Massumi would call "parables" of affective experience.[5] Inevitably framed and structured within some form and genre, they model bodily experiences and their rise to awareness in a partial, aestheticized fashion. In examining these early- and mid-twentieth-century works, I therefore do not aim to explore what affects are in their essence, but to increase our intellectual flexibility in engaging with the paths by which they make their way into our consciousness and our forms of representation.[6]

In so doing, I also offer novels and poems (these specific ones, but also their genres in general) as especially fruitful grounds for inquiry into such intersubjective dimensions of our self-knowledge. This is paradoxically not because they disclose our inward selves more clearly than other forms of expression, but because they help us address these introspective selves' partial artifice (an artifice that the novels and poems I examine question with particular commitment). At the same time, as a form of engagement with literature, *Spaces of Feeling* inverts many of the reasons why and modes in which we might conventionally turn to works of literature for insight into intersubjectivity. I see novels and poems not only as paths toward exploring the radical otherness of other people, but also as ways of considering how vulnerable and open we are to (and how intensely desirous we sometimes are of) having our bodily and mental states discerned and interpreted by others. These literary works also help me highlight alternative strategies of social subversion— or alternative means of diagnosing the structural effects of homophobia or racism—that depend both on affirming the feelings of the disenfranchised and on stressing and generalizing from the inconsistency of a person's capacity to interpret her affects on her own.

These questions of affective awareness and its intersubjective dimensions are related but irreducible to the moral issue of how we manage our affective expression in consideration of the presence of others. My approach to affects is, of course, indebted to the work of moral psychologists and philosophers such as Paul Bloom and Martha Nussbaum, who ask how we incorporate feelings—little as we can often do to control them—into our sense of ourselves. But the range of confusing affects in which I am interested is also far greater than just the ones that produce measurable communal effects. Indeed, I argue that we are often unable to involve other people in taking stock of our feelings as fully and intensely as we need them to be—and this inability is one of the points of difficulty in our relations to others that I emphasize.

In its regard for such more fleeting and apparently inconsequential affective experiences, *Spaces of Feeling* responds more directly to discussions that are ongoing in the field of affect theory. These discussions concern the subject position of a person who seeks to describe the larger meanings and stakes of mental and bodily experiences that she also believes to exceed and precede her capacity to become aware of them. Affect theory may at first appear merely to continue the long twentieth-century critical tradition of mining personal experiences for political or critical insights: one might see it as simply shifting the scale of these personal experiences to the microlevel of fleeting moods and ambiances. But in its increased emphasis on the partial unknowability of our bodily and mental responsiveness, this branch of theory also invites questions about how one can reliably put such uncontrolled, transitory, and only belatedly and partly cognized experiences to broader critical use. These questions become most pressing when the affect theorist does not adopt the safer, if somewhat patronizing, role of other people's unsolicited analyst and includes her own body and mind among the inspirations of her affective reflections. To think of our affects as potentially exceeding our immediate awareness offers a strong argument for why examining them might add to our understanding of ourselves; however, to admit to the confusion into which affects throw us also casts doubt on our capacity to tell idiosyncratic affective experiences apart from socially pervasive ones, or contingently from structurally triggered ones, given that they can all be hard for us to notice and untangle. Once we acknowledge how unaware we are of many parts of ourselves, we do not just increase the amount of unknown forms and content we might discover in ourselves. We also draw heightened attention to the unreliability of the consciousness within which such affective self-discoveries take place and receive interpretations: an unreliability that becomes even more troubling when we propose that the outcomes of a particular person's affective self-analyses are important to the self-understanding of others whether or not her expression impacted them directly. One might respond that, in this sense, the proof of affect theory is always in the response it elicits in its audience, who may or may not recognize themselves in a given theorist's picture of affective experience. But such an answer merely obscures the disjuncture between this profession of selflessness and the more personal needs for clarification by which the theorist is often also driven. It also refuses to engage with the kinds of judgments—or refusals of judgment—that go into deciding that explicating one's particular affective confusions might have intrinsic broader significance and stakes.

This last point could be put—and has been put—much more harshly. "If you can't understand, just try to feel. According to Massumi, it works," is the quip with which Ruth Leys opens her critique of affect theory in a 2009 issue of *Critical Inquiry*.[7] As suggested both by this first jab and the more sustained argument that follows, insisting on gaps between affect and cognition makes affect theory vulnerable to relatively easy criticism. To admit that we do not always know how to articulate our affects, but should nevertheless be trusted as sources of insight into their significance, can be read unfavorably as narcissistic intuitionism. It could even make the study of affect sound like an unquestioned demand that others attend to one's inner life—and take one's word for its contents and importance—based solely on its immediate, often inarticulate intensity.[8]

To some extent, *Spaces of Feeling* agrees with Leys's critique of affect theory. I show that most key affect theorists merely skirt the question of how we manage to bring our affects to conscious awareness and how this process impacts our critical subject position. However, I argue further that this seeming weakness of affect theory can become the foundation for a more nuanced kind of affective inquiry. The antinomies that Leys sees as fatal contradictions offer us clues into affect theory's potential to illuminate the processes by which we become aware of, and ascribe significance to, our affects. Affect theory has long defined itself as a means of appreciating the surprising expressiveness of our bodily and mental states. I combine this mode of analysis with noting the unpredictably and uncontrolledly interpersonal nature of the means by which we take stock of this expressiveness and draw conclusions about it. I look to Baldwin's protagonist David—as well as Proust's overstimulated narrator Marcel, Plath's paranoid lyric speakers, and other literary figures—for ways of representing affects that insist on the inseparability of these two perspectives and on its consequences for a person's sense of herself. Further, I show that this insight can ground a metatheory of affective awareness through which the notion of intersubjectivity itself may be rethought. To study affect, as I see it, is to confront not only the mysteriousness but also the potential outward transparency of one's mind and body. It is to consider not only how much hidden richness our embodied presence might hold but also how rarely and contingently we are able to take stock of the affects that surge within us on our own. It is, finally, to appreciate our never fully controllable or 'repayable' reliance on other people and our surrounding spaces for the means by which we ensure our affects' intelligibility day by day and minute by minute. This uncontrolled reliance does not reduce itself to these people's and spaces' manipulativeness or to our submissiveness to them. It also stems from the physical impracticality of other options, appealing though the notion of infinitely prolonged, fully autonomous affective self-scrutiny might theoretically be.

The notion of intersubjectivity has hitherto figured within affect theory primarily in accounts of affects as amorphous, aromalike "ambiances" by which several minds and bodies can be moved all at once—or in theorists' attempts to put themselves in the position of other people's or communities' affective analysts. Without disputing the possibility and value of such relations, I propose that the experience of bringing our affects into conscious awareness illuminates the process by which we negotiate mismatches between what we ourselves and others discern and focus on within our bodily responsiveness. I argue further that such recalibrations are necessary to a nonsolipsistic way of inhabiting the world we collectively share. They help us recognize the multiplicity and contingency of the sources from which what we come to describe as our awareness of ourselves actually emerges. By drawing attention to these discrepancies and dependencies, the study of affect undoes our sense of ourselves at least as deeply and provocatively as it does by merely asserting the belatedness of our inward insights. It also leads us more acutely to appreciate our cognitive debts to, and needs from, our communities and environments: fleeting and unstable, and occasionally unhelpful, as their responsiveness to us might be.

A brief reading of a poem by John Ashbery can offer one example of what such an expanded approach to affect might look like. Here is the ending of "Wet Casements," first published in 1976. In this poem, Ashbery's speaker wishes he could see himself from a perspective at once his own and someone else's. "I want that information very much today," he says,

> Can't have it, and this makes me angry.
> I shall use my anger to build a bridge like that
> Of Avignon, on which people may dance for the feeling
> Of dancing on a bridge. I shall at last see my complete face
> Reflected not in the water but in the worn stone floor of my bridge.
>
> I shall keep to myself.
> I shall not repeat others' comments about me.[9]

The speaker whimsically imagines building a bridge out of his anger; and then he also imagines himself and many other people dancing on it. "I shall at last see my complete face," he says, "reflected not in the water but in the stone floor of my bridge." For a moment, this speaker appears to fulfill his wish, and—through an act of poetic imagination—sees himself in a context that is not only personal but interpersonal. But by the end, this fantasy frightens him to the point that he seeks to diminish the sense of openness that it created. "I shall keep to myself," he decides. "I shall not repeat others' comments about me."

An affect theorist analyzing this poem might focus only on this speaker's brief euphoria. She could treat the poem as an expression of the speaker's hope for a future community of people who will care about him, highlighting how the speaker's affects temporarily allow him to see this sense of belonging as a real possibility. But such a reading would overlook the fact that Ashbery's speaker likens his dreamt-of bridge to that of Avignon—which, famously, leads nowhere. It would also ignore the ending of the poem, with its suggestions of rapid, fearful withdrawal—and gloss over the puzzling emergence, within this seemingly escapist poem, of "others' comments" as a main source first of the speaker's desire and then of his trepidation. Who are these "others"? And why would "the stone floor of my bridge" be reduced, in its disenchanted version, not to a solipsistic fantasy, but to malicious gossip? This surprising metonymy underscores that the bridge represents to the speaker not a dream of having one's preexisting inward self-understanding recognized by someone else, but one about other people making "comments" on which this self-understanding could depend. As I show more extensively in the chapter devoted to Ashbery, his poems conjoin daydreaming with the hope of being known and even cared for by one's surroundings; of feeling safe among other people because they are already privy even to one's most unconscious bodily and mental secrets. To notice how often Ashbery's speakers alternately fantasize about and rage against imagined knowledge held by the people around them leads one to appreciate how much importance these poems place not only on the act of disclosing one's affects but also on its context. The question is not just "Will I be able to name my affect?," but "What would others say about it?"—and indeed, the presence of these others seems crucial to the speaker's ability to give this affect any name at all. The affective effusions of Ashbery's speakers remain disconcerting because even those who could potentially recognize and respond to them often do not pay them much attention. In the minds of other people these speakers' affects might exist as nothing more—the speaker of this poem fears—than irrelevant chatter.

Ashbery's speaker in "Wet Casements" is neither coherently self-consistent nor completely self-knowing; he is isolated, but not cognitively autonomous in any other sense. His lyric expression carries with it the knowledge that he might be just cursorily interesting to the people to whom he looks for validation, even as their responses are vitally important to his sense of himself. *Spaces of Feeling* takes such represented characters or speakers—highlighting moments of their self-doubt such as the one quoted above—as models for what it would mean to recognize the way our partly unconscious affects shape our practices of awareness and to take greater note of the unreliable outward ties on which this awareness depends.

Throughout this book, I define the term "affect" broadly. I understand it, with Charles Altieri, as "the entire range of states that are bounded on the one side by sensation and on the other by thoughts . . . immediate modes of sensual responsiveness to the world accompanied by an imaginative dimension."[10] With both Altieri and Massumi, I identify the delay between the presence of an affect and one's capacity to became aware of or interpret it as an important aspect of what distinguishes affects from emotions or feelings.

Each chapter of *Spaces of Feeling* sets the authors I examine in conversation with a contemporary affect theorist: Brian Massumi, Charles Altieri, Sianne Ngai, Lauren Berlant, and Eve Sedgwick (and, more briefly, Sara Ahmed). The qualities of affects to which these poems and novels draw attention are generally well known to these theorists, who often describe affective experience as involving forms of confusion, inarticulacy, risk, and helplessness.[11] By engaging with their work in greater detail, I show how each of their approaches to affect could be transformed by the intersubjective angle of affective awareness on which I focus here.

In the process, *Spaces of Feeling* also revisits the challenges that modernist and later twentieth-century writers encounter when they turn their attention to first-person experience. Among these writers, I highlight a group of poets and novelists who locate the difficulty of representing first-person experience in moments such as the one with which this chapter begins: moments when, even though one cannot count on another person to fully know one, this person's presence is necessary to reaching some insight about oneself. These writers create represented worlds in which such contingent relays of knowledge seem inevitable, and one is pressed to integrate them into one's self-understanding. Their depictions of personhood and interpersonal interaction doubtless bear the marks of the long tradition of lyric and narrative first-person expression, on the one hand, and the contemporaneous rise of psychoanalysis, on the other. But they also cannot be reduced to such concurrent traditions because they cast doubt on these other practices' frameworks of independent, or reliably dependent, introspection. In psychoanalysis, the analysand trusts the analyst's attentiveness and insight; more traditional forms of lyric or narrative expression measure the strength of a represented voice by its independent capacity for complex self-awareness. In the novels and poems I examine, one cannot consistently count either on others or on oneself for affective awareness and attentiveness: the possibility of such a strong, reliable center of interpretation is very tempting, but constantly called into question. These writers do not suggest that the characters and speakers they represent understand each other, or are understood by other people, with as much attentiveness and directedness as the notion of empathy presupposes. And while their characters and speakers often wish that people saw them as inscrutable, mysterious beings, they find it extremely hard to sustain this aura of inscrutability and reliable self-knowledge or, indeed, to believe in it themselves. The aesthetic innovations through which these novelists and poets represent such changing balances of awareness have been underappreciated both as potential objects of affective inquiry and as rhetorical practices in their own right.

The fact that psychoanalysis and phenomenology develop right around the time these novels and poems are being written is, of course, crucial to my choice of them as representations of affective awareness. These works emerge as first-person experience gains renewed cultural and scientific interest, but theories of how it can best be known and described are still hotly and unresolvedly debated. They thereby help us see more clearly that practices such as psychoanalysis, or later twentieth-century affirmations of the intrinsic interest and value of self-expression, attempt to resolve not only questions about unconscious or less conscious parts of ourselves but also hesitations about how we access these parts of ourselves in the first place—and how we should cope with the fact that others might recognize them more easily than we ourselves do. By designating the poems and novels examined here as my points of entry into these latter questions, I do not mean to imply that their authors do not also have other political and aesthetic interests—or, indeed, that mimetic strategies similar to theirs could not be found in novels and poems from other regions and periods. I am much less committed to arguing for these works' exceptional status than I am to highlighting questions about subjectivity and awareness that I find them to be good at representing.

My mode of engagement with these early- and mid-twentieth-century poets and novelists is formal. I uncover the narrative and lyric strategies by which their works orient their representations of affect toward the immediate, spatiotemporally circumscribed present and to the people who surround one in that moment. I show how these authors' shared interest in affective experience gives rise to structural and stylistic principles that shape their represented worlds, in ways that often cut across the generic divide between poetry and the novel. The importance these writers attach to representing affects is part of the extensively studied early- and mid-twentieth-century reorientation of literary mimesis away from social conventions and toward particular people's immediate experiences. (This reorientation itself has its origins in even earlier, nineteenth-century literature.) It also emerges from this period's well-documented fascination with what Sigmund Freud described as the unconscious, and William James as automatic or involuntary mental activity. The works I examine focus on inconsistently conscious affective states as a fundamental aspect of first-person experience around which an understanding of individuals' needs and capacities could be reshaped. These writers also ask what purpose should attend the representation of feelings if they are no longer treated—the way they typically were in the nineteenth century—as generalizable social or biological patterns or symptoms thereof, but instead as experiences that might give rise to entirely new questions about the kinds of knowledge of which a person might be capable.[12]

The interpersonal dimensions of these representations of affective awareness are reinforced by these affects' unusual spatial expression. These novels and poems depict affects primarily through the relationships of human bodies to their surrounding social and physical environments. At the same time, the scale on which the representation of these affects takes place often makes more familiar critical terms such as "map" or "network"—both first applied to depictions of affect by Jonathan Flatley—inappropriate to them.[13] At the very least, it shows that a fundamental disjuncture exists in modernist poetry and fiction between this more urban, expansive understanding of space (to which some of the writers I examine do occasionally turn), and the smaller, more enclosed spaces in which the characters and speakers they represent try to gather their subjectivities into something like coherence and order. Unlike in Flatley's *Affective Mapping*—which describes early twentieth-century representations of affect as spanning city- or society-wide networks of relation—the spaces of feeling represented in these novels and poems are relatively small. These small spaces highlight the immediate environments in which their characters and speakers try to make sense of themselves. Their feelings take place in close quarters where another person's partial access to them become all the more difficult to question, and where the tensions between these people's presence and the main characters' and speakers' wish to see themselves as cognitively autonomous, become very apparent.

Many accounts of space in early- and mid-twentieth century literature—including Joseph Frank's famous essay, "Spatial Form in Modern Literature"—describe the period's novels and poems as translating temporal relations into spatial ones in order to make time seem more synchronously accessible.[14] In the novels and poems I examine, this sense of accessibility is frequently absent. Also absent, or at least very hesitant, is the air of detached third-person objectivity that Frank associates with the spatial forms he finds in Ezra Pound or T. S. Eliot. Instead, the works I examine represent space in ways that highlight an awareness that their characters and speakers cannot have access to, or instant cognizance of, everything around them, including their own minds and bodies. They also use these small spatial confines to suggest that the object of their characters' and speakers' self-scrutiny is often just their own, affectively driven self. The narrowness of the walls and doorways in which these speakers and characters find themselves further highlights the immediacy with which anyone else present in this space might be able to witness these characters' or speakers' confusion. (In this sense—to push this metacritical point a little further—the critic might also see the spaces represented in these novels and poems as skeptical models of the experience of repeated reading and rereading and of the dream of a simultaneously well-circumscribed and total awareness to which it gives rise.)[15] For instance, Proust's narrator retreats from living rooms to bedrooms because he finds that the presence of even one other person suffices to make him lose confidence in his capacity for affective self-awareness. In Woolf's *Mrs. Dalloway*, it is in living rooms that Peter Walsh discovers how easy it is for others to notice his affects and how hard it is for him to control their interpretation. These relatively intimate and narrow enclosures represent one's lack of complete independence from outward contexts as unquestionable and disarming: as a relation not between a private person and an impersonal social network, but between this person and her familiars who often also turn out to be equally vulnerable, knowable beings.[16]

I name successive chapters of this work after the enclosed or semienclosed domestic spaces to which the writers I examine turn as guiding metaphors for their represented beings' struggles between a sense of affective exposure and solitude. Each of these works has a slightly different relationship to such spaces. Some return to them overtly and insistently; others mention them more obliquely, or only at the beginning or at the end of their narratives. I do not argue for these spaces' overall structural dominance in these works, but I do highlight their particular importance for the way these poems and novels orient their representations of affect toward a narrowly construed physical and interpersonal context and for the larger points about interpersonal awareness they make on this basis. For example, Proust's and Baldwin's characters obsessively retreat into bedrooms. They emphasize their protagonists' difficulty in understanding their affects, or even in becoming aware of them, if they do not physically isolate themselves from others. Stevens and Plath represent their speakers on thresholds, whether literal or existential. These speakers try to figure out what their affects would look like from both a private and an interpersonal perspective and what it would mean to interpret them, at once, as possibly trivial personal matters and as events of potentially shareable philosophical or political import.

The innovativeness with which the writers of this period represent first-person experiences has long been the subject of scholarly research.[17] T. J. Clark aptly describes early- and mid-twentieth-century art and literature as "always pulled to and fro between private (defensive) and public (expository). Always *dreaming* of the public life."[18] My book builds on prior work done on early- and mid-twentieth-century attitudes toward affects and on this period's modes of representation in general. I am indebted to the longer school of criticism, inaugurated by Frank's "Spatial Form," that shows the means by which, and reasons why, the writers of this period represent subjective experiences in spatial terms. I am also inspired by Ann Banfield's description of the British modernists' engagements with notions of object persistence in *The Phantom Table*, Douglas Mao's arguments about modernism and materiality in *Solid Objects*, Georges Poulet's analyses of spatial form in literature, and many other studies with which later chapters will engage at greater length.[19]

In my successive readings, I acknowledge the differences among the various political or philosophical allegiances of the authors I examine, while highlighting how their strategies for representing affects bring them together. Ellison's and Baldwin's novels represent forms of racial discrimination. Woolf's and Plath's works comment on gender inequalities. Baldwin, Proust, Woolf, and Ashbery are frequently described as gay, lesbian, or queer writers. Scholars also sometimes group Proust with Stevens as philosopher-aesthetes. Without neglecting the particularity of these authors' aims and subject matter, I show that affects and their intersubjective rise to awareness are among their most significant preoccupations. I see figures such as Woolf and Fitzgerald, or Plath and Stevens (as my chapters pair them together), not as each other's equivalents, but as authors who end up reaching for surprisingly similar aesthetic forms from starting points that, in many other ways, could not be more different. I treat these authors as united in their shared view of affective awareness—of its manifold sources and the constant tension that exists between one's own stakes in understanding one's affects and these various sources' attitudes toward them. From the thresholds of Stevens's and Plath's poems—which invite the reader from a more public space into a more intimate one—through the social spaces of Woolf's and Fitzgerald's fiction, to the bedrooms represented by Proust and Baldwin, Ellison's basement, and Ashbery's mirrors, the sense of constraint represented in these works grows ever more acute, and the kinds of enclosures required to hold a self together become extreme. At the same time, their characters and speakers go ever further in abandoning a belief in the secrecy of their affects or their autonomous capacity to make sense of them. They articulate the distributed, interpersonal nature of affective awareness, and their hopes for the alternative forms of relation we could build around affects, ever more boldly, turning domestic spaces from metaphors for subjective coherence to models of something like extended cognition.

In my first chapter, "Threshold," I show that Stevens's and Plath's poems stall in realizations that a person's mind and body do not themselves, even upon reflection, provide her with sufficient clues about the content and causes of the affects that move them. These poems' speakers try, and fail, to imagine or conjure into being a world in which the affects that emerge within them are always already clear and articulable. The speakers' sense of themselves and of the genre in which they express their feelings is undone by this inability.

The second chapter, "Living Room," follows Woolf's and Fitzgerald's protagonists through social settings in which such a clarifying audience is sometimes present: another person's word or gesture inadvertently assuages their affective confusions. The contingency of these moments of elucidation drives their characters to frustration and even despair. It also makes them overidealize these random encounters as forms of deep connection and empathy that both novelists ironize with varying degrees of gentleness and optimism. These characters are depicting as half-intuiting, but mostly missing, the instability of the ways in which their self-awareness relates to the presence of other people around them. The affective clarity they occasionally derive from others is made to seem all the more miraculous for the confusions and misinterpretations amid which it is given and received.

"Bedroom" follows characters of Proust's and Baldwin's novels who retreat from forms of uncertain dependence such as the ones explored by Woolf and Fitzgerald, into ever smaller and secluded physical spaces. Only in such spaces does their sense of themselves seem autonomous and complete. Both novelists affirm the value of the insights their characters gain in such constrained settings; yet they also highlight the difficulty with which such insights can be brought back into a larger, more dispersed social sphere. Proust and Baldwin end up representing the novel as an intensely private space of self-expression of the sort that their characters continually seek: as a means by which, instead of bringing himself out into a more distracting and confusing outside world, a person can invite into her more confined sense of herself an equally solitary reader.

In the penultimate chapter, "Basement," I show that Ellison's *Invisible Man* takes its political edge from turning the tables on experiences of interpersonal affective disempowerment of the kind that Baldwin's and Proust's characters intensely fear. Its narrator begins by trying, much like the protagonists of Woolf's and Fitzgerald's fiction, to look to the people and objects around him for confirmations and clarifications of how he feels and how historically and socially important his feelings are. Yet he eventually realizes that the social structures he opposes are disrupted much more effectively by his destabilizing other people's affective awareness and showing them how much this awareness depends on his cooperation. The basement offers this narrator a model of such an absorptive but not readily responsive attitude toward others.

My final chapter, "Mirror," returns to the lyric, while inviting its readers into the most constrained of the spaces of feeling I examine. Ashbery's poetry explores anxieties about lyric expression's dependence on its audience that are analogous to those voiced by Plath and Stevens. But like the novels I examine in earlier chapters, Ashbery's lyrics also implicitly accept their speakers' reliance on their self-awareness, on audiences whose presence and attentiveness they cannot control. The mirror serves these speakers as a model for the intense, careful outward scrutiny that they constantly dream of but cannot consistently secure. As Ashbery's speakers mistake paintings, daydreams, and natural landscapes for such mirrors, they reflect on the imperfect self-knowledge they can attain in a world from which such forms of outward support are not forthcoming—as well as on the way this desire for self-knowledge clouds their capacity to relate to their surrounding world. Ashbery also takes these poems as opportunities to emphasize that the yearning his speakers feel for outward elucidation and recognition is inalienable to their sense of themselves, impossible as it might be to fulfill sustainedly and consistently.

The questions raised in *Spaces of Feeling* frequently build on the argument of my first book, *Flat Protagonists: A Theory of Novel Character.*[20] *Flat Protagonists* describes a form of character construction that seeks to illuminate the surprising simplicity and nongeneralizability of any person's experiences. *Spaces of Feeling* similarly takes the poems and novels it examines as a space of reflection about the ease with which we might be wont to over-state the completeness and autonomy of our affective self-awareness. If my first book relies on novel protagonists' surroundings mostly as sources of de-flation and disenchantment, this second one explores depictions of aware-ness as an inherently (if vulnerably) interpersonal process in order to appre-ciate our inevitable partial transparency to and dependence on others. It thereby also highlights the critical value of allowing other people's attentive-ness or inattentiveness to calibrate our trust in how good we are at interpret-ing the weight and significance of our feelings on our own. I argue that such interpersonal negotiations ought to be seen not simply as our environments' dismissals of our unique perspectives, but as processes that are intrinsic to combining our individual phenomenologies into a world that we can share and explore with others—as well as to appreciating where our own self-awareness comes from in the first place.

In both my first and this second book, I revisit relatively old-fashioned subjective aspirations toward social exemplarity, autonomy, and self-knowledge in order to suggest that, even in this post-human day and age, it still takes us much effort to shed them. The partial redundancy of our belated efforts at self-understanding and the potential obviousness of this redundancy to others might be particularly difficult to admit for someone claiming to be a theorist, philosopher, or critic. Through fictionalized and lyricized models of introspective thinkers beset by doubts about the speed, range, and inde-pendence of their inward reflections, I here reframe these liabilities as new points of entry into what we mean by self-awareness and what our stakes are in attaching (or refusing to attach) value to it. *Spaces of Feeling* argues that, in order to continue expanding our notions of critical reflection and of affects as one of its shaping forces, we need to desist from pursuing confir-mations of our capacity to both succumb to affects and reliably elucidate them or of the striking, universal interest of the feelings by which we are troubled. By backing out of these slippery goals, we find ourselves in a space of inquiry that is both more welcoming and more flexible, one in which our current preoccupation with affects can itself be addressed with greater lucid-ity and conceptual breadth.

Chapter 1

Threshold

Wallace Stevens and Sylvia Plath

"How does one stand / To behold the sublime?" asks Wallace Stevens's speaker in "American Sublime." To answer this question, the speaker looks up at a statue of Andrew Jackson. "When General Jackson / Posed for his statue," he says, "he knew how one feels." "But how does one feel?" he repeats open-endedly.[1]

"American Sublime" voices a concern that runs through many (though by no means all) of Stevens's works. His speakers occasionally claim that their minds do not give them consistent clues about what causes their affects to emerge, and toward what objects these affects are directed. As they try to interpret their affects by attaching them to a variety of potential sources and aims, these speakers are haunted by their slow, incomplete self-cognizance. They eventually begin to fantasize that an experience of affective articulacy and certitude could somehow descend on them from the outside, in a way that would not require much conscious effort on their part. Sylvia Plath's poetry revolves around similar fantasies, in a way that at times brings these poets together across their many formal and thematic differences.

My book begins with two poets in whose work concerns about our incapacity to become aware of our affects on our own are articulated with open-
ended abstraction as well as great longing for outward input. Stevens (in my
admittedly selective reading of him) and Plath (more consistently) tread the
line between a continued insistence that something like a coherent speaker
is present in their poems and an emphasis on the ways in which this air of
subjective coherence dissolves within their chosen genre. They represent
these speakers' subjective dissolution as something that comes as an unwel-
come surprise—disrupting the form of their poems midway through their
utterance—and as a process that retroactively turns out to have always
already been inscribed into their self-expression.[2] What precipitates these
subjective crises is not just the instability of language in general, but, more
specifically, the speakers' increasing desire and ever clearer inability to describe their affects in a way that they could stand behind for more than a
moment, and that did not feel like merely a temporary, wishful solution.
The poetry I read in this chapter places its speakers in almost total solitude: they rarely address an interlocutor who is actually present or actively
listening. This sense of isolation soon becomes a burden on their introspective efforts. The speakers constantly, vainly search for some outward anchor
in which the forms and the felt urgency of their affects could be reflected.
They are confused both by the readiness with which their minds and bodies
occasionally settle on such anchors, and by the equal ease with which these
anchors suddenly cease to convince them.

These speakers' solitude gives these confusions a speculative air in which
public and private spaces frequently blur into each other surreally. They are
overwhelmed by reminders of the world beyond them, but they also fear that
they cannot describe their relations to this world very clearly. The image of
the threshold—which the speakers often imagine themselves crossing—
functions both as a model for their preoccupation with personal boundaries
and as a fantasy of knowing where their selves, and the affects that move
them, begin and end. It also signals these speakers' inability to confidently
look beyond, or express much concern with, anything but their own incom-
prehensible embodiment, in a way that lends their introspective meditations
an increasingly, helplessly comic air.

Unlike many other poets from their respective periods—such as Stevens's
contemporaries H. D. (Hilda Dolittle) and Ezra Pound or Plath's contemporary Adrienne Rich—Plath and Stevens frequently refuse to resolve

the ambiguities these affects create and to posit their speakers as voices of larger historical or social transformations. Instead, they make the process of lingering in these affective uncertainties into its own object of aesthetic representation. Indeed, as these two poets' speakers cannot decide what it is that they feel so strongly about, a more conventional process of lyric expression often cannot even get started. The poems recurrently search for their occasion and for the tone with which this occasion ought to be addressed, in a way that is usually depicted with mild bemusement or disappointment in Stevens's work, and with frustration and despair in Plath's. This double uncertainty contributes to the speakers' subjective fragmentation. It also deprives the poems themselves of a center of gravity to which the stakes or even the names of the affects they convey could be tethered. The many potential valences that Plath's and Stevens's poems speculatively attach to affects offer these poets means of investigating the potential philosophical (for Stevens) or political (for Plath) significance of their inner lives, as well as the leaps of faith that an affectively driven, not fully self-cognizant, body must make in order to pronounce on an emergent affect's significance and import.

I examine Stevens's and Plath's poetry in conversation with Charles Altieri's writings about affect. Altieri praises affects for their resistance to our staid, conventional notions about ourselves. Affects reveal that our impulses and attachments are always more diverse and changeable than our stated values and beliefs make them seem. Following an affect allows the self "to feel itself able to make all the turns and twists necessary to stay connected with where thought and speech might lead it."[3] It helps a person recognize a wider range of possible positions she can adopt toward the world and incorporate more of these positions into her self-understanding. Stevens and Plath similarly explore the multitude of successive objects and goals onto which each surging affect can be imagined to latch. Their poems follow what Altieri calls "the turns and twists" of their speakers' affective experiences, treating their changeability as an important object of representation.[4]

However, Altieri's approach toward affect also presupposes a capacity for detachment from oneself, or what he calls "an ideal of generous irony." "We need the irony," he says, "because we are never entirely in control of our conative drives or our propensity to be moved by what we cannot rationalize. And we need irony even more desperately because expression is an inexact art, where what is symptomatic lies down with what agents manage to give a distinctive shape."[5] I argue that Plath and Stevens do not always take for granted our capacity for what Altieri calls irony, especially not with the self-evidence Altieri assumes here. Instead, occasionally in Stevens and frequently in Plath, affects serve as reminders about how little awareness we have of ourselves by our own lights, even when we accord much time and energy to efforts at introspection. As their speakers test out the various potential outward correlatives for their affects, they cannot always find a stable point beyond them from which they could gaze upon their affective confusions with self-mocking distance. They also begin to feel increasingly claustrophobic within their bodies and minds, which constantly require but do not quite repay their cognitive efforts.

Stevens's poetry edges toward occasionally articulating this perspective from a position that is, at first, much more ambitiously open-ended. Many of Stevens's early poems represent a sensitivity caught midway in its effort to express its values and interests, as yet unable to fully define the objects of its attention but trusting in its eventual success. "Earthy Anecdote," *Harmonium*'s first poem, thus creates a tension between its confident acuity on the level of sounds and particular words, and its almost childlike vagueness on the semantic level. The poem conveys the experience of being buoyed by a confident enthusiasm about one's bodily and mental faculties. Its lines flow with a beautiful, melodious rhythm that the small number of words Stevens recycles stanza by stanza highlights prominently. But the propositions these words string together do not hold up to the kind of intense attention this poem's finer particles invite. These propositions are not yet pieces of new knowledge, or even visualizable images, but mere suggestions of what the objects of these pieces of knowledge might be. Reflecting this outward ambiguity, the speaker of the poem himself remains difficult to articulate. He hovers somewhere between a third-person observer and a voice telling a parable about itself. The animal with which this speaker half-identifies is an imaginary, unvisualizable "firecat."

Stevens begins with a grand generalization:

> Every time the bucks went clattering
> Over Oklahoma
> A firecat bristled in the way. (3)

This stanza's assonances and alliterations make it seem tight and controlled, aware both of its intent and of its joyous power. The second and third stanzas then unpack the bucks' and firecat's movements through parallel syntactic structures and expanding repetitions. They savor the poem's central image and thought in ever new semantic and syntactic constellations:

> Wherever they went
> They went clattering,
> Until they swerved
> In a swift, circular line
> To the right,
> Because of the firecat.
>
> Or until they swerved
> In a swift, circular line
> To the left,
> Because of the firecat. (3)

Stevens's speaker expresses himself with crisp, geometric precision. His repetitions, over which he lingers ever longer, make the poem seem precise and formal, concerned with nothing but small sharp-edged sounds and shapes. But at the same time, the propositions these melodies and geometries compose are hard to take in as bits of insight: the mimetic work they begin to announce is incomplete. The first stanza could not conceivably sum up what goes on in an entire state. And even though the second stanza's grammar is geometrically precise, the physical movement "to the right . . . or to the left" that it traces remains vague. Instead of representing this firecat's movement, these stanzas merely sketch out the initial verbal and auditory components and prospective aims of such a representation and slowly test the skills the speaker will put toward it. Rather than show the speaker's knowledge of firecats, bucks, and Oklahoma, they gesture toward such knowledge as a point somewhere on the horizon, an objective that this poem chases much like the firecat chases his bucks.

   In the fourth stanza, Stevens recompresses this represented world into a burst of melodious sounds and rapidly accumulating lines:

> The bucks clattered.
> The firecat went leaping.
> To the right, to the left,
> And
> Bristled in the way. (3)

This is the third time the speaker returns to the same scene. He has framed it as an assertion and as a pair of alternatives. Now he articulates its few components in a long list. One might interpret this speaker's voice as forcefully confident. As Altieri puts it, "it is as if the language were miming the force of the firecat, even to the extent of not having to reveal anything about itself or about the allegorical situation except what manifests itself as quiet confidence in how it can produce effects on other beings."[6] And yet this list again reveals very little about these animals' movements toward each other. The speaker does not even say exactly where, respective to the bucks, the firecat bristles. Stevens draws attention both to the clarity his speaker achieves in defining his poem's smallest components and to the large-scale discoveries toward which his sensitivity has not yet worked its way. As if to emphasize this tension, the poem ends in an image of exhaustion, as the firecat eventually falls asleep: "Later, the firecat closed his bright eyes / And slept" (3). The firecat has not hunted anything down. He seems to be resting so that the hunt may resume sometime else. If one takes this firecat—as critics often do—for a figure of the poem's lyric speaker, the world it sets out to explore is both vast and only partly imaginable even to the voice that strings together its descriptions. To say this is not to imply that the environment and experience this lyric voice conjures up should dissatisfy the reader. But it is to suggest that this poem enacts and describes a mental effort whose strenuousness has, pointedly, not yet been rewarded.

Stevens's later poetry delves deeper into this combination of yearning for, and uncertainty about, the objects and contexts of his speakers' affects. These later poems represent affects through ever more rapid changes in the scope and stakes of what their speakers consciously attribute or attach them to. Stevens himself describes his speakers' vacillating interpretations of their inner states as a capacity "to believe in a fiction, which you know to be a fiction, there being nothing else."[7] Simon Critchley speaks of them as "intuitions overflowing concepts without the source of the intuition."[8] For Altieri they are experiences of "breaking through to [a] sense of force or necessity and finding it gorgeously intricate."[9] For both Critchley and Altieri, such experiences arise as one falls in and out of different kinds and directions of potential affective expression, living them out in what is at once an earnest and a hypothetical mode. I propose that the unsettled quality of these speakers' self-expression at times also leads Stevens's poetry to speculate about what these affective vacillations reveal about the speakers' capacity for self-awareness. They draw attention to affects as experiences that origi-nate in a particular human body: a body that they surprise, exhaust, and confuse in a way that Stevens represents as disjointed from, and not neces-sarily predictable through the outward triggers and resonances of such un-settled inward states.

In poems written in the 1940s, Stevens often defends these issueless acts of mental self-scrutiny. The difficulty with which we take stock of our affects, these poems suggest, enriches our experience more than the sense of clar-ity to which we aspire would do on its own. "The Poems of Our Climate" constructs and then rejects a vision of unquestioned and unperturbed self-transparency. The poem conveys a sense of longing or malaise for which the speaker tries to imagine a peaceful, definitive resolution. "Clear water in a brilliant bowl," this speaker begins. Within this water float "Pink and white carnations." The room shimmers with light caught in reflective surfaces. This image (whether actually seen or merely imagined) leads him to formulate a more abstract hope for an effortlessly lucid and tranquil existence. "Pink and white carnations," the poem repeats wonderingly. And then, across the fol-lowing line break, the tone changes without warning: "one desires / so much more than that." The speaker recoils from this setting; he experiences it as "cold," "simplified," and merely empty "with nothing more than the carna-tions there" (193).

Marie Borroff claims that Stevens's poems contain climates rather than arguments.[10] But to make this distinction underestimates the intensity with which the speaker of this poem quarrels with his immersive, seemingly wel-coming environment. Even as he goes on to call the self that rejects this peaceful image "evilly compounded" and imagines that this all-encompassing sense of clarity might have the power to "[strip] one of all one's torments," he also defends his right to remain dissatisfied with the cool, unperturbed "cli-mate" of this real or imagined interior:

> Say even that this complete simplicity
> Stripped one of all one's torments, concealed
> The evilly compounded, vital I
> And made it fresh in a world of white,
> A world of clear water, brilliant-edged,
> Still one would want more, one would need more,
> More than a world of white and snowy scents. (193)

In the last stanza this speaker celebrates his continual urge to "escape" any such spotlight of lucid stillness (194). Indeed, he describes an "imperfect" relation to his world as "paradise," defending his right to "come back to / what had been so long composed." This last, initially ambiguous statement soon turns out to refer to the poem itself, as the fruit of the speaker's extensively documented affective confusion. The speaker reframes this pursuit of cognitive and expressive imperfection as the explicit task of the poet. "Since the imperfect is so hot in us," he says, "delight . . . lies in flawed words and stubborn sounds" (194).

Even as this poem celebrates the kind of sensitivity first explored in *Harmonium*, it also changes the terms of this celebratory gesture. The imperfection for which this speaker yearns does not necessarily belong to the world beyond him. Instead, it is a quality that the self nurtures and maybe even generates on its own. The restlessness with which he refuses to settle into calm and clarity is now depicted as a conscious choice. Stevens's speaker here does not simply, as Altieri suggests, discover new ways in which the surrounding world can seem insightful or valuable to him. Instead, he begins to unmoor affects, as experiences of unresolved unrest, from his initial desire to reduce this confusion to clarity. The imperfect is "hot" in us, and we should affirm the indeterminacy of our minds and bodies without regret or embarrassment.

But what would happen if one did not defend the worth of this imperfection so strenuously? A few of Stevens's poems eventually turn to this issue. Even as these later poems find ever more ingenious ways of dramatizing the meandering cognitive speculations with which their speakers respond to their surging affects, these poems also dissociate such speculations from any narrative of cognitive satisfaction or progress. Trying to give appropriate names and contexts to our affects, Stevens suggests there is an endless and often comically fruitless, circuitous task. This task takes place within the narrow bodily circumferences of a single human being, who alone appears to be particularly interested in or concerned about its fluctuations—and whose inward impulses often exhaust or resolve themselves with embarrassing ease.

In some of his extended later poems, Stevens dramatizes not merely the variety of the objects to which his speakers might relate their affects, but also the various possible lengths and rhythms of their interludes of cognitive certitude. "Notes toward a Supreme Fiction" highlights that its speaker's sense of confidence in his affective awareness sometimes wanes very quickly and sometimes lingers in his mind and body for a long time; furthermore, even within an unchanging environment, his body can suddenly prove his affective self-assessments entirely wrong. I examine two sections of "Notes" in which such shifts are particularly striking. The first comes from around the middle of the poem:

> To discover winter and know it well, to find,
> Not to impose, not to have reasoned at all,
> Out of nothing to have come on major weather,
>
> It is possible, possible, possible. It must
> be possible. (404)

The speaker has been describing the joy of discovering a preexisting order to his inner world, which he metaphorically represents as a landscape torn by inexplicable shifts of weather. On one level the first of these stanzas continues this description. But the poem's images also begin to shift in ways that undercut this joyful confidence. Rather than seek or celebrate a knowledge of summer—with which this section began—the speaker starts to wish for a knowledge of winter, with all the overtones of desolation and blankness this season holds in Stevens's poetry. The next line brings two negations: "Not to impose, not to have reasoned at all." These negations restate Stevens's distinction between the imposed and the discovered but also make this distinction seem effortful. Instead of merely stumbling on winter, the speaker now needs to prevent himself from "imposing" on it or "reasoning" about it. The third line continues this change of perspective. The word "weather" repeats and summarizes his prior list of the seasons, but much more vaguely and immediately, in a way that implicitly involves considerable interpretative effort. The following two lines: "It is possible, possible, possible. It must / be possible" openly recenter the poem on the now troubled speaker. This speaker finds himself half demanding, half begging, for an inner world that will allow itself to be discovered by him, a world whose order he can trust himself to not have merely invented. As in "The Poems of Our Climate," the progression this sequence stages depends on rapid shifts in the scope, intensity, and objects of the speaker's affects. First, the speaker describes the delighted surprise of finding a plausible interpretation of his inner world. Then he lets himself fall into the fear that this interpretation will not, in the long run, hold his belief.

This section is part of the poem's longer meditative course around the possibility of such a plausible long-term form of awareness, which Stevens calls a "supreme fiction." The power of this fragment within this larger context does not come from the newness of the twist it stages. The whole prior part of the poem has been, in various ways, outlining and rehearsing what Helen Vendler calls "a constant motion back and forth . . . or else a recurrent convergence" between "the subjective and the objective."[11] The passage I quote here stands out amid these oscillations because the pace of Stevens's shifts between these two perspectives quickens. He retraces within five lines a hinge in thought the poem previously unraveled over the span of two sections. These lines themselves echo this shift in speed. Their rhythm is clipped in the last couplet even while this couplet does little more than repeat a single word, drawing attention to how much less space its iterations occupy from one line to the next.[12]

Such passages highlight the dissonances between the longer and briefer expressions of the speaker's affect. Reiterating the speaker's shifting trust in his capacity for awareness in such various longer and shorter ways, the poem decouples it from the sense of urgency or ponderousness that its more or less extended durations might respectively suggest, as well as from the notion of progress or transcendence that a single iteration of this movement might be taken to signify. Instead, this feeling's changeability foregrounds the unpredictable inward fluctuations in the speaker's attitude toward and sense of control over himself and his environments. It also draws attention to the speaker's unresolved cognitive uncertainties as sources of this sense of uprootedness. To say this is not simply to propose, with Critchley, that Stevens exposes our isolation from the elusive things in themselves among which we live.[13] The revelation that this poem stages also focuses on its speaker's incapacity to predict how convinced he might be by each successive formulation he finds for his sense of himself.

The second section, entitled "It Must Change," occasionally lifts the speaker out of this experience of confusion: at several brief, unpredictable moments, his body and its outer environments harmonize with each other. These experiences of harmony surprise the speaker with their relative conventionality. Thinking suddenly ends, in these poems, not because an affect has been explained or accounted for, but because this affect itself changes just as unexpectedly as it first emerged:

> The old seraph, parcel-gilded, among violets
> Inhaled the appointed odor, while the doves
> Rose up like phantoms from chronologies.
>
> The Italian girls wore jonquils in their hair
> And these the seraphs saw, had seen long since,
> In the bandeaux of the mothers, would see again.
>
> The bees came booming as if they had never gone,
> As if hyacinths had never gone. We say
> This changes and that changes. Thus the constant
>
> Violets, doves, girls, bees, and hyacinths
> Are inconstant objects of inconstant cause
> In a universe of inconstancy. This means
>
> Night-blue is an inconstant thing. The seraph
> Is satyr in Saturn, according to his thoughts.
> It means the distaste we feel for the withered scene
>
> Is that it has not changed enough. It remains,
> It is a repetition. The bees come booming
> As if—The pigeons clatter in the air.
>
> An erotic perfume, half of the body, half
> Of an obvious acid is sure what it intends
> And the booming is blunt, not broken in subtleties. (389–90)

This passage explicitly describes the persistence and inconstancy of affects. I focus on its two affective shifts—the movement from pleased interest to "distaste" in the first four stanzas, and then the turn back to intoxication in stanzas five and six. The first two stanzas begin with several changes of perspective. Each line break marks an addition to its landscape. Yet another human or animal presence moves within it; yet another dimension emerges in which this scene coalesces into a pastorally self-contained, self-perpetuating sphere of scents, movements, bodies, and gazes. But an undercurrent of doubt or boredom echoes in these descriptions. One could argue that this undercurrent starts, subtly, with the early mention of the word "appointed." The adjective is itself affectively neutral, but it begins the poem's slow shift from an evenly joyful to a frustrated, probing tone; what had at first seemed like a boon becomes an imposition. This shift in emphasis culminates in stanza four. The speaker lists the components of this pastoral with cool detachment. In the next two lines, he repeatedly accuses this scene of being both "inconstant" and, paradoxically, too "constant," at once "withered" and insufficiently changed. The night sky is at once "constant" and "inconstant" because "the seraph is satyr in Saturn." The sky moves forward, but it does so in a predictable cycle. His world can never "change enough" because one always keeps returning to states one already knew. At the beginning of this section this predictability soothed him. Now the same rhythm leaves the speaker repulsed and exasperated.

The last two stanzas do not resolve these questions. But unexpectedly they bring the speaker a spark of the delight for which he has been steadily losing hope since the beginning of this section—a delight that the poem now also sexualizes. The steady sound of bees, whose description is about to repeat the exact line with which the section started, gives way, mid-phrase, to a "clattering" of pigeons. Both are repetitive undulating sounds, so similar to each other that in the final line these sounds all fuse in the same gerund, "booming," that the poem previously associated only with bees. This booming now no longer bores the speaker; indeed, it intoxicates him. The speaker absorbs it with an erotic delight that "is sure what it intends." His "body," as he experiences it, becomes indistinguishable from the "obvious acid" of the vitality with which this landscape stings or inflames him. As Vendler puts it: "Whatever our determinist metaphysics, . . . the experience of energetic free feeling flaunts its own truths, as spring, however predictable in theory, brings golden furies rising in us."[14] The speaker can no longer, as he did before, list the fine differences among the ways this scene repeats itself. He experiences it as a throbbing, unbroken cocoon.

The irregularities of pacing that were crucial to the first passage from "Notes" I analyzed again come to the foreground. This time, what changes are the affective stakes and meanings that the speaker attaches to an unaltered pace and rhythm of sensation. The same resonant booming first beats out his peaceful happiness, then his aggravation, and then his intoxicated sexual pleasure. The form of this section highlights that these rapid shifts of affect are irreducible to any significant changes in the environments to which he is responding, or in his conscious attitude toward them. Its stresses remain prominent and prominently regular, as steady in the first pastoral stanzas as in the later distressed or delighted ones. Phrases such as "the seraph / Is satyr in Saturn," in which the same stress pattern, and a pattern of near-identical sounds, leads us through three drastically different frames of reference, enact these stanzas' surprising shifts within apparent rhythmic predictability.

Such phrases in which complicated metaphors glide into the same simple rhythm or assonance also draw attention to another feature of these sudden affective alignments: their surprising conventionality. The poem's speaker searches for adequate tools of self-expression as if uncovering a great, inscrutable secret. But in this moment when his affects and his environment synchronize with each other, the tie between them—and the apparent urge behind this tie—become extremely, almost embarrassingly simple and immediate, as if, to cite the poem's earlier section, the speaker's frustration had in fact required no "reason[ing]" at all. Now that the speaker has found a way to connect to his environment, he also discovers that he has nothing particularly new or insightful to say about it; indeed, he cannot even properly explain how his body and mind got there.

Altieri praises Stevens's poems from this period for "combining temporal, qualitative, and psychological registers for staging events so that there is simultaneity in events, parallelism in qualities, and opportunities for expressing the manner of one's interactions with objects."[15] These simultaneities and parallelisms, he claims, transform Stevens's poetry into "an elaborate phenomenological enterprise exploring states where one feels oneself responding to what engages our sense of values."[16] Altieri rightly points out that, for Stevens, affects are aesthetically interesting to the extent that they encourage one to consider, and come to the threshold of, many different kinds and categories of attachment. Yet their open-ended indeterminacy does not merely, as Altieri argues, give Stevens's speakers a sense of greater flexibility in and mastery over their "mortality." These affective experiences at times also lead the speakers toward a heightened awareness of how unpredictably their minds and bodies respond to their surroundings and how often they fail in their attempts to predict or even retroactively account for these responses. Rather than help these speakers attain a sense of imaginative independence from their world and their immediate physical presence within it, affects paradoxically make them increasingly, uncontrolledly dependent and responsive.

These explorations of affects as unpredictable patterns of bodily responsiveness finally resurge in several of Stevens's last poems. These are poems at once, as Vendler puts it, of the mind effortfully "coming out to see"[17] what is left out there and, as Altieri observes, of "drowsiness," now finally accepted as the speaker's way of communing with the world. "Not Ideas about the Thing but the Thing Itself" stages such a drowsy affective revelation. Alone, sitting beside his window, its speaker returns to an excitement about the world that he had not thought he could still feel. "It was like / A new knowledge of reality," he says of the cry of a bird he hears at sunrise (534). This is a cry that the speaker has heard many times before. Now that the sound reaches him once again, it unfolds into a choir of associations. They bind the bird to the rising sun and make this sun, though "still far away," seem to approach him as directly as the bird's voice (534). He describes the bird's "scrawny cry" as

> A chorister whose c preceded the choir.
> It was part of the colossal sun,
>
> Surrounded by its choral rings. (534)

A chorister plays a note to set all of the voices of a choir in tune. To the speaker's mind, this bird similarly announces to the world a timbre and ambiance with which everything around him harmonizes in triumphant C major harmony, in which this speaker hopes he himself is also included.

"It was not from the vast ventriloquism / Of sleep's faded papier-mâché . . . ," he emphasizes. "The sun was coming from the outside" (534). For the speaker to stress that he is not asleep draws attention to how self-consciously he orients himself around this newly noticed sound. It also highlights how many details of this vision, including the sun's approach toward him, do in fact resemble a dream. The way the line breaks and stanza breaks fragment his description into short phrases makes it seem all the more slow and effortful. These rapid breaks also remind the reader that the original event that startled this speaker was very brief. By setting up these tensions, Stevens stresses his speaker's cognitive effort while suggesting that his awakened sensitivities are struggling to make sense of a commonplace sensation whose habitual details this aged speaker may have temporarily forgotten. To follow this feeling leads one to discover not only its great philosophical ambition but also the small bit of experience around which its generalizations emerge, whose smallness the poem alternately highlights and obscures. Stepping back out onto the threshold between his mind and a world from which he will soon withdraw permanently, Stevens's speaker depicts this experience as a reflection of the heightened, incompletely self-knowing effort with which he still tries to explain his ties to his surroundings.

Plath's poetry shares with this strand of Stevens's a preoccupation with the potential objects and scopes of her speaker's surging affects. Stevens cares most about complicating our efforts to treat the mind and body as objects of philosophical inquiry; Plath's speakers wonder how their partial awareness of their affects troubles their understanding of their expectations of and relationships to others. I argue that Plath's poems are not—as some critics have suggested—direct political statements,[18] nor are they best understood as demanding a psychoanalytic interpretation.[19] Instead, these poems dramatize a state of awkward uncertainty about the causes of their speakers' affective turmoil. Amid this uncertainty, their speakers express the recurrent fear that they might not be able to derive any articulable insight or profit from the attention they devote to how they feel. Especially in her later work, Plath turns this self-doubt into her main object of representation and into the main constitutive principle around which she constructs her implied speakers. Rather than try to free themselves from these uncertainties, Plath's speakers—who become increasingly incoherent and fragmented—place them front and center in the way they define their shifting, incompletely self-knowing personhood.

Despite highlighting similarities between Plath's and Stevens's poems, I do not attribute to Plath Stevens's generally more self-accepting attitude toward affect. However, I do suggest that this comparison helps one notice, in both poets, an interest in similar ways of dismantling a more conventional notion of the affectively introspective self. The moods within which Plath's and Stevens's aesthetic operates differ considerably. In Plath, they tend to range between frustration, humiliation, and anger; in Stevens, they remain somewhere between mild irritation and surprised, comforted complacency. Both poets probe these moods in order to highlight both their speakers' high stakes in achieving some stable form of affective self-awareness, and their inability to do so through their introspective efforts. Their poems represent the self as struggling with, and eventually as defined by, this gradually acknowledged failure of self-cognizance. Plath comes to depict her speakers as not just exposed, but positively undone, by the pressure they put on bodily and mental experiences that refuse to resolve their apparent complexities or yield their secrets.

In her earliest poems Plath's speakers often strive to imagine in what kind of world their affects would find validation and recognition. Plath dramatizes both their affects' urgency and the speakers' inability to picture them as embodied in, or focused on, coherent, articulable objects. Instead, these affects fade in and out of varying degrees of apparent grandeur and reality. Her speakers alternately embrace and mock their own continual attempts to articulate and express them.

Ted Hughes recounts that Plath's youthful "evolution as a poet went rapidly through successive molts of style, as she realized her true matter and voice."[20] Many of her early poems self-consciously stage the artificiality of such "molts." "Rhyme" brings out what Robin Peel diagnoses as Plath's youthful "admiration for Nietzsche and her celebration of artistic individualism."[21] It also conveys Plath's uncertainty about how much of this self-celebratory confidence can be hers. The name of this poem already carries this ambivalence. It sounds very ambitious, presenting as nothing less than a poem *about* making poems. But this ambition is undergirded with self-mockery: perhaps we are reading nothing more than a metrical exercise. "Rhyme" anticipates both its reader's potential dismissal of, and his potential admiration for, itself. As it tries to forestall both responses, its successive lines create ever more ambiguity about what actual event, if any, this poem responds to and what kind of person, if any, is being described there.

The implied speaker of "Rhyme" tries and fails to curb a violently impatient greed. She owns a goose that does not lay golden eggs though she believes it could. In the course of the poem she grows frustrated and disembowels her bird. This macabre scenario seems to take place at once within and beyond the speaker's daydream, on the physical and on the verbal level. Plath makes her reader struggle to sort out how the affect the poem represents is shaping its speaker's perceptual experience, as well as to understand why this affect needs sorting out in the first place.

Plath's speaker compares her goose to an old, rich woman who buys sex with her wealth. "She . . . struts / the barnyard like those taloned hags / Who ogle men / And crimp their wrinkles in a grin, / Jangling their great money bags" (50). The metaphor roams far from how a goose would normally be described. A goose's feet are webbed, not taloned. Geese have no wrinkles; they cannot grin. It is as if the speaker were not merely describing her environment but conjuring up a world that would better match her affects' intensity. This obstinate, precious goose seems at once like part of her environment and an elaborate daydream. It could also be read as a metaphor for the poem itself as the speaker tries to make it seem valuable for her own and her reader's benefit.

When the speaker finally kills the goose, its "gut" is not, as the first stanza promises, "honeycombed with golden eggs." Instead, there "exit from a smoking slit" not gold but "ruby dregs" (50). This macabre jewel produces a moment of surprising sensory vividness: the poem finally applies its meticulously crafted language to what a goose's shiny entrails could look like. But it thus also reaches a high point of solipsism: she still refuses to see the goose as anything else than treasure, now that the animal's sheer existence has become doubtful. The speaker's final act of violence at once reaffirms her daydream and undoes it. Even as it foregrounds the intensity of the affective experience described here, it leaves the stakes of this experience indeterminable. To the extent that this poem reflects on its own making—which its title, "Rhyme," suggests—it refuses to represent writing as the process of parsing out a complicated affect. Instead, the speaker's intellectual and aesthetic work goes mostly toward acknowledging how little she can know about the objects and stakes of this affect based merely on its immediate, confused sense of urgency.

As Plath's poetry matures, she represents such uncertainties with increasing insistence. Her later poems highlight that their speakers have great difficulty in finding reliable names or outward correlatives for their surging affects. These poems also linger with such confusions as entry points into the speakers' troubled sense of themselves. Plath's later work does frequently depict processes of affective introspection. However, it reflects less on affects in themselves than on uncertainties about how much one's momentary interpretations of them correspond to the stakes these affects might hold for an imagined, detached other or even for a later version of oneself.

Plath's path toward this broader poetic range passes through a series of failed elegies. "Parliament Hill Fields" and "Tulips" are two major poems from this period. In both, Plath's speakers stall in an attempt to accept a disempowerment or loss: the passing of an unborn child and the speaker's spell of unconsciousness during illness. These poems represent their speakers' apparent eagerness to articulate their affects' objects and their tragicomic inability to decide—even after the poem has run its course—with what greater or lesser personal or political conundrum these affects are associated. Unlike in "Rhyme," in both later poems the speaker finds herself among a crowd of potential (though silent) observers. She fears that these observers know too much about her and also do not care about her affects nearly as much as she does. Their presence provides a model for the kind of knowing attitude Plath's speakers desire, as well as confirmations of her confinement to a confused first-person perspective. These elegies represent affects as intrinsically, almost necessarily, generative of such forms of uncertainty and vulnerability. They also depict their speakers as ripped apart by affective experiences in a way that they cannot assuage or resolve.

"Parliament Hill Fields," a poem about a miscarriage, takes its pathos from the speaker's combination of paranoia and uncertainty about whether anyone notices, let alone cares about how she feels.[22] To represent this paradox, Plath puts together a lyric world that is eerily anthropomorphic as well as intensely indifferent to her speaker. This environment seems capable of seeing through her and of showing no interest in anything that it might see. "The round sky goes on minding its business," says Plath's speaker in the first stanza. "Your absence is inconspicuous; / Nobody can tell what I lack" (152). At first, the sky seems all-knowing: it is "minding its business," as if it knew of the speaker's bereavement but chose not to prod her about it. By contrast, in the next two lines the unborn child becomes so "inconspicuous" that only the speaker herself knows about its absence. Between these two opening phrases the speaker describes herself as not merely grieving in private or grieving in front of an indifferent public, but taking stock of a grief whose intersubjective resonances remain indeterminate. This latter ambiguity—irrelevant as it may initially seem to the process of mourning—soon becomes central to the way the speaker understands her loss as well as herself.

The poem stages a series of encounters in which such degrees of communion or isolation remain uncertain. The speaker's "eyes wince / and brim," but she blames it on the sunlight (152). The wind "stops [her] breath like a bandage," which could describe both the wind's outward effects and memories of the hospital, as well as the speaker's efforts to keep herself from sobbing (152). "A crocodile of small girls / . . . / Opens to swallow" her, and "One child drops a barrette of pink plastic." "None of them seem to notice," writes Plath, making one wonder if what they do not notice is the speaker's bereavement, her motherliness, her unfitness to be a mother, or merely the absence of the pink barrette (152). Gulls fly above her as what Vendler calls "surrogate spectators," put in this poem for no apparent end beyond making the speaker seem more exposed.[23] For Perloff, this speaker urgently wants to and cannot be claimed by her environment.[24] But such a reading sells short the oscillation between the public and the private that makes Plath's depiction of this walk so unbearable. This speaker appears at once to hope and fear that the beings around her could potentially help her understand her grief. She is moved both by their indifference and by the intensity with which this indifference registers as a lacuna within her attempt at articulating how she feels.

The poem ends with an unfulfilled vision of a small world of private objects and associations in which the speaker could express her grief more comfortably. "The day empties its images / like a cup or a room," the speaker comments (153). Plath telescopes the day-lit park in which her speaker has been walking into the bedroom of her surviving child. She transcribes these hills, fields, and radiances into the curves and angles of nursery plants, furniture, and family photos: "the little pale blue hill / In your sister's birthday picture starts to glow" (153). This smaller space, where she could be alone again, might let her speaker parse out less ambiguously the ways her unborn child has been with her throughout the day.

But the last stanza reverses this resolution. "The old dregs, the old difficulties take me to wife. . . . / I enter the lit house" (153). Rather than ending in this house, the poem's final line leaves us on its threshold. Plath's speaker, it turns out, was not in a nursery but in a fantasy about a nursery. The poem has expressed only a hope of grounding the speaker's daylong grief in a familiar, cognitively manageable external setting. To the "dregs" of her reality Plath's speaker is not mother but "wife," which the transitive "take" turns into an unequal partnership. As she enters the house she describes neither its interior nor any resolution to the grief that has ambiguously racked her throughout the poem. The ending occludes the next way in which the speaker's grief might find its indeterminate, continually revised expression. This ending also suggests that this speaker might only be able to trust these affects unself-consciously in a space where she could somehow—in a way that by now sounds self-mockingly escapist—forget about her potential knowability to her surroundings, and about her inability to represent to herself the knowledge they might have about her.

In "Tulips" Plath's speaker assesses her affective uncertainties on an immediate bodily level. The poem expresses a mounting anger and irritation, until a climax in which the speaker finally acknowledges and tries to accept her sense of vulnerability and cognitive disempowerment. When "Tulips" begins, Plath's speaker is succumbing to anesthesia. She claims that she has relinquished her body and mind to others. "I am nobody; I have nothing to do with explosions. / I have given my name and my day-clothes up to the nurses / And my history to the anesthetist and my body to surgeons" (160). As "Tulips" progresses, its speaker fears that she has become fully transparent to her hospital surroundings, and also that she cannot fully picture to herself the way she comes across to them. Her "patent leather overnight case" and "husband and child smiling out of the family photo" (160) are staring at her, she announces. This irritation escalates in a steady crescendo. "The tulips are too red in the first place, they hurt me," the speaker states dramatically (161). She accuses the tulips of conspiring against her and weighing her down like "a dozen red lead sinkers round my neck" (161). They finally become a "loud noise" around which her sensations center "the way a river / Snags and eddies round a sunken rust-red engine" (161).

As these accusations intensify, they become ever less credible, and the poem becomes overtly conscious of it. Its rhetoric shifts from confident assertions of the speaker's needs, into a gradually dawning, humbling recognition that no one besides herself is actually interpreting or even taking note of her affective self-expression. Plath's lines loop back into descriptions of the speaker's recovering body. She refolds her speaker's hospital room into a ribcage that encloses a flowerlike heart. "And I am aware of my heart: it opens and closes / Its bowl of red blooms out of sheer love of me" (161). As the poem ends, she seems to "taste" blood in her mouth: "The water I taste is warm and salt, like the sea, / And comes from a country far away as health" (161). Plath's speaker metaphorically envelops herself in this hospital room, whose distractions she fuses into a collage-like image of herself. Its images of the sea and faraway countries again measure how vaguely this speaker can discern how her affects appear to anyone, including herself. These metaphors at once aggrandize and mock the kind of self-awareness to which she aspires, which she can only depict as a drugged daydream.

Plath achieves what most critics call her mature style when her poems embrace this state of vague indeterminacy as a necessary, unresolvable condition of her speakers' sense of self. In this regard—unlike in Altieri's framework—Plath's poems reach their fullest potential by eliminating, rather than increasing, a sense of "generous irony" and "third-person distance" in their speakers' affective experiences.[25] These poems capture the urgency with which their speakers strive for greater affective awareness. They also underscore the speakers' suspicion that they cannot achieve the kind of awareness they desire on their own, however much knowledge and cultural capital they might try to muster to their aid.

"Ariel," the speaker's famous self-portrait, enacts this sense of self-loss with reckless aplomb. In its drowsy emphasis on an overwhelming sense of oneness with the speaker's surroundings, it bears comparison with Stevens's "Not Ideas about the Thing but the Thing Itself." The ostensible context for the poem is an early morning ride on a horse named Ariel. The speaker fuses her ecstatic, near-orgasmic joy at this ride with the joy of writing poetry. She contemplates both the pleasures of these activities and their inevitable, disappointing brevity: celebrating the cosmic, boundaryless self she becomes within them and fearing for what will happen to her when this self melts away. For Jacqueline Rose, poems like this one showcase the "provisional, precarious nature of self-representation": they highlight that the body and its urges resist any verbal labels.[26] Christina Britzolakis counters that "Ariel" systematically "forges its own myth" out of its shifting images. It creates a narrative of the speaker's loneliness into which this restless speaker finally settles.[27] In a sense, both Rose and Britzolakis are right—and much of the poem's power comes from this duality. Hypnotized by a rapid physical or mental movement, the speaker feels her body reshape itself. As in "Tulips," this speaker does not distinguish between her body and what this body's changing states remind her of or make her feel recognized by. Yet, unlike in "Tulips," this confusion is defiantly embraced; and unlike in "Not Ideas about the Thing," Plath focuses both on her speaker's episode of seemingly cosmic ecstasy and on her fall away from it. "Ariel" challenges its reader to see its speaker as someone whose hopeful sense of harmony with her world collapses around her even as she also realizes that nobody else is implicated in her crisis. Plath's focus is not just on her speaker's confusion, but also on the loneliness amid which this confusion takes place; the poem eventually rejects as both unachievable and unsatisfying the dream of being an autonomous, reliable source of one's own self-understanding.

"Ariel" begins with "Stasis in darkness. / Then the substanceless blue / Pour of tor and distances" (239). Plath enacts this transition from stasis to blurred movement visually and aurally. "The substanceless blue / Pour[s]" into "substanceless blue pour" after the line break, and the sounds of "blue," "pour," and "tor" meld into each other. But even as she renders this transition melodiously vivid, she also draws attention to the gap between its formal precision and the haziness of these lines' content. The self to which this poem gives voice is at once acutely, self-controlledly subtle and blindly intoxicated. The speaker applies her refined sensibility to an experience whose limits she cannot discern.

These abstractions soon reappear as more recognizable cultural tropes. "God's lioness, / how one we grow," the speaker exclaims, apparently speaking not only for herself but also for the broad signifiers (God's lioness is what "Ariel" means in Hebrew) in which she finds a model for her inward states. As Heather Clark puts it, the speaker "is a wild animal in motion, shape-shifting, . . . eluding both reader and writer who seek to capture its essence."[28] This speaker depicts herself as creative but also strikingly passive: it is as if, like many of Stevens's speakers, she has finally found herself on the receiving end of an "order" she did not herself invent. Various disparate conventions embrace her, and she lets herself be caught up in them. A few lines later, "nigger-eye / Berries" surround her; they "cast dark / Hooks" and leave a taste in her mouth that is "black" and "sweet" despite resembling "blood" (239). These shifts in register, from the biblical to the crudely racialized, parallel an insistent increase of intimacy between this speaker's body and the concepts she invokes. She does not merely inhabit, but ingests them. All these wild transformations lead to the speaker's being hauled through air, flaking away into a "White / Godiva," turning to "foam," to "glitter," and finally to "dew" that will steam into air with the coming sunrise (239–240). As Vendler observes, these final lines obsessively repeat the pronoun "I." It appears first in its proper meaning, then in puns ("the red / eye") and in assonances ("flies," "suicidal," "drive"; 240).[29] These puns embody the affectively driven fusions also enacted by the poem's metaphors. The speaker's "I" at once encloses the entire world of this poem and fragments into a variety of metaphors for the significance and intent this "I" might hold. In this last image, Plath's lines metaphorically unravel not only the speaker's body but also the tropes with which she identifies: her passage from a woman into foam, glitter, and dew inverts the familiar myth of Aphrodite.

A single person could not, of course, take the whole of her culture down with her: and that is part of the point of this dramatic ending. Rather than trying to gain some distance from her intense angers and frustrations, Plath's speaker pursues her loss of distance to its logical extreme. At this extreme, individual self-expression and age-old linguistic and mythic production begin to seem to her like one and the same thing. We are left with neither a particular person nor a coherent abstraction whose expression we might affirm or whose passing we might mourn. This fragmentation paradoxically marks an apex of the poem's affective realism: the speaker refuses to bring back an order and a sense of perspective into an experience centrally defined by their absence. The fact that the myths she claims to dismantle do, of course, remain intact and ready for other people's use after the poem is over, underscores the distinction between these myths' capacity for coherence and persistence, and the kind of intermittent, incoherent attention the speaker can give to her own bodily and mental states.

"It is quite important," Altieri argues, "that I try to understand why I love someone or take pleasure in certain company. But it is even more important not to let the difficulties of understanding prevent my letting myself perform those states for myself to see what I become within the affects they allow."[30] Altieri sees such "difficulties" as necessary transition points toward insights about our affective needs and attachments that we might not otherwise be willing to face. For Plath and Stevens, experiences that Altieri describes in these terms can be sources of insight in themselves. Rather than merely affirming a state of solipsism—a term both writers' work has occasionally evoked—the poems I examine here depict their speakers as trapped within the realization that they need outward perspectives and responses to make sense of their affects: they have no idea how these affects would come across in their surrounding world, nor are they able to construct a coherent notion of themselves without such external input. These speakers are fragmented by their affective experience in a way that also blurs their awareness of the inward and outward events to which their minds and bodies respond.

What would happen if someone else were indeed present for such a moment of affective confusion? This question is addressed by the series of novels to which I now turn, beginning with those of Virginia Woolf and F. Scott Fitzgerald. On the one hand, as is well known—especially of Woolf—these novels often highlight the ways in which another person's presence can enrich our understanding of our affects and help us accept them. On the other hand, they underscore the uncontrollable contingency of such forms of sudden interpersonal insight—and the rarity with which both of the parties involved recognize these moments of insight as meaningful or profound, or agree on the aspects of such exchanges that were most significant to them. In Woolf, these constant misunderstandings, in the midst of what otherwise seems like empathy and mutual comprehension, give her characters' exchanges a comic undertone. In Fitzgerald, the irony of these misunderstandings is considerably darker and tinged with tragedy: he represents his characters as, more often than not, squandering or misinterpreting the opportunities others give them for recognition or insight.

Chapter 2

Living Room

Virginia Woolf and F. Scott Fitzgerald

Midway through Virginia Woolf's *Mrs. Dalloway*, Richard Dalloway gives roses to his wife, Clarissa. He intends these flowers to show Clarissa that he loves her. "She understood; she understood without his speaking; his Clarissa," he rejoices as she arranges the roses in vases.[1] Joking about how busy she seems, he leaves. Woolf's free indirect discourse then switches from channeling Richard to Clarissa—and it turns out that his romantic confession has not reached her. Instead, all she can think of is the "unpleasant feeling" with which she is left as her husband exits. What is this feeling? she wonders. "Her parties! [Richard] had criticized her very unfairly, laughed at her very unjustly, for her parties" (120). What Richard intended as a stray remark escalates in her mind into sharp criticism; meanwhile, she rapidly forgets about, or perhaps does not even notice, the love he wished to confess.

Amid these quid pro quos, both characters also leave this interaction realizing that the other person has helped them understand themselves, in a way that Woolf's narration does not ironize. On seeing Clarissa receive his flowers, Richard is moved anew by the depth of his feeling for her. Richard's joke leads Clarissa to acknowledge a long-standing unease about the purpose of her busy social life. She will only be able to dispel this malaise when she hears about and reflects on Septimus Smith's suicide.

In Woolf, attempts at divining how one's affective expression comes across to others usually backfire. At the same time, as in the quoted passage, her characters cannot achieve any form of introspective affective clarity without external (usually accidental and unwitting) help. F. Scott Fitzgerald's characters are similarly astounded by how difficult it is for them to predict how others will respond to their self-expression, or even to describe their affects to themselves coherently. Both novelists' engagements with affective experience continue their long-studied subversion of older, nineteenth-century norms of character construction: the characters they depict are not defined by stable outward characteristics, but by inward states that they strive to articulate to themselves. But paradoxically, these characters' inward selves turn out constantly to require other people's attention and interpretation in order to seem understandable and meaningful—even as such outward acts of care are only inconsistently and unreliably forthcoming. As do the lyric speakers of Plath and Stevens, the characters of these novels experience such dependencies as challenges to their sense of themselves as self-knowing beings. Woolf's and Fitzgerald's novels also undercut notions of empathy or interpersonal affective communication that depend on a belief in our autonomous affective awareness. Woolf's *Mrs. Dalloway* depicts episodes when a character is suddenly able to glean some form of self-knowledge from someone else, despite this person's unawareness of the support she has just provided, as near-miracles in which the precarious coherence and sustainability of their sense of themselves is suddenly saved. Fitzgerald's *The Great Gatsby* and *Tender Is the Night* focus, instead, on the personal and social crises that arise when their characters fail to obtain such outward cognitive support from others, even when it is being openly offered to them. In a way that resembles the fragile, controlling speakers of Plath's poems, his protagonists paradoxically lose touch with reality because of the urgent intensity with which they try to explicate their relations to it.

Woolf's and Fitzgerald's characters experience surges of affect during teas and parties. *Mrs. Dalloway*, *The Great Gatsby*, and *Tender Is the Night* do not take place uniquely inside living rooms. But they do consistently focus on characters' attempts to become aware of their affects in densely social environments for which both novelists take the living room as a metonymy.

What is it like to have a feeling in the immediate presence of others—indeed, of people whom one has invited into one's home? Both novelists take this question as a point of departure for acknowledging, first, how belated and context-dependent one's access to one's affects often is; and, second, how much one depends on other people for any sense of affective clarity at all.

For both novelists, one inspiration for these representations of affect comes from the experience of the modern city. Woolf and Fitzgerald stress that even casual, anonymous interactions facilitate brief forms of interpersonal support when a person's accidental word or gesture elucidates someone else's affects with unexpected depth. These surprising encounters highlight the comparative contingency of their characters' attempts consciously to share their affects with people with whom they are already intimate. Both in Woolf and in Fitzgerald, the experience of trauma or shell shock occupies a central place in these affective reflections. They treat it as a radical example of a form of unself-conscious affective expression that lays one's body and mind open to other people's interpretations. For Woolf, these depictions of extreme affective exposure provide a way of stressing that her characters depend on the fortuitous presence and responsiveness of others to make themselves feel in control of their affective expression. Fitzgerald uses these representations of intensely uncontrolled affects to subvert his characters' confidence in their self-awareness and—especially in *Tender Is the Night*—in their ability to orchestrate how they come across to people they love. Psychoanalysis looms large in this last novel as a false discourse of supposed affective self-knowledge and intelligibility that his characters vainly hope might overcome these difficulties.

In the course of this chapter, I set these novels in conversation with the writings of Brian Massumi. Massumi describes affects as processes of emergence that inevitably catch one's conscious self unawares. His notion of affect—with which Woolf's and Fitzgerald's character construction has much in common—hinges on the concept of the "virtual." The virtual, for Massumi, is a dimension of our bodily existence whose effects we can access only indirectly and after considerable delay. He defines it as "the 'real but abstract' incorporeality of the body."[2] Affects constitute one example of the virtual because they emerge within our bodies and begin to shape them before we are able to notice their presence: any attempt to register their incipience is futile. Within this context, affects confront their bearers with "unpossibilized *futurity*: pure potential."[3] Affective experience leads one into a perpetually surprising process of self-discovery; there is no telling what one's body might come to express or respond to.

Like the scientific subjects Massumi invokes, the characters of Woolf's and Fitzgerald's fiction frequently behold their minds and bodies in astonishment. At times, these minds and bodies surprise them by how intensely they respond to the presence or absence of another person. At other times, they suddenly become indifferent to a prior object of longing or frustration. Woolf's and Fitzgerald's novels turn the delays between the emergence of characters' affects and those affects' rise to intelligibility into a marked feature of their narrative structures. They emphatically differentiate between the effects that emergent affects have on their characters and these characters' capacity to discern these effects or integrate them into their pre-existing worldviews and interactions.

But Massumi's account can also be complicated and redirected by a consideration of Woolf's and Fitzgerald's characters. Massumi represents such affective surges as taking place either in solitude, or in a relatively controlled quasi-scientific context. He describes affect theorists as catching themselves feeling something or as observing someone else's affects—the affects of children, in the opening example of *Parables for the Virtual*—over which the scholar hovers in a position of authority. Departing from a similar premise about the belated relationship between affect and cognition, Woolf and Fitzgerald focus on the inevitability with which such delays force their characters to look to others in order to make their affects controllable and intelligible. In the work of these novelists, such gaps and delays in affective self-knowledge become means of interrogating the ways in which a person tries to shore up, over and against the "virtual" dimensions of her mind and body, a sense of control over and awareness of herself. These writers show less interest in affect itself than in the mockery it makes of one's pretenses to coherent and independent self-knowledge, as well as in the contingent, interpersonally distributed forms of awareness with which it replaces one's supposed subjective autonomy.

Woolf's novel begins with a series of discoveries about its characters' affective inarticulacy.[4] To have an affect, *Mrs. Dalloway* suggests, does not in itself give one the ability to name it. Indeed, even when Woolf's characters feel ready to offer up their affects to others in a purposeful expressive gesture, they refer to these offerings clumsily and vaguely. In *Mr. Bennett and Mrs. Brown*, Woolf famously regrets the brevity of time she has to get to know the woman she calls Mrs. Brown or to express herself to her. "I had no time to explain why I felt it somewhat tragic, heroic, yet with a dash of the flighty, and fantastic, before the train stopped, and I watched her disappear, carrying her bag, into the vast blazing station." "And I have never seen her again," Woolf adds, "and I shall never know what became of her."[5] Being moved by someone or something, as Woolf depicts it here, sends one into a flurry of mental activity as one tries to discern one's reaction to this thing or being. It is, above all, an experience of cognitive belatedness: a temporary state of ignorance that holds in suspension even one's capacity to articulate the stakes of this encounter. A similar air of confused urgency animates *Mrs. Dalloway*. Woolf's characters experience their affects as revelations of how much they can be made to care about certain people or events. But having these affects does not in itself allow them to describe their significance to others or even to themselves. *Mrs. Dalloway* depicts its characters' occasional affective self-awareness as resulting someone else's (usually inadvertent) ability to provide some satisfactory, ready-made account of this affect in a way that does not require its bearer's own cognitive effort. These flashes of insight are, of course—as many critics before me have stated—expressions of Woolf's optimism about the possibility of harmony and interpersonal support in the communities she represents. But what Woolf depicts as such fortuitous moments do not usually correspond to more conventional notions of what it means to communicate with someone intimately or to be known by them. In Woolf's represented world, characters rarely discern the profound echoes that a word or gesture of theirs has in the mind and body of another. They pull each other out of their confusion and helplessness in a way that Woolf depicts as both much needed and vulnerably accidental, and as emphatically not tantamount to an actual, two-way act of mutual recognition or communication. Whether her characters would be capable of such genuinely empathic forms of mutual awareness is a question that *Mrs. Dalloway* does not, in the end, really address: these characters are too busy continually restoring their own selves to coherence and articulacy.

In early parts of the novel—as Clarissa prepares her party—her characters begin to reexperience their past affects toward the people they are going to meet there. They try to imagine what it will be like to see these people again, and wonder how these other people will feel up on seeing them. *Mrs. Dalloway* begins with Clarissa heading to the florist shop. As she walks through London, her body and mind fill with one affect after another. "What a lark!

What a plunge!" she famously exclaims in the opening line, and as she continues her walk this feeling of joy only increases.

Critics have long stressed the importance such surging affects have for Woolf's characters' sense of themselves. Jane Duran notes that, in Woolf's fiction, a person's life events only seem "real" to the extent that they spark such intense feelings: "What is real for a given character has a great deal to do with the importance of a given moment in the character's internal construction of self and time."[6] I follow Duran in arguing that these powerful affective experiences anchor Woolf's character construction. However, Woolf's representations of affects also highlight the sense of partiality that hovers on the margin of these acts of articulating a meaningful affective attachment. Massumi describes suddenly emergent feelings as inarticulable in the moment, but eventually illuminating. Woolf does not suggest that her characters' inarticulacies eventually dissipate on their own. Her narrative focuses on the awkward, always only partly satisfying means by which her characters rush to understand and express themselves. As characters try to make sense of their affects, they look around rather than into their minds and bodies, even though other people are not usually interested in elucidating their inward states or in communicating their impressions of them. Even an indifferent and inattentive other, *Mrs. Dalloway* suggests, often helps us understand our affects better than we ourselves are able to do despite the intense attention we often bestow on them.

Soon after the novel's opening, Clarissa feels a wave of affection for Peter Walsh, whom she saw briefly earlier that morning. Clarissa sometimes thinks she should have married Peter instead of her husband, Richard. She wonders: "For they might be parted for hundreds of years, she and Peter, she never wrote a letter and his were dry sticks; but suddenly it might come over her, If he were with me now what would he say?—some days, some sights bringing him back to her calmly" (7). The way Clarissa describes her continued attachment to Peter highlights that this affect can reemerge in her mind without any predictable cause. It suddenly makes him an important, continued part of her life, which can overwhelm her long after their original romance has ended. This passage also highlights that her former lover comes back to her not as a beautiful body or face, but as a trusted observer. Clarissa insists that—well as she might know Peter after so many years—she still cannot easily answer the question she poses herself here. The question enters her monologue between a dash and a comma, continuously with her ongoing train of associations. Yet the narrator also capitalizes it as a separate sentence, as if carried over from a different time and place. The answers that it might elicit in this new context remain unimaginable to her. Clarissa finds that she cannot reproduce the perspective Peter used to add to her sense of herself despite her fresh recollection of him: they saw each other earlier that morning.

The inarticulacy of Clarissa's affects and her felt need for someone else to make sense of her experiences return with even greater force toward the end of Clarissa's walk. Clarissa tries to imagine her life, as her current bodily and mental states illuminate it. She instantly begins to picture it as a gift that she could present to her parents. "For she was a child," is how Woolf's narrator channels her perspective, "throwing bread to the ducks, between her parents, and at the same time a grown woman coming to her parents who stood by the lake, holding her life in her arms which, as she neared them, grew larger and larger in her arms, until it became a whole life, a complete life, which she put down by them and said, 'This is what I have made of it! This!'" (43). At the end of her inward expression of feeling, Clarissa tries to give it more specificity. "And what had she made of it? What, indeed? sitting there sewing this morning with Peter" (43). Clarissa pictures her life as a coherent whole that she can carry around and give to others. Yet when she tries to describe the content of this life, all she can think of is the conversation she had with Peter a few hours earlier. Again, the presence of other people who might behold her life for her grounds Clarissa's fantasy of understanding herself. In the composite image she draws of her condensed experiences as an offering to her parents, Clarissa is standing beside her parents as a child and also approaching them as a grown woman. This doubling frames her past as something that is at once accessible and distant, as something that she both has within her and has yet to receive. The feeling that overwhelms her here is less a link to coherent memories and more an unfulfilled urge toward such a sense of coherence and completeness that only someone else's approving attention could give her.[7]

In the course of the novel that develops out of these opening scenes, Woolf represents this sense of dependence as a need that her characters have neither the capacity to do without nor to satisfy consistently and reliably. Their inarticulate anticipatory surges of affect soon find reflection in a series of unsuccessful acts of affective communication. When Woolf's characters draw someone else's attention to themselves, their exchanges are rarely comforting or illuminating as actual acts of mutual recognition. As the novel progresses into a series of meetings and lunches among Clarissa's party guests, these characters express their feelings toward each other through gifts of flowers, cakes, or expensive voyages. Clarissa's daughter Elizabeth tries to show her governess that she cares for her by buying her tea and pastries. Mr. Dalloway gives his wife a bouquet of roses in what he hopes to be a clear confession of love. The inner monologues in which these characters engage during such exchanges reveal that all these gifts—conventional though they are—fail to convey what they were intended to. Permanently dissatisfied with her ward's affections, the governess pours out onto the pastries torrents of inward insecurity. She takes Elizabeth's attempt to care for her as an act of indifference, and her disappointment comes through to Clarissa's daughter as petty, selfish hostility. As I mention in the opening of this chapter, Clarissa responds to her exchange with Richard with frustration at her domestic life. Focusing on incompatible details of their mutual expression—and failing to suspect the depth of this incompatibility—these characters absorb strikingly disparate interpretations of what they communicated to each other. In a mockery of confession, when these characters try to consciously open themselves up to someone else, they rarely succeed.

Peter Walsh, one of the more anxious characters in the novel, often notices these discrepancies and worries about them. He puzzles over how he might come across to others, as well as over his affects' general lack of clarity. When Peter leaves Clarissa's house after visiting her that morning, he wonders about the amount of affection that he may have shown her. The feelings that overwhelmed him when he saw Clarissa were incomprehensibly intense and urgent given how rarely they write to each other. He has traveled all the way from India to London for the sake of his young fiancée Daisy. The time and effort spent on this voyage should prove how much he loves her; he never went to such material lengths for Clarissa or anyone else. And yet, "For hours at a time (pray God that one might say these things without being overheard!), for hours and days he never thought of Daisy" (79). The balances of what he used to give or now gives to each of these women cannot explain the felt experience of how much Clarissa and Daisy matter to him from one moment to the next.

Peter's feeling of disempowerment peaks—and unexpectedly resolves itself—during an accidental encounter that follows his rumination. As he attempts to weigh his affects, Peter gives alms to an old woman. The woman is singing a popular tune: "With the bird-like freshness of the very aged she still twittered 'give me your hand and let me press it gently . . . and if some one should see, what matter they?' she demanded" (82). This song echoes with eerie precision the way Peter and Clarissa pressed each other's hands a few pages earlier. Does this woman begin to sing this song because she noticed Peter's distress, and guessed its origins? Woolf's novel does not suggest that as a plausible interpretation. But it does show that this accidental, anonymous encounter offers Peter a much more direct articulation of his feelings for Clarissa than he could have come up with on his own. Such fortuitous accidents—when an appropriate correlative of one's affect miraculously appears before one could have thought of it and even though the other person did not intend to provide it—usually give Woolf's characters much more clarity about themselves than do their extended attempts at introspection or self-expression. However much relief Woolf's characters take from such momentary acts of apparent understanding, these acts bear little resemblance to empathy or analysis in the conventional sense. These are not moments when—as in Charles Dickens or even in Woolf's more psychoanalytically minded contemporary D. H. Lawrence—an affect and its personal or archetypal significance travel directly from a person to another or from a surrounding environment into the self. In different people's minds, various facets of this affect's expression assume varying degrees of prominence and significance; even if two of her characters sometimes agree that a meaningful exchange took place within them, they would be surprised—as Woolf depicts them—to discover exactly why their interlocutor was moved by it.

Mrs. Dalloway stresses the importance of such interpersonal dependencies—contingent as they are—in its depictions of Septimus Smith. Woolf represents Septimus's descent into madness as caused by his enclosure in a set of inward affective correlatives that he cannot modify in response to the new people and places that now surround him. When we are introduced to him, Septimus struggles with intense guilt and remorse caused by his war experience. His wife, doctors, and friends have affective responses to his plight and often catch glimpses of Septimus's affects, given how little control he has over their expression. But these other people do not appreciate how complicated a personal mythology Septimus has constructed around his affects, and Septimus fails to grasp the incompatibility of this inward mythology with the middle-class domesticity that surrounds him. He eventually

falls into despair and then commits suicide because—as Woolf depicts him—
he trusts too naively that the meanings and contexts he associates with his
affects can be understood by others, and he cannot integrate other people's
presence into his sense of himself.

Throughout the novel, Septimus feels intensely watched. His guilt and
sadness surround him from all sides. Each gesture he makes refers back to
the war in which he let down his friend Evans. In each new space he enters,
he discovers reasons why he should be regretful or fearful: "The world
wavered and quivered and threatened to burst into flames. It is I who am
blocking the way, he thought. Was he not being looked at and pointed at;
was he not weighted there, rooted to the pavement, for a purpose? But for
what purpose?" (14–15). In a way that an analyst might call psychotic (in
contrast to Peter's neuroticism), Septimus tries to make amends of cosmic
proportions for having once fallen short of someone's expectations. Much
like Plath's speakers in *Ariel*, he lets the incompleteness of his affective self-
cognizance draw him into widening circles of associative thinking. He acts
as if not only his deceased comrade, but the whole "world," were still burning and shaking because of some mistake he might have made, about
which everyone must already know. His frantic attempts to figure out how
he came across to Evans in his moment of failure and how he could repent
for it prevent him from accommodating within his self-awareness the ways
he is perceived by anyone else. He cannot recognize how diminished the
current, immediate contexts of his affective expression have become; nor
does he acknowledge that their original significance is presently unintelligible. Instead, Septimus insists that the situations and objects around him
should be seen as complete expressions of the exaggerated fear and remorse
that haunt him. In his frustration, he eventually writes impassioned trea-
tises to share the grand meanings he attaches to his affects with the general
public.

These misrecognitions bear an added pathos because Septimus' affects
have their origins in major historical tragedies and debates of Woolf's time:
the First World War, psychoanalysis, trauma, changing gender stereotypes.
Septimus expresses more confidence than any other character in his capacity
to cognize this broad history and express it to others, along with larger
philosophical or political questions this history raises. But his inner world
also engulfs him so completely that he loses track of the possible impact that
his affects' immediate expression might have on anyone else, as well as of the

partial means by which he interprets and communicates them. The historical legitimacy of his feelings continually clashes with his unawareness of the contexts in which and means by which he unsuccessfully articulates them.

Septimus's struggle to resolve these disjunctures culminates in the scene leading up to his death. In this scene, a commonplace object he and his wife Rezia make together unexpectedly gives shape to his urge to commit suicide. Septimus and Rezia pick out patterns with which to decorate a hat. Rezia sees this as a moment of hope that they can once again share their lost marital intimacy. "How it rejoiced her that! Not for weeks had they laughed like this together, poking fun privately like married people. What she meant was that if Mrs. Filmer had come in, or Mrs. Peters or anybody they would not have understood what she and Septimus were laughing at" (143). Even as Rezia "rejoice[s]" at how small and private a thing they are doing together, Septimus veers into unchecked self-aggrandizement: "It was wonderful. Never had he done anything which made him feel so proud. It was so real, it was so substantial, Mrs. Peters' hat" (144).

When Septimus decides to kill himself a few pages later, he subjects his own body to the kinds of middlebrow, domestic considerations that he and Rezia previously applied to Mrs. Peters's hat. He hurriedly deliberates which part of the world he ought to mark, and how, with his suicide. "He considered Mrs. Filmer's nice clean bread knife with 'Bread' carved on the handle. Ah, but one mustn't spoil that. The gas fire?" (149).[8] In the end, right as Rezia returns to the room with his doctor, Septimus jumps out the window. Rezia and the doctor behold the suicide with shock and incomprehension. The effect of this scene comes, in great part, from its eerie resemblance to Peter's self-recognition in a popular song. Septimus finds some definite shape for his affective expression not through careful introspection, but by joining in and imitating someone else's acts of expressive competence. This self-discovery is chilling in its randomness, especially since Rezia has been trying to help her husband become more aware of his affects for weeks on end, in the hope that they might resume a happy life together.

Clarissa's party, which comes soon after this scene, does not resolve these issues of incomplete, not fully controlled, affective self-knowledge. However, it shows perhaps most emphatically that these characters' inability to agree on the significance of each other's affective expression does not prevent them from being nurtured by each other's presence. In a way on which the later novels and poems I examine build considerably, Woolf launches into something of a celebration of her characters' accidental, outwardly induced flickers of self-awareness. Though the irony with which she represents these fortuitous accidents does not dissipate, they are emphatically depicted as her characters' best chance at a less fraught and confusing sense of themselves.

Throughout the party Clarissa tries to make others happy; she calls it her "offering" (122). Woolf describes the effects of Clarissa's skills as a hostess, but never shows her exercising these skills directly. Instead, the narrative jumps between Clarissa's consciousness and the minds of others in whom her presence evokes alternate feelings of irritation and pity. Clarissa herself does not discern how she comes across to all these people, or she recognizes their reactions only retroactively and partly. She wanders around the room, believing that this party is a great success, even as most of those around her stew in incompletely articulated resentments and annoyances.

Amid this gathering, Clarissa hears about Septimus's suicide. She observes the ripples of discomfort and shock it creates in her guests. Picking up on this changed social ambiance, she finds herself thinking about his death and the affects that might have accompanied it. Clarissa begins by imagining the physical experience Septimus must have gone through: "Always her body went through it first, when she was told, suddenly, of an accident." Then she speculates about Septimus's possible motivations: "Death was an attempt to communicate; people feeling the impossibility of reaching the center which, mystically, evaded them; closeness drew apart; rapture faded, one was alone. There was an embrace of death" (184). By the end of this inner monologue, she finds between herself and Septimus a feeling of kinship: "She felt somehow very like him, the young man who had killed himself" (186). Septimus's death, she also discovers, reaffirms the joy she felt earlier that morning: "She felt glad that he had done it; thrown it away. The clock was striking. The leaden circles dissolved in the air. He made her feel the beauty; made her feel the fun" (186).

Septimus "made her feel the fun": this inner monologue is obviously cruel to him, and the narrator reports it with considerable irony. Septimus, who "threw away" his life, apparently makes Clarissa feel reconciled to having 'thrown away' an afternoon of questionably successful party preparation. News of Septimus's suicide, and the effect it has on others, give Clarissa an unanticipated opportunity to reinterpret the affects she has felt throughout the day—including ones of partial loss and isolation—as positive and self-affirming. Hearing about Septimus's despair from the guests around her lifts her up more than receiving formal expressions of joy and gratitude from them. Woolf's narrator does not, of course, represent Clarissa and Septimus here as understanding each other from beyond the grave. Clarissa's capacity to take up Septimus's affects and interpret them in this fashion affirms his suicide as a source of a potential life philosophy for her, as well as showing casual indifference toward what his inward sense of himself might have been.

Susan Bennett Smith and David Neal Miller, following many other critics, propose that this scene highlights Clarissa's capacity to feel for a man whose experience is drastically different from hers.[9] Martha Nussbaum makes an even stronger—not merely epistemic but ethical—claim about these affective resonances. She argues that, in such moments of empathic closeness, characters momentarily overcome their selfishness and form a community within this otherwise isolating social space: "The mysterious grand problem of other minds thus has, here," Nussbaum claims, "a mundane humble tentative answer . . . [:] by working patiently to defeat shame, selfish anxiety, and the desire for power, it is sometimes possible for some people to get knowledge of one thing or another thing about some other people; and they can sometimes allow one thing or another thing about themselves to be known."[10]

I agree with Nussbaum that questions of empathy and connectedness are at stake in this passage. But Woolf makes it suspect to believe that these characters direct their inward efforts primarily to getting to "know" another person better. Woolf's novel also does not suggest that one could describe such forms of engagement as empathy, even though her characters often take comfort in believing that. Instead, such passages highlight the eagerness with which a character might notice someone else's affective expression and use it as a means of supplementing her own insufficient awareness about how she feels. The picture of interpersonal communication that emerges from such episodes emphasizes these characters' interdependence, even as it depicts this interdependence as far less voluntary and knowing than Nussbaum proposes. It stems not only from the kind of open-mindedness that Nussbaum lauds, but also from attempts to deal with cognitive delays of the kind described by Massumi. These characters look to each other because they need such outward reflections and models to help them feel more in control of their own selves.

A final instance of such affective interdependence occurs at the very end of *Mrs. Dalloway*. Only a few hours after Peter has decided that Clarissa is "false and wooden," he feels toward her the elation with which the novel ends: "What is this terror? what is this ecstasy? he thought to himself. What is it that fills me with extraordinary excitement?" Peter asks. He looks for a source of the "terror," "ecstasy," and "excitement" he feels and finds it at the top of the staircase. "It is Clarissa, he said. For there she was" (194).

Throughout the day, Clarissa and Peter could not express their feelings for each other satisfyingly. Now, when Peter—and arguably also Clarissa—least expect it, and when the party is basically over, he brims with a happiness that he finally, unapologetically, attributes to seeing her. We do not know if Clarissa notices Peter's radiance or why his feelings toward her are reignited now, in particular. Peter's thoughts fly not only toward Clarissa but also toward his own mind and body, of which he can now finally, triumphantly make sense: "For there she was."

The vertigo pervading Woolf's final description of Peter echoes Massumi's accounts of bodily experience in *Parables for the Virtual*. Massumi stresses that our bodies are fragmented and reshaped by our always retroactive and partial access to them. "In a very real sense," he says, "the body is always-already obsolete, has been obsolete an infinite number of times and will be obsolete countless more—as many times as there are adaptations and inventions."[11] By centering her representations of affective experiences on questions of intersubjectivity, Woolf reveals an interpersonal dimension of these experiences that Massumi's account—which focuses on solitary, retroactive self-knowledge—does not probe. Disconcerted by their inability to take independent stock of their affects, Woolf's characters find that these affects make them dependent on other people in unpredictable ways. The living rooms in which her characters gather provide a model both of the inevitability of such dependencies and of the naïveté of believing that a person can fully control or orchestrate them—or that the seeming insights her characters draw from each other amount to mutual knowledge and care in a more conventional sense. They paint a picture of the compromises and contingencies on which a person must depend in order not to succumb—as the solitary speakers of Plath and Stevens sometimes do—to a sense that her affective conundrums are simply, universally unresolvable.

Like Woolf's, Fitzgerald's fiction centers on questions of mutual and introspective affective awareness. Ambiguities about how much of one's own affects or their effects on others a person can notice give form and focus to his character construction. Fitzgerald's novels highlight their protagonists' limited capacity to control how their self-expression comes across to other people or to impose on others their own interpretations of their ongoing affective exchanges.[12] Fitzgerald infuses his depictions of these affective exchanges with a cruelty and bitterness that Woolf's fiction generally lacks. Woolf celebrates the possibility of any interpersonal support at all in one's efforts at understanding one's affects. For Fitzgerald, whose main characters are generally less adept than Woolf's at garnering accidental bits of insight from others, a person's inability to know how he appears to those around him, and especially to incorporate into his self-awareness the weaknesses and blind spots other people see in him, is a source of constant, frequently tragic affective overreaches and miscommunications. His protagonists are surrounded by other people's responsiveness to them as by a halo of goodwill that they cannot properly discern as they fixate on one or two individuals whose affects they cannot calibrate to theirs. These missed opportunities are made to seem all the more unfortunate because of the vapidity of most of these characters' life goals: Fitzgerald's characters inhabit a superficial world of upper-class snobbery in which their affects mostly come into conflict with other people's pleasures and pastimes.[13]

Like Woolf, Fitzgerald represents his characters as aspiring orchestrators of social gatherings. His protagonists treat these gatherings as potential opportunities to wrest control over their affects' meanings and outward effects. As they invite others into their living rooms and ballrooms, Jay Gatsby and Dick Diver aspire to become stage managers of how their guests feel about them: "His voice, with some faint Irish melody running through it, wooed the world," Fitzgerald's narrator says of Dick in *Tender Is the Night*.[14] Much like Clarissa Dalloway, Fitzgerald's protagonists carefully set up the environments in which they want their acts of affective expression and communication to take place. They are then confused by their interlocutors' capacity to disregard the affective narratives imposed upon them and shocked by the ease with which bystanders notice fears, confusions, and vulnerabilities they were trying to hide.

To bring out these inconsistencies in inward and interpersonal affective awareness, *The Great Gatsby* frequently draws attention to the slapdash quality of the objects on which Gatsby leans to express his feelings. When *The Great Gatsby* begins, Gatsby's lavish weekly parties charm and mystify Fitzgerald's narrator Nick Carraway. Nick wanders into Gatsby's library at one of these parties and hears another man describe the volumes his host has collected. "What thoroughness! What realism!" this other man exclaims because the library is walled not merely with imitations of book spines, but with real books. "Knew where to stop, too—didn't cut the pages" (46). These uncut books provide an ironic counterpart to Gatsby's insistence that he was once a student at Oxford. Despite their cost, Gatsby's attempts at refashioning himself as a gentleman bear marks of inattentive haste that others easily see.[15] They highlight the grand ambition of Gatsby's displays of his worthiness of Daisy. However, they also begin to hint at the facility with which these displays will be dismantled by the Ivy League–educated Tom Buchanan, whose polish is the work of many communities and generations. The rushed, comic grandeur of these bookcases bears a kind of inarticulacy that might remind one of the imagined "gift" that Mrs. Dalloway tries to give to her parents at the beginning of Woolf's novel. But unlike Woolf's protagonist, for whom the act of showing this gift to someone else is a crucial component of how she hopes to make it intelligible, Gatsby refuses to admit that he might not have fully understood and controlled all of the undertones and shades of his affective expression.

T. Austin Graham finds a similar sense of unsounded, incomplete overlap between characters' feelings and their sensory correlates in the music that plays in the background of *The Great Gatsby*'s love scenes. When Gatsby and Daisy first meet at Nick's, Gatsby puts "Three O'clock in the Morning" on the gramophone. The song's lyrics—the story of a couple reunited after a long absence—ostensibly resonate with the melancholy and romantic mood of this scene. But as Graham describes it, this resonance is only superficial: "By the time McCormack [the soloist] delivers his full-throated, chivalric plea—'say that there soon will be a honeymoon'—the song has come in many ways to seem too flashy, too extravagant, and, above all else, too literal for what is otherwise a brooding and ambiguous scene." To have chosen this music reveals Gatsby's blindness both to the current state of his relationship with Daisy, and to his affects' own darker undertones of fear and self-hatred. Trusting the terms and expressions he enthusiastically gives for his love, he is swept up by them into a sense of himself and his world that is ever more divorced from reality.

The novel brings out these various aspects of Gatsby's inward and intersubjective unawareness poignantly when Daisy finally visits his home and he showers her with his shirts in Nick's presence. The colorful pile of fabrics constitutes yet another lavish display of the lifestyle he can now afford to give her. In Gatsby's mind, it also represents the many days he has spent longing for her, as well as the long future he hopes they might have together: "He took out a pile of shirts and began throwing them, one by one, before us, shirts of sheer linen and thick silk and fine flannel, which lost their folds as they fell and covered the table in many-colored disarray," Nick says. "While we admired he brought more and the soft rich heap mounted higher—shirts with stripes and scrolls and plaids in coral and apple-green and lavender and faint orange, with monograms of Indian blue" (94).

These shirts have a powerful effect on Daisy. "Suddenly, with a strained sound, Daisy bent her head into the shirts and began to cry stormily" (94). Her crying is the first dramatic expression of feeling she has allowed herself since she was reunited with Gatsby. "'They're such beautiful shirts,' she sobbed, her voice muffled in the thick folds. 'It makes me sad because I've never seen such—such beautiful shirts before'" (94). Daisy and Gatsby laugh and cry like children, admiring each other's beauty and affluence. But as W. T. Lhamon Jr. points out, this scene reveals perhaps most clearly that Gatsby does not know how to fit himself into Daisy's class background, or to imagine for his love a sense of stability and permanence. Instead of the upper-class order that Daisy's circles create around themselves, he only knows to display his wealth in disorganized, massive piles; in Lhamon's words, "When Gatsby attempts to emulate with his hotel the series of gestures that elaborate the Buchanans, the result is a heap of shirts, of rooms, of guests—expensive disarray."[16] This "disarray" further prefigures the vagueness and ephemerality of the promises that Daisy and Gatsby go on to make to each other, and which Gatsby assumes to be both clear and binding.

Ross Posnock calls this display of love "duplicitous": "The use of language to establish or present one's identity to another tends toward the duplicitous, the indeterminate, and nowhere more so than in moments of supposedly sincere revelation."[17] But to describe this scene and others like it merely as a sequence of lies overlooks the earnestness with which all three characters—Nick, Gatsby, and Daisy—temporarily give in, amid these shirts, to intense feelings of sadness, love, and admiration. It also overlooks the way in which Nick's retroactive eloquence and sensitivity is being contrasted with Daisy's inarticulate, shallow outburst. This scene instantiates not simply a failed, but a multiply misinterpreted and miscognized expression of feeling. Gatsby does not realize whose enduring attentiveness and admiration he is winning through his awkward displays of wealth. Nor does he notice—as Nick does—how transparently such showy gestures reveal his inability to give his passions a more coherent future-oriented articulation.

As the novel progresses, Fitzgerald's tone in narrating these affective exchanges grows darker. After investing great amounts of attention and wealth in his beloved, Gatsby attempts to cash in on this investment. He then finds that the grand gestures through which he tried to prove his love to Daisy did not seem nearly as definitive or all-encompassing to her. In a climactic sequence of confrontations between Gatsby, Daisy, and Tom Buchanan, Gatsby tries to make Daisy say she never loved her husband, and she refuses to do so: "'Oh, you want too much!' she cried to Gatsby. 'I love you now— isn't that enough? I can't help what's past.' She began to sob helplessly. 'I did love him once—but I loved you too'" (132). In response to this outburst, Tom insists that "there's things between Daisy and me that you'll never know, things that neither of us can ever forget" (132). Gatsby falters; as the narrator puts it, "The words seemed to bite physically into [him]" (132).[18] As Fitzgerald depicts him, he is at least as shocked by the ease with which Daisy lets go of him as by the intimate mutual awareness Tom still shares with Daisy: an awareness that Gatsby's lavish parties were supposed to render irrelevant, and about which by this point he seems to have entirely forgotten.

In the end, Gatsby's passionate attachments do not find recognition among people to whom he intended to communicate them; but they are partly noticed and appreciated by other, secondary characters, to whose attentiveness to him he was oblivious. Nick and Gatsby's father are distraught by his death, even as Daisy retroactively pretends never to have associated with him in the first place. "So we beat on, boats against the current, borne back ceaselessly into the past," Nick comments lyrically on his friend's death in the novel's last, and perhaps most famous, lines. The pathos of this ending lies partly in how much Gatsby has come to mean to the narrator: Nick elevates his fate to the level of a grand philosophical exemplar of effort and loneliness, implicitly also making his own friendship with Gatsby sound like a major, momentous landmark in his own life. These last lines also take their eerie power from how little Gatsby ever relied on or inquired about the insights that Nick painstakingly collected about him, many of which so greatly exceeded the eloquence of his own self-expression. Like Woolf, Fitzgerald represents his characters as sources of potential affective support and inspiration for each other, but also as consistently unaware of whom their presence in any given environment touches most. Unlike Woolf's characters, Fitzgerald's are depressingly ignorant of how much their accounts of their feelings would benefit from such outward responses or models.

Tender Is the Night continues this engagement with incomplete, belated forms of affective awareness.[19] The couple at its center is bound by a long-standing marriage, which raises the stakes of their failures of mutual recognition. The man in this couple believes himself to be highly aware of his own affects and capable of knowing and controlling those of his wife. His inability to succeed at either of these self-appointed tasks becomes all the more obvious and humiliating because he is a psychoanalyst and his wife is his former patient. This sense of humiliation is further deepened by the tone with which Fitzgerald narrates this story: under this narrator's cold, ironic gaze, Dick's narcissistic failures to reach beyond the narrow limits of his affective awareness accumulate into a didactic thesis about his cognitive incompetence and the many occasions he squanders to transcend it with the help of others.

Fitzgerald introduces his main characters, Dick and Nicole Diver, during a party at the beach. Rosemary, a young ingénue through whose perspective we first see them, instantly lets the couple occupy center stage in her narrative of herself. "Rosemary felt that this swim would be the typical one of her life," the narrator comments as Rosemary steps into the water with Dick and Nicole; "the one that would always pop up in her memory at the mention of swimming" (19). The novel then follows these characters' interactions at more or less crowded parties, teas, and meals, during which Dick and Nicole—and especially Dick—constantly court and often also attain such outbursts of unconditional admiration from others. It seems, at first, as if we witnessed in this couple a more successful version of the hypercontrolled social success Jay Gatsby yearned for: Dick seems aware of, and very much in control of, the self-image he projects toward others and the ways others interpret it.

But this initial impression topples quickly: and indeed, the novel devotes most of its rhetorical energies to showing exactly how and why it fails. In a series of increasingly ironic third-person descriptions—which give the plot that follows a quasi-scientific air of inevitability—Fitzgerald's narrator diagnoses Dick as a person with a surprisingly narrow scope of affective awareness, combined with exceedingly specific, high expectations about how others should feel about him. Dick, as the narrator near-caricatures him, cares about little beyond reinforcing and confirming his overblown, fragile self-love; he is unable to absorb any experiences or events that might contradict it. The narrator asserts this superficial narcissism of Dick's attachments in a long passage only a few sections after the novel's triumphant opening:

> To be included in Dick Diver's world for a while was a remarkable experience: people believed he made special reservations about them, recognizing the proud uniqueness of their destinies, buried under the compromises of how many years. . . . So long as they subscribed to it completely, their happiness was his preoccupation, but at the first flicker of doubt as to its all-inclusiveness he evaporated before their eyes, leaving little communicable memory as to what he had said or done. (28)

Tender Is the Night is, arguably, less aesthetically successful and certainly less suspenseful than *The Great Gatsby* because of how often it resorts to such paraphrases, in which Dick's eventual demise is detachedly and insistently predicted. In a way that constantly undercuts Dick's perception of himself as Nicole's omniscient analyst, Fitzgerald's narrator circumscribes and mocks the limits of Dick's capacity for awareness. As the narrator insists in this early passage, Dick's sensitivity has a surprisingly small radius: he seeks in others little except reflections of his own preexisting high self-regard. His attentiveness to other people is, the narrator further points out, contingent on their willingness to let him feel in control of the narratives they live out together. When this willingness is withdrawn, Dick simply "evaporates," without even leaving his former friends any precise memories of himself: a detail that captures at once Dick's lack of deep, lasting commitments and the generic nature of the support he provides to other people, keen as they often are to perceive this support as highly particularized. Much of the story that follows elaborates on this early description as if on a thesis that its plot illustrates. If *The Great Gatsby* reckons with Gatsby's blinding passions somewhat nostalgically and with marked sympathy, *Tender Is the Night* is poised to dismantle Dick as an ever-flatter avatar of irredeemable cognitive overconfidence and solipsism.

Dick's capacity to stage and orchestrate his interactions with others falls into crisis when he begins to overextend himself: as he tries to elicit unwavering admiration and submissiveness from too many different people at once, the repetitive nature of the gestures he extends toward them and the vagueness of his perception of them begin to cause him to lose touch with reality. It becomes increasingly clear that Dick cannot discern other people's responses to him very clearly. He misses both these other people's warning signs of dissatisfaction and their attempts to show toward him an empathy that is not simply adulation. Amid these aggregating misapprehensions, a widening gulf emerges between Dick's inward sense of himself as an admirable person and others' perceptions of him as alternately annoying and pitiable. In a way that might remind one of Woolf's Septimus Smith, he becomes defined by an increasingly naïve, desperate insistence that he knows himself and his relations to the world beyond him completely and precisely. Meanwhile, his practiced social graces start to seem ever less effective and ever more undiscerningly mechanical.

Dick's love affair with Rosemary—a young actress whom he and Nicole meet at the beach—illustrates his deterioration midway through the novel. As the narrator depicts it, Dick cannot tell his pleasure at being loved by Rosemary and by Nicole apart from each other. Instead, every new expression of Dick's infatuation with Rosemary blurs it with his love for his wife— and the two relations congeal, in Dick's mind, into closely related ways of managing his need for intimacy and self-control. Rosemary begins her film career by starring in a film called *Daddy's Girl*, and she makes Dick and Nicole watch this film with her. She is much younger than Dick; he also frequently calls her a child. These details make this relationship resemble a Freudian enactment of Nicole's trauma (as if Dick were attempting to become a version of Nicole's sexually abusive father), which is also how critics have frequently read this subplot. Yet, in the actual rhetoric Fitzgerald uses to depict it, Dick's infatuation with Rosemary merely makes both his old and his new love seem uncannily generic. Here, for instance, as Rosemary and Dick finally consummate their attraction, the narrator follows Dick's impression of Rosemary's face and limbs as they draw closer to him: "He breathed over her shoulder and turned her insistently about; she kissed him several times, her face getting big every time she came close, her hands holding him by the shoulders" (155). The description fragments Rosemary into disjointed body parts. These body parts absorb and reflect Dick's breathing, becoming surprisingly, almost grotesquely large as they draw near. The narrator's phrases, which channel Dick's perspective, are determinedly vague. Dick becomes fully immersed in his affects without showing much awareness of their origins and effects. His phenomenological account of this encounter, as the narrator channels it, leaves no room within it for anything like Rosemary's own self-expression or even her individual features, except in the most impersonal terms. It does not even carry within itself a sense of Dick's own stakes in this encounter.

The progress of this love affair does not lead Dick to an increased cognizance of Rosemary or Nicole, or of his attitudes toward either of them. But it does reveal that, the more urgently he tries to clarify and stabilize his affects, the less often he succeeds at making these affects intelligible to others or even to himself. Shortly before Nicole divorces Dick, the police have to restrain him from assaulting a taxi driver. The drunken, indignant Dick calls out, "I want to make a speech! . . . I want to explain to these people how I raped a five-year-old girl" (235). Pamela Boker reads this as a crucial moment of psychoanalytic transference: "By accepting Nicole's transference love, Dick has become psychologically engaged in her incestuous drama and, through identification with her father, has become the perpetrator of the original act of violence against her."[20] I partly agree with Boker that this Freudian reading is not far from the narrator's mind. But I further draw attention—as another important focus of this scene—to the way in which the guilt Dick expresses easily fizzles out into a non sequitur. The people around Dick do not understand what he is talking about, and everyone's attention turns to his current misbehavior. Even Fitzgerald's readers cannot know, based on this description, whether Dick is referring to Nicole or Rosemary. He might be mockingly chastising himself for a brief affair with a younger woman, or melodramatically taking the whole weight of Nicole's trauma onto himself—and the inarticulacy of this confession is at least as striking and chilling as either of these possibilities in turn.

Amid these vague attachments, Dick fails to notice that his wife has begun to tire of him and that the hold he used to have on her is slipping. "That he no longer controlled her—did he know that?" Nicole asks herself. "She felt as sorry for him as she had sometimes felt for [their friend] Abe North and his ignoble destiny, sorry as for the helplessness of infants and the old" (301). Turning the tables on Dick—who frequently referred to both her and his lover Rosemary as children—Nicole expresses her concern for him in ways that show how easily she sees through his performances of confidence and how far she is from being seduced by them. Soon after she leaves him for a lover, Dick is also astonished to realize that Franz, his collaborator at the hospital he runs, has noticed his deepening depression and the drinking problem into which it propelled him. This collaborator asks Dick to resign at very short notice, assuming that Dick already knows about the precariousness of his professional standing. But "Dick had not expected to come to a decision so quickly," the narrator comments; "nor was he prepared for Franz's so ready acquiescence in the break" (256).

In a way that deepens this sense of narrative irony or malice even further, Fitzgerald also stresses moments when Dick's self-expression does make him seem likeable again to other people, although he is usually unable to benefit or learn from it. These surprising connections—of which Nicole's pity, expressed above, is one example—redirect the novel's attention to contingent forms of interpersonal affective awareness in parallel to the progression of *The Great Gatsby*. As Dick's career and marriage unravel, he does not simply lose the affection of the people he loves. Instead, in an echo of the reactions that Gatsby's passionate attachments find after his death, he elicits flickers of recognition and attentiveness from others through certain aspects of his affective expression that he cannot consciously control and does not seem to acknowledge as parts of himself. Shortly before the ending of the novel and Dick's final breakup with Nicole, he tries to make himself attractive to her by lifting a man at the beach: "When the men had ridden long enough to find their balance, Dick knelt, and putting the back of his neck in the other man's crotch, found the rope through his legs, and slowly began to rise" (283). The trick fails and Dick and this other man both fall back into the water. Dick cannot hide his embarrassment. At that point, Nicole finally attends to him: "Nicole watched for a sight of Dick's face. It was full of annoyance as she expected, because he had done the thing with ease only two years ago" (284). As Dick attempts the trick a second time, the narrator starts to focalize this passage through Nicole, turning what had been a description of her detachment from him into an expression of increasing, surprised intimacy: "He could not rise. Nicole saw him shift his position and strain upward again but at the instant when the weight of his partner was full upon his shoulders he became immovable" (285).

Fitzgerald's narrator has never before described Dick lifting anything besides the body of a young lover. Dick has also never before used physical force except, unsuccessfully, when being overpowered by a group of policemen. In effect, strength has not figured as his particular character trait. Here—after Dick has lost his credentials as a faithful husband and a potentially brilliant doctor—a random, failed bodily exercise makes his humiliation unexpectedly present to others.[21] The scene gains its pathos both from the triviality of its occasion and from Dick's failure—once again—to notice the opportunity it gives him to reestablish a bond to the two women who watch him. Preoccupied as he is with the approval-seeking trick that he cannot accomplish, he lets this brief moment of respite lapse as everyone returns to their separate hotel rooms for the evening.

The final sequence of the novel reads similarly. After the breakup of his marriage, Dick continues to repeat the same social and personal errors in strikingly parallel circumstances. He never completely loses his ability to become admired, however diminished (and given the prior course of Dick's life, unsatisfying) a form this admiration takes; yet it also becomes quite clear that he cannot revise his repertoire of social graces, let alone his life goals, in response to the poor effects they ultimately tend to elicit in others:

> Dick opened an office in Buffalo, but evidently without success. Nicole did not find out what the trouble was, but she heard a few months later that he was in a little town named Batavia, N.Y., practicing general medicine, and later that he was in Lockport, doing the same thing. By accident she heard more about his life there than anywhere: that he bicycled a lot, was much admired by the ladies, and always had a big stack of papers on his desk that were known to be an important treatise on some medical subject, almost in process of completion. He was considered to have fine manners and once made a good speech at a public health meeting on the subject of drugs; but he became entangled with a girl who worked in a grocery store, and he was also involved in a lawsuit about some medical question; so he left Lockport.
>
> After that he didn't ask for the children to be sent to America and didn't answer when Nicole wrote asking him if he needed money. In the last letter she had from him he told her that he was practicing in Geneva, New York, and she got the impression that he had settled down with some one to keep house for him. She looked up Geneva in an atlas and found it was in the heart of the Finger Lakes Section and considered a pleasant place. Perhaps, so she liked to think, his career was biding its time, again like Grant's in Galena; his latest note was post-marked from Hornell, New York, which is some distance from Geneva and a very small town; in any case he is almost certainly in that section of the country, in one town or another. (314–315)

Tracing an asymptotic course of minor failures, Dick vainly seeks to restore his prior sense of self-importance within diminishing communities.

Meanwhile, unbeknown to him, his estranged wife keeps track of these successes and mishaps. Needless to say, this is not a happy ending. It highlights Dick's inability to recognize and nurture the ways in which other people do care for him. This ending also models perhaps most forcefully the notion of personhood around which Fitzgerald's novel oscillates. Fitzgerald's protagonists flounder in their mistaken belief that they are privileged, reliable centers of insight into their affects and these affects' expression. Their fatal flaw—played as tragedy in Gatsby's case and as farce in Dick's—consists not only in the indifference that those they love are capable of showing them but also in their own inability to benefit from potential moments of responsiveness or recognition that they had not expected or solicited.

Within the "living rooms" to which Woolf and Fitzgerald return throughout the plots of these novels, both authors depict affects as experiences that make one's mind and body partly open to, and dependent on, others in ways that cannot be controlled through efforts at independent self-awareness. Within these networks of never fully overlapping forms of cognizance, the flickers of clarity that Woolf's and Fitzgerald's characters achieve about themselves remain rare and contingent. Departing from a premise much like Massumi's—that affective experiences are often not immediately and completely noticeable to the bodies and minds experiencing them—the two authors develop from this basic insight an exploration of the degree to which even our most basic affective sense of ourselves and our affects' ties to reality depend on the witting or unwitting cooperation of others. Living rooms also provide Woolf and Fitzgerald with means of showing that the forms of affective awareness to which their characters aspire are not consistently achievable even in very familiar and structured settings. Though Woolf responds to these realizations with cautious optimism—and Fitzgerald with an angry resentment that deepens in his successive works—the kinds of cognitive dependency and disempowerment on which these writers focus are analogous.

Proust and Baldwin, whose novels I examine in the following chapter, explore a similar suspicion about our incomplete autonomous affective awareness. Unlike either of these preceding novelists, they represent this suspicion as inducing an increased desire for withdrawal from social life. Their protagonists are drawn to the rare and contingent contexts in which they can avoid having their affects exposed to, and complicated by, others. They privilege these moments, which they can usually only attain in small, very constrained settings, as instances when their minds and bodies temporarily seem up to the task of making sense of themselves. These protagonists wonder what it might say about themselves that they only find moments of cognitive respite—when they seem entirely aware of their affects—in tightly enclosed spaces that afford them total or near-total solitude and freedom from outward stimuli. Lingering with a dream of introspection as something one could undertake entirely on one's own, Proust and Baldwin depict the extremely constrained and controlled outward conditions under which one might believe oneself to be such an independently introspective being. For both writers, this sense of exceptionality and dependence becomes all the more fraught because they refuse merely to dismiss such solitary insights as insignificant. They are sources out of which a new form of aesthetics or politics can take shape, vulnerable as these aesthetics and politics are made to seem by their necessary reliance on such outward constraints.

Chapter 3

Bedroom

Marcel Proust and James Baldwin

When Marcel Proust's *In Search of Lost Time* begins, the narrator is waking up inside a bedroom. In semidarkness he tries to recall the shapes of the
objects that surround him. From these shapes he begins to divine in what
room—of the many rooms he has known—he has now found himself. For
a brief period—before he is quite awake and before the sun has risen—his
mind and body totter on the brink of many past and present chambers: "I
had seen first one and then another of the rooms in which I had slept during
my life . . . rooms in winter . . . rooms in summer . . . or sometimes the Louis
XIV room . . ." (1:7–8).[1] These walls enclose Marcel's easily ignited affects
and help elucidate them. They also serve to keep out other people, whose
presence often confuses this narrator's self-understanding. Bedrooms allow
him to inhabit a world in which his consciousness encounters no resistances
or rivals to interpreting the affects expressed or experienced there.

Whereas Woolf's endlessly generous hostesses and Fitzgerald's frivolous
socialites pride themselves on curating spaces of social intercourse, Proust's
and James Baldwin's more introverted protagonists frequently retreat into

the privacy of their bedrooms. These narrow confines give their affects more coherence than they could ever have in a crowded salon, let alone in an open public sphere. Small rooms allow these characters to maintain the temporary illusion that their minds and bodies are easily, autonomously self-knowing. Within these rooms they also reach insights about themselves that they could not hold onto in a wider social space. Even as they affirm the value of many of these insights, Proust and Baldwin dismantle their characters' illusions of independent self-knowledge by showing how many favorable outward conditions they require to make this experience temporarily sustainable. Like the authors I explore in the two earlier chapters, Proust and Baldwin depict their characters as holding onto a relatively conservative notion of subjectivity and introspection. But unlike these other authors, they do not merely subject this notion to skeptical critique. Indeed, they complicate the issue of affective self-awareness by suggesting that sometimes one's communities might be not just indifferent but openly hostile to an affect in whose resolution one has great stakes. The partial forms of affective awareness that a person achieves in isolation from others might not simply be wrong, or discardable. However, the effort it requires to develop such an awareness, and hold onto it, is unsustainable for their protagonists outside of highly favorable conditions of confinement and comfort that are very difficult for them to find. The autonomously introspective self is, in both authors' novels, an artifice that requires careful outward maintenance; while Proust and Baldwin highlight the benefits that can come from maintaining this artifice, they also stress its precariousness and its intrinsic limitations.

I read these forms of ambivalence as important undercurrents to what is otherwise rightly perceived as these authors' insistence on affirming idiosyncratic and socially rebellious forms of self-expression. Proust is indisputably a self-confident, effusive aesthete; and Baldwin just as indisputably asserts the value of generous self-love and mutual love. But alongside these better-known preoccupations, both authors are also concerned with the circumstances under which one can hold such a view of oneself in one's mind and believe in it; they also see these circumstances as much more contingent and beyond one's control than it might seem. To go out into the larger world, they both suggest, is to instantly let one's self-awareness mingle with, and be reshaped by, other people's responses. Even as such distributed self-awareness is necessary for any sense of orientation within a broader social and material sphere, it also restricts their characters' capacity to embrace things about themselves that other people do not care about. Both novelists insist on the precariousness of their protagonists' capacity to see themselves as independent, reliable arbiters of their affective states. They also express concern with how trifling these protagonists' more socially subversive or uncommon affects frequently seem because their rise to awareness cannot take place anywhere except in a very narrow and isolated space. The books these authors write are, in this sense, idealistic efforts to create a space that is both private and companionate, into which the narrator can invite a reader but in which he can also remain undisturbed by anyone—and in which the various foreshortenings that the illusion of autonomous affective self-awareness requires can thus be somehow acknowledged and partly neutralized.

I examine Proust's and Baldwin's novels in conjunction with Sianne Ngai's notion of "minor" affects. Ngai studies a group of affects such as paranoia, anxiety, and envy, that superficially come across merely as cognitive distortions of their surroundings.[2] She claims that these ostensibly marginal affects need to be examined in their own right because even "minor" affective experiences can teach us much about ourselves and the environments that shape us. This chapter does not assimilate the affects Proust and Baldwin represent to Ngai's particular categories, which also include disgust and animatedness. However, it engages with Ngai's insistence on the specter of triviality as an important, frequently overlooked dimension of affective experience. I ask what happens when the critic-figure herself—rather than just her subjects—fears that she might be moved by, and maybe even in thrall to, an affect that can only find affirmation and clarification in very constrained settings that actively forestall the possibility of other people's challenges or counter-perspectives.

Ngai treats minor affects from a detached, third-person perspective. She describes them as experiences that the texts and art objects she studies can represent and induce in their audience, but not as aspects of the condition of the person who analyzes them. Studying minor affects from such a third-person viewpoint allows Ngai to defend these affects as oblique insights into their bearers' social condition. As she puts it, quoting Virno, "for all its pettiness, the feeling calls attention to a real social experience and a certain kind of historical truth."[3] Proust and Baldwin attribute this quality of minorness to the thinker himself and his internal affective landscape. Their novels highlight the disconnect between the effort it takes to articulate one's affects and the small number of stimuli that even one's most heroic introspective endeavors can compass at any moment. They also showcase the limited, simplified contexts to which one might need to resort to explicate one's affective experience on one's own. Such simplifications make one's affects—however intense they might be—difficult to relate back to a larger social world. Proust and Baldwin struggle to find ways of acknowledging these problems without quite letting go of the insights that forms of isolation allow their protagonists to reach.

One way to understand the trajectory of Proust's *In Search of Lost Time* is to think of it as a process of heightening attentiveness to self-enclosed spaces, both as necessary conditions for and as limits to his narrator's cognizance of his affects. These spaces mark the difficulty Marcel experiences in incorporating into his affective self-knowledge even another person's presence, let alone her attitude toward how he feels. The rooms through which he passes also provide immediate tests of his affective awareness: is he sufficiently aware, he asks himself, of his responsiveness to each of a room's particular parts? Marcel ponders shades of difference in his relationships to each room he enters. He notes moments when a room gathers and then loses its appeal; he puzzles over his failures to affectively catch up with these rooms' changing components and over the mood swings that they sometimes trigger in him. Proust's narrator also becomes ever more conscious—in ways that are at first self-mocking and then more affirming—that he can only make sense of his affective experiences by mapping them out onto contained, small spaces and the habits he maintains within them. Marcel discovers this seclusion to be a necessary condition of describing what his experience feels like to him. He also comes to realize that these experiences of inward clarity come at the cost of rendering fundamentally uncertain the degree to which anybody else might share in his perception of himself. Indeed, the very urgency with which he needs to retreat to solitude in order to clarify his affects on his own signals to him how deep the gulf between his own perception of these affects and anybody else's attitudes toward them might be.[4]

Of course, *In Search of Lost Time* does not take place only within rooms. But the *Search* does pay meticulous, disproportionate attention to rooms and particularly bedrooms, in a way that makes them apt representations of the aesthetic strategies I highlight here. Rooms are used throughout Proust's novel to define his protagonist's shifting affections and the progress he makes in satisfying them. They also lend a sense of immediacy to Marcel's preoccupation with time, as he tends to map out his memories onto the particular spaces he is visiting or revisiting. Marcel expresses and tests his feelings toward his past and present not against the full span of years he might recall, but against his surrounding physical environment and the particular memories or sensations this environment incites. Over two thousand pages of the *Search* pass before we hit on a single date. But we always know whether Proust's narrator has woken up in his own bedroom, in Albertine's, or in Saint-Loup's. Whenever he walks into a salon we are never left wondering whether this might be the salon of the duchess or the princess of Guermantes, that of Madame Swann or Madame Verdurin.

Proust structures narratives of Marcel's loves and longings around the kinds of rooms through which he passes in the course of each day. His narrator makes sense of his affects by noting how each of these rooms inflects these affects and how much he longs to be in each of them. Marcel describes his adolescent love of Gilberte as a desire to follow her into the chambers she will enter once she has left their meeting place. He understands his love of Albertine as an increasingly obsessive need to keep her in his bedroom. After Albertine has left him, his anguish becomes most vivid when Saint-Loup lists the rooms in which she now stays without him. "How I repeated to myself these words, shed, passage, drawing-room, renewing the shock at will, after Saint-Loup had left me! In a shed one girl can hide with another. And in the drawing room, who knew what Albertine did when her aunt was not there?" (5:480).[5] The narrator notices how much a person has changed, or how differently he has come to feel about her, when she appears in a new and unexpected salon—as, for instance, when he sees the middle-aged Gilberte at the Princesse de Guermantes's. This aristocratic setting, in which he would never have expected to see his childhood love (whose mother used to be a courtesan), prevents him from recognizing her. Proust's narrator also often discovers ambiguities in his relationships to others on the brink of rooms: it is no accident that Charlus gestures toward his attraction to the narrator while standing in the latter's doorway.

Throughout the novel, Proust's narrator seeks to articulate fine distinctions between the kinds of enclosure offered by a bedroom, a salon, a church nave, an opera hall, an artist's studio, a train compartment, a room in one's home, a hotel room, or a room in a brothel. Many of the novel's early turning points are staged as discoveries of new rooms that Marcel finds hard to assimilate into his existing experiences. For example, in *Within a Budding*

Grove,[6] visiting Elstir's studio makes him realize how much natural beauty one can condense into a single, private space. This studio also helps him see the relationship between rooms and the temporality of feeling in a new way: Elstir's paintings show him how a series of momentary sensations could be condensed into a rich history of affective upheavals.

These forms of spatial and temporal enclosure pervade even the basic features of Proust's style. His sentences foster an experience of dwelling rather than of linear progression. They make present to the narrator, as he elucidates his feelings, not merely the form of these feelings but the experience of lingering in the limits of his awareness of them and of allowing these limits to shrink ever further. These increasing contractions do not result in an unambiguously deepened or enriched experience of his surrounding spaces. Instead, they markedly circumscribe the incidents from which Marcel draws even his grandest conclusions about himself and others. We see this process in the following fragment, in which he works himself up to declaring that Charlus is acting like a woman. He moves toward this conclusion in two long motions. First he describes Charlus's momentary appearance as it coalesces moment by moment and trait by trait, from a set of sensations into a series of adjectives: "Blinking his eyes in the sunlight, he seemed almost to be smiling, and I found in his face seen thus in repose and as it were in its natural state something so affectionate, so defenseless." Then, in similarly sweeping fashion the narrator takes the reader through all that he knows of Charlus's attitudes toward femininity and women: ". . . that I could not help thinking how angry M. de Charlus would have been could he have known that he was being watched; for what was suggested to me by the sight of this man who was so enamored of, who so prided himself on, his virility, to whom all other men seemed odiously effeminate. . . " In the final phrase these observations are summed up by a condensed list of the various aspects of Charlus's appearance that now definitively single him out as female: ". . . what he suddenly suggested to me, to such an extent had he momentarily assumed the features, the expression, the smile thereof, was a woman" (4:5).[7] Proust's parallel clauses rephrase their precedents ever more forcefully, creating an aura of increasing enclosure and certainty. As these clauses become shorter and more conclusive, Proust represents the narrator's thought process as a centripetal motion in which the thought he expresses gradually spirals down from a long sentence to a single word. The ongoing contraction of these clauses enshrines Marcel's observation in an air of generality and certainty.

Eve Sedgwick has described Proust's novel as a path toward realizing, as did Plotinus, that the outward enclosures of our world and the inward enclosures of our minds are identical to each other.[8] I would argue that Proust, in fact, inverts this Plotinian parallel. For Plotinus, this comparison means that our minds and bodies reflect the divinely ordained structures of the universe. Proust's narrator eventually realizes that the world he experiences is circumscribed by the bodily and mental limits of what he is able to absorb and become aware of. Proust's depictions of the narrator's well-enclosed affective self-discoveries ring with an irony that grows more explicit as the novel progresses. It becomes increasingly clear that the forms of enclosure sought out by Marcel merely shield him from how unknowable and unpredictable his affects seem in any more open or more social space. In a way that recalls the belatedness Massumi discusses in *Parables for the Virtual*, Proust's narrator depicts himself as comically slow to make any affective induction about himself or anybody else. Not only an open space but also any larger, less familiar room easily overwhelms him. Marcel is also frequently taken aback by the incompatibility of his own understanding of his affects with other people's. These other people often show more awareness of how he feels than he expects them to or than he does himself. They also care much less about these affects than the narrator: treating them not as grand discoveries of love and beauty, but as instances of idiosyncratic, somewhat annoying obsessiveness.

In the second volume of *Search*, such a moment of noticeable, disempowering affective delay occurs when Marcel sees Albertine in Elstir's studio. The narrator has been following her around Balbec for days on end; now, he has finally persuaded Elstir to introduce him to her. He walks into Elstir's studio shortly after the painter made this promise, and his eyes fall on Albertine. The narrator hardly knows what to do with her, or with himself. As he beholds her, he feels none of the longing he developed while following her all over Balbec. "There was certainly a girl sitting there in a silk frock, bareheaded, but one whose marvelous hair, whose nose, whose complexion, meant nothing to me, in whom I did not recognize the human entity that I had extracted from a young cyclist in a polo-cap strolling past myself and the sea." The narrator marvels that, despite his total sense of estrangement, "nevertheless it was Albertine," the person he has longed to see for the past weeks. His numbness renders him all the more helpless because he now encounters her not on a crowded beach, but in a studio that secludes them from other distractions. Meanwhile, Albertine and Elstir continue talking to each other and to him with an effortless courtesy that shows, at once, that they enjoy the narrator's company and that they treat this interaction as much less eventful and overwhelming than the love-struck narrator perceives it to be.

Confused and awkward, the narrator lists Albertine's features to himself one after another. Still they do not add up to "the human entity" with whom he fell in love. He cannot process the pleasure these sensations give him until he retreats into his bedroom later that day: "So far as pleasure was concerned, I was naturally not conscious of it until some time later, back at the hotel, and in my room alone, I had become myself again" (2:615–616).[9] Retroactively, the narrator recounts this interaction with exceptional acuity and sensitivity; yet he only comes into this sensitivity long after this encounter, when entirely alone.

In a similarly comic scene, Marcel describes the ease with which his mother recognizes and dismisses his infatuation with their neighbor, the princess of Guermantes. He has been following Madame de Guermantes's movements whenever he can: watching for her departures and returns home, letting himself be transfixed by her when they attend the same opera, taking walks down the Champs-Élysées in the hope of seeing her there and maybe even saying hello to her. Throughout this period of infatuation, he frequently expresses dismay because it seems that the princess has not noticed his efforts or his presence at all. Meanwhile, as it turns out, his mother has been embarrassed by the transparency of her son's attachment. "You really must stop hanging about trying to meet Mme de Guermantes," she tells him one day. "You're becoming a laughing-stock. Besides, look how ill your grandmother is, you really have something more serious to think about than waylaying a woman who doesn't care a straw about you."

When he hears this revelation, the bubble of his fantasies bursts all at once. "Instantaneously—like a hypnotist who brings you back from the distant country in which you imagined yourself to be, and opens your eyes for you, or like the doctor who, by recalling you to a sense of duty and reality, cures you of an imaginary disease in which you had been wallowing—[my mother] had awakened me from an unduly protracted dream" (3:428).[10] Retroactively laughing at himself, the narrator describes his obsession as nothing more than a "dream" or an "imaginary disease"; it suddenly seems irrelevant and solipsistic, nothing more than a hindrance to actually getting to know the person about whom he claimed to care so much.[11]

The retroactive irony with which Marcel recounts such disillusionments makes the *Search* oscillate precariously between unquestioningly indulging in the narrator's purposeful self-isolation and dismissing his inner life. As the novel progresses, the constrained conditions under which the narrator's affects seem meaningful to him in themselves become a significant object of his attention. Ngai shows that minor affects can indirectly highlight a person's forcibly marginalized position within a larger social system. They do so by exposing this person's failures to relate to this system as a larger entity: staging, time and again, "a certain failure on the part of the subject to *conceptualize* a social whole."[12] Marcel is not always actively marginalized by others, but his affects do analogously build toward a sense of his affective life—and by extension, of his painfully achieved affective self-knowledge—as something that might only seem momentous to him or to a person similarly ensconced in solitude. He also starts to represent this withdrawal from other people as the necessary prerequisite of feeling in control over his affective self-scrutiny.

The *Search* focuses on the means by which Marcel translates his surrounding world into more manageable and private enclosures that he can then commit to his awareness. Whenever he encounters large, open spaces, the narrator attempts to contain them in smaller ones. Here, he imagines contracting a vast and sublime natural landscape into the back garden of a mansion and then into the sitting room from which he looks onto this garden. Marcel describes "the garden at La Raspelière" as "a compendium of all the excursions to be made in a radius of many miles. . . . [these resting-places] assembled round the chateau the finest views of the neighboring villages, beaches, or forests, seen greatly diminished by distance, as Hadrian collected in his villa reduced models of the most famous monuments of different regions" (4:541).[13] He is awed by the natural beauty that lies beyond the Verdurins' summer salon. But going on excursions around La Raspelière ultimately leads him to decide that he might be able to relive these excursions in a garden. Watching these landscapes from within the garden further lets him imagine that they could be replicated in decorative models and kept indoors. Rather than describe these contractions with a sense of loss, the narrator offers them as signs of his deepening relationship to the surrounding nature. These diminutions ironically remind us of the narrator's fragile health and of his tendency to become overstimulated. Descriptions such as this one also highlight the extent to which the narrator's aesthetic sensibility depends on constantly contracting—or, as he puts it in a prior passage, on "extracting" himself from—any larger and potentially more social environment.

The narrator's automobile, which ostensibly increases his mobility, turns out to have a similar foreshortening effect:

> We realized this as soon as the vehicle, starting off, covered in one bound twenty paces of an excellent horse. Distances are only the relation of space to time and vary with it. We express the difficulty that we have in getting to a place in a system of miles or kilometers which becomes false as soon as that difficulty decreases. . . . it was easy to go in a single afternoon to Saint-Jean and La Raspelière. Douville and Quetteholme, Saint-Mars-Le-Vieux and Saint-Mars-Le-Vêtu, Gourville and Balbec-le-Vieux, Tourville and Fêterne, prisoners hitherto as hermetically confined in the cells of distinct days as long ago were Méséglise and Guermantes, upon which the same eyes could not gaze in the course of a single afternoon, delivered now by the giant with the seven-league boots, clustered around our tea-time.[14] (4:537–538)

As Georges Poulet puts it, "For Proust the ideal voyage is one which abolishes distance all at once, placing side by side, as if they were contiguous and even in communication with each other, two of those places that had seemed distinctive precisely because they had always seemed to exist apart from each other, without any possibility of such communication. It is in this sense right to say that the experience of movement changes the laws of the universe."[15] However, Proust describes traveling not only—as Poulet rightly points out—as an increasing experience of simultaneity but also as the fusion and contraction of spaces that previously seemed vaster and more separate. The narrator's greater mobility does not make him feel freer within the world he used to know. Instead it creates a new, separate world onto itself, which he once again needs to redescribe to himself as relatively small and circumscribed.[16]

Diane Leonard shows that Proust, inspired by John Ruskin, sought to understand architectural spaces as models of their inhabitants' inner lives.[17] The extent to which such models also highlight Marcel's cognitive limitations—which have little to do with Ruskin's more confident aestheticism—becomes most striking when he tries to fit into these rooms another, actually present person. To reassure himself of his love of Albertine, he arranges for other women to come to his doorstep—to almost, but not quite, enter the space he and Albertine share, giving him premonitions of what it would be like to inhabit this space with another woman. These brief encounters with milk-maids or flower vendors soon become an obsession. Marcel tries to picture to himself exactly how much pleasure he could have with each of these visitors. "To estimate the loss that I suffered by my seclusion, that is to say the riches that the day had to offer me," the narrator writes, "I should have had to intercept in the long unwinding of the animated frieze some damsel carrying her laundry or her milk, transfer her for a moment, like the silhouette of a mobile piece of stage décor between its supports, into the frame of my door, and keep her there before my eyes (5:177).[18] He represents his attraction to Albertine in architectural terms as a "frieze" of gifts and sacrifices that surrounds him from all sides.

By describing his enveloping longing, the narrator also begins to reveal—in a way that is, here, retroactively ironized—how flat and oversimplified a notion of Albertine and these other women he finds to be fully immersive and satisfying. Even in the passage just quoted, he does not appreciate this young woman herself, but her framing in the entryway and the ease with which this framing makes her seem like a bibelot. Retelling this incident many years after, the narrator retroactively highlights the naïveté of using a room as a tool for thinking about his relationship to a person whose life extends considerably beyond it, and who can leave it at any time. Ngai describes minor aesthetic experiences as "call[ing] attention to their own weakness."[19] A similar process takes place in Proust's novel: what Ngai terms the "incon-sequentiality" of minor affective experiences—the way in which they do not measure up to their full surrounding world—becomes an object of representation in and of itself.[20] Proust foreshadows that Marcel's affection will easily become uncontrollable and unintelligible once Albertine decides to leave his apartment, making him realize with tragicomic terror that she was not a permanent fixture of it after all.

In *Time Regained*, Proust depicts even the adult, aging Marcel as unable to transcend these limitations. Marcel returns to the salon of the princess of Guermantes after the First World War. He is baffled by how much his friends have aged: many of them are altered in ways he could not have imagined, so that he has to puzzle over these people's identities. He also wonders what his confused feelings toward these strangers whom he only half-recognizes might tell him about abstract concepts such as time and space.

One of the people Marcel meets is Argencourt, who used to despise him but now treats him with weary politeness. The narrator is taken aback. As he continues to look at Argencourt, this now elderly man becomes doll-like. He seems, as Marcel puts it, like a puppet in a children's morality play. It is as if, he continues, this aged frame had been projected onto Argencourt's former body the way Golo, the figure from his childhood magic lantern, would have been projected against the walls, doors, and doorknobs of the narrator's bedroom. Reimagined in this fashion, the body he sees before him reveals the qualities not of any specific person, but of "time" itself. Argencourt's presence explains the whole history of the narrator's relations to all the people he has been meeting here. "As immaterial now as Golo long ago on the doorknob of my room at Combray, the new, the unrecognizable Argencourt was there before me as the revelation of time, which by his agency was rendered partially visible" (7:342).[21]

In the narrator's mind, Argencourt turns first into an inanimate prop within a shadow-puppet theater and then into a doorknob. Once his body forms part of the imagined bedchamber of Marcel's childhood, it becomes merely a spot of darkness imposed on that backdrop. By recasting his feeling toward Argencourt as a sensation that is at once wholly immersive and capable of circumscription, he generalizes this affect as an experience not merely of Argencourt, but of temporality itself, and as a source of insight that might prove not just locally but universally true. In the next paragraphs, Marcel starts to apply this observation to everyone in the salon. This thought process helps him explain the sense of estrangement that overwhelmed him when he first entered. By using an entire physical space—rather than just an object—as a model for his immersive affects, Marcel emphasizes the philosophical ambition with which he reflects on them. Yet this description also highlights the foreshortenings required by this narrator's affective reflections. Even at his most philosophical, he only accesses and relates to a strikingly limited sphere of time and space; indeed, only in such a circumscribed space does his affective awareness begin to seem like a philosophy at all.

Sedgwick and many other critics read the *Search* as a narrative of closetedness.[22] It is possible to see the constricting circumferences of these bedrooms as an ever more explicit, and ever more inevitable, expression of Marcel's repressive withdrawal. In this sense, one could interpret the *Search* as responding to its narrator's feelings with little more than self-hatred, failing to fulfill their political potential in the way queer affect theorists eventually do. I do not disagree with this assessment to the extent that it exposes Proust's adamant refusal to formulate more hopeful, future-oriented visions of his narrator in which he could go on to lead an openly queer life or at least a life unhindered by anxiety and illness. But for Proust, it is just as important to hint that Marcel's affective struggles might point to some significant, repressed aspect of his psyche as it is to suggest that probing these aspects of himself necessarily occludes much else about the surrounding world, including other people's actual or potential responses to his affective expression.

Toward the end of the novel, the narrator explicitly turns these forms of withdrawal into the basis of his self-understanding as an artist. Most critics have interpreted the involuntary memories with which the novel starts and ends as tipping points at which Marcel is finally able to relate to something more than his immediate environments and obsessions, taking stock of his life as a whole. Even though that is basically right, involuntary memories also mark the point at which this narrator becomes most strongly committed to the privacy of the affective self-knowledge that matters to him—and to a state of relative ignorance about any sensations or beings that his hard-won, secluded self-awareness is not able to include.

In both his initial remembrance of Combray and his later involuntary memory of Venice, Marcel first forms a clear mental image of a room or a chamber: the baptistery of St. Marc's cathedral, the bedroom of his aunt Leonie, his hotel bedroom in Balbec. Out of these rooms emerge further recollections of the paths he used to take toward and away from them. "Immediately the old grey house upon the street, where her room was, rose up like a stage set to attach itself to the little pavilion opening on to the garden . . . and with the house the town . . . the Square where I used to be sent before lunch, the streets along which I used to run errands, the country roads we took when it was fine" (1:64).[23] The madeleine, bells, and cracks in the pavement give rise to memories of familiarly small, confined spaces and of his habitual ways of dwelling within them. Marcel begins to hope that these small rooms could all be reconnected and brought together into an image not just of each such room in turn, but of the world in which they all existed.

These flashes of remembrance open Marcel up to a greater range of affects than he thought possible—and he, in turn, responds to them with a heightened awareness of the isolation he will need properly to make sense of them. He realizes that his affectively charged memories again require an enclosed, small space for their consideration. He retreats to a single chamber, alone, and locks himself within its confines as tightly as he can. "I shut out every obstacle, every extraneous idea, I stop my ears and screen my attention from the sounds of the next room," he says after tasting the madeleine (1:61).[24] In the last volume, his series of involuntary memories causes him to rush to his host's library instead of directly joining the party he has come to attend. Within these confines, he believes that he has reached a state of self-understanding based not on momentary appearances but on essences; he also claims that he has found a way to transform his feelings into larger laws of thinking and feeling, and his life into a form of art. "This being which had been reborn in me," he says, "this being is nourished only by the essences of things, in these alone does it find its sustenance and delight" (7:264).[25]

These passages have often been read as an at least partly convincing philosophical account of time and memory.[26] I highlight that these revelations depend on Marcel's withdrawal to a constrained space in which little can distract or contradict him. His ability to hold on to his involuntary memories and represent them to himself hinges on his well-practiced habits of shielding his body and mind from excess stimulation and other people's interference. Even the terms in which he describes these recalled memories—as rooms around and out of which larger networks of relations are created—affirm his tendency to relate to his environments as a series of small enclosures that separate him from others.

As he progresses from experiencing these affectively charged memories to writing them down, Proust's narrator insists on these forms of physical and cognitive confinement ever more forcefully. Soon after the social occasion where his final series of involuntary memories take place, he has a slight stroke that leaves him, as he claims, unable to care much about the world beyond these memories: "Since the day of the staircase, nothing in the world, no happiness, whether it came from friendship or the progress of my book or the hope of fame, reached me except as a sunshine unclouded but so pale that it no longer had the virtue to warm me, to make me live, to instill in me any desire; and yet, faint though it was, it was still too dazzling for my eyes, I closed them and turned my face to the wall" (7:522).[27]

This ending powerfully asserts his work's totalizing ambition. The bedroom in which he has locked himself models how completely he now devotes his attention to recreating the past course of his life. But only in the absence of any alternative perspectives or stimuli is Marcel able to recall these prior triggers and spans of his sensitivity. Involuntary memories do not liberate him from this room, or from the past rooms he inhabited. Instead, they remind him of his dependence, even in his greatest moments of insight or creativity, on such processes of deliberate self-isolation in which he is as shielded from potential interferences as possible. These affective explorations might only matter and make sense to his own self or to someone who wholly aligns himself with his constrained viewpoint. The process of articulating his feelings in solitude does not, for Marcel, simply affirm his affective autonomy. In parallel, it also gradually uncovers the narrowness and contingency of the outward conditions under which he can feel satisfactorily aware of his affects and in control of them, so that they can give rise to the work of art of which he dreamed. While the *Search* is a space in which this narrator's reflections are collected and made available to others, it also perpetuates their circumscription: we are invited into them as equally solitary, silent readers.

Compared to Proust, Baldwin engages with affective and cognitive self-enclosure in a much more social context. This is partly because Baldwin's characters rarely have a free bedroom at their disposal, but also because Baldwin insists that a person's affective self-discoveries cannot be kept secret in the long run. They soon become known to others even if they initially happen in a very secluded space. In moments of relative isolation, Baldwin's characters discover aspects of how they feel that might not bear being narrated in public, for fear of derision or even of violence. They then struggle to preserve these insights and share them with others.

As Henry Louis Gates, Jr., describes it, Baldwin's fiction strives to represent forms of self-understanding that do not merely repeat prevalent stereotypes.[28] His characters mine their experiences for alternative notions of who they are or could be. His fiction focuses on pairs of lovers rather than solitary individuals, and these love affairs frequently break racist or homophobic social norms. Baldwin depicts such romantic encounters as precarious not only because they invite other people's scorn but also because the characters he depicts themselves have a hard time holding on to their feelings in the presence of any third person. In the society he represents, such affects are confined to being 'minor' because of the tight, only contingently lifted, restrictions imposed on their rise to awareness even in the people involved in them, let alone in the communities among which they live. As in Proust, these restrictions have to do with the instantaneousness with which—once a person enters a larger social space—this space begins to shape her affective self-awareness, in a way that Baldwin also represents as both potentially repressive and physically inevitable.

Baldwin's commentators have sometimes accused him of political quietism or naïveté. For Langston Hughes, Baldwin's lyrical style is intrinsically unable to capture his social conditions. "The surface excellence and poetry of his writing did not seem to me," he argues, "to suit the earthiness of his subject matter."[29] Eldridge Cleaver sees this lyricism, more extremely, as an expression of racial self-hatred.[30] I argue that we can better appreciate Baldwin's aesthetic if we read his novels as narratives of discovering our partial affective un-self-awareness and isolation. His characters lock themselves in an incompletely self-knowing individualism because they rarely dare speak their affects' names, but also because they typically do not know all their affects' names in the first place. Like Proust, Baldwin devotes as much attention to depicting moments of isolated self-discovery, as to instances when—in the absence of more favorable conditions—his characters lose track of what their affects mean to them. In *Giovanni's Room*, experiences of discovering viable spaces of affective self-recognition rapidly give way to experiences of losing them. In *Another Country*, many of Baldwin's characters can only dream of a small space in which their affects could become articulable. Even as Baldwin continues to affirm the value of the insights his characters reach in such spaces—insights that sometimes become almost utopian in their apparent generality and idealism—he also insists that this generality is persistently undercut by the precarious, narrow conditions required for its expression. In these representations of affect, one can thus see quite clearly the narrow path Baldwin tries to tread between completely entrusting himself to his contemporaries' self-affirming liberalism, and casting wholesale doubt on the validity and potential broad value of individuals' personal accounts of themselves. The insights that we reach about ourselves in solitude can have profound, life-changing impact on our sense of ourselves, and maybe even on the lives of others; but to transpose these insights from their immediate, secluded settings into a larger social world constitutes in his novels no easy or obvious task.

With a structural persistence that recalls Proust's *Search,* the plot of *Giovanni's Room* hinges on the rhythms with which characters inhabit rooms, claim them, and are confined in or thrown out of them. Baldwin's narrative marks shifts in its characters' affects by recording changes in the kinds of rooms where they meet, the length of their stays within these rooms, or the number of people who visit them there. Like Proust's novel, *Giovanni's Room* begins and ends with the narrator waking up and reminiscing in a bedroom. Its two major narrative turns occur when this narrator—David, an American living in Paris—moves into the room of his lover Giovanni, and then moves back in with his fiancée Hella. In both cases, David's move from one room to another marks an implicit choice between the affects he wants to act on, and those he prefers to forget. His ability to keep faith with either of his lovers is measured by the persistence with which he returns to the room each person occupies.

For David, as for Proust's narrator, rooms and especially bedrooms provide precious safe havens in which their affects temporarily become more intelligible and manageable. David's transitions among different enclosed spaces immerse him in a series of unexpectedly illuminating, understandable feelings. At the same time, his affects can only ever retain such clarity when he shuts himself in a small space that forestalls any other distractions. At the beginning of the novel, as David ponders his guilt, he describes his love for Giovanni as a presence within his hotel suite that stares back at him from every corner.[31] When Giovanni and David meet at a bar, David feels that everyone there knows that he and Giovanni are flirting. David then realizes that he cannot leave the room to which he and Giovanni retreat at the end of the night. "I thought, if I do not open the door at once and get out of here, I am lost. But I knew I could not open the door, I knew it was too late; soon it was too late to do anything but moan" (64). Near the end of the novel, David confronts his guilt toward Hella in similar fashion. She enters the gay bar where he has just met a sailor, and he sees her reflection in the mirror, juxtaposed against the sailor's face.

Within and in response to these spaces, David begins to name his affects with a precision and confidence that he otherwise cannot attain. F. W. Dupee rightly describes the eagerness with which David and Baldwin's other characters formulate their feelings in these settings as excessive. "Nobody else in democratic America writes sentences like this anymore," Dupee remarks of Baldwin's style. "It suggests the ideal prose of an ideal literary community, some aristocratic France of one's dreams."[32] Indeed, David narrates the layers of his affective experience with an almost painful earnestness: "Beneath the joy, of course, was anguish and beneath the amazement was fear," he says of his early relationship to Giovanni. "But they did not work themselves to the beginning until our high beginning was aloes on our tongues. By then anguish and fear had become the surface on which we slipped and slid, losing balance, dignity, and pride" (75). David previously acted on this feeling obliquely and vaguely—by befriending an older gay man, expressing tolerance toward homosexuals, agreeing that his fiancée should take a long holiday without him. Now he names this feeling as precisely as if it were a quality of his surroundings. Indeed, David physicalizes his affective state until it becomes like a room in itself. He describes this feeling as the very foundation on which he stands.

Kathleen Drowne claims that such immersive experiences lead David to recognize that he will carry his affective life with him wherever he goes and act on it in any environment that allows him to do so.[33] These florid generalizations do convey an initial hope that such affects could be transposed beyond the small spaces in which they first find expression. David thus reaffirms his love for Giovanni by noting that it leads him to find other men attractive. "At that very moment," he narrates, "there passed between us on the pavement another boy, a stranger, and I invested him at once with Giovanni's beauty and what I felt for Giovanni I also felt for him. Giovanni saw this and saw my face and it made him laugh the more" (83). When David and Giovanni live together, David believes that Giovanni wants him to express his affection by "destroy[ing]," and thus opening up, this shared space. "I understood why Giovanni had wanted me and had brought me to his last retreat. I was to destroy this room and give to Giovanni a new and better life" (88). In all these passages, the rooms David inhabits seem like temporary stages in the expression of an affect that, ideally, would be much more flexible and expansive. The clarity with which Baldwin's characters experience their affects in such enclosures inspires them to imagine these affects as potentially expressible and intelligible anywhere.

Such small spaces make these characters' affects seem temporarily transparent and earth-shattering. However, Baldwin also highlights his characters' difficulty in finding and holding onto these narrow enclosures. He also stresses the considerable gap between finding for one's affects such a temporary, highly personal set of correlatives, and being able to make these affects articulable in one's social life, or to predict the way in which their presence might change one's ties to other people. These characters' affects remain minor both because of the smallness and rarity of spaces in which they find satisfying expression and because of how inarticulate and out of place they seem within any other environment. As soon as David leaves a particular room, his affections seem ambiguous and scattered. To put it in Ngai's terms, these represented affects are plagued by a "non-cathartic" quality that makes the insights to which they give rise perpetually suspect and ephemeral.[34] Their ephemerality stems, in great part, from the extreme paucity of communities or contexts in which these affects can be safely and clearly recognized. In Proust's *Search*, the narrator's dependence on rooms makes him aware of how much he needs to narrow down his world to begin to discern the scope and forms of at least some of his feelings. Occasional experiences of small, enveloping spaces show Baldwin's characters that their affects inevitably lose their coherence without such forms of outward containment. Beyond each such enclosure, his characters rapidly lose sight even of the people and goals that they thought mattered to them most. The discoveries they made about themselves in private easily give way to more conventional and socially acceptable choices.

Baldwin models the fragility of his characters' affective self-understanding through images of dirt, dust, and litter. On a day-to-day level David and Giovanni show their affection, while it lasts, by letting a layer of dust and flaked paint cover all their belongings as a sign that they are still working on their bedroom together. They make explicit their anger, fear, and joy at each other's presence by staining their room and by littering both inside and outside of it: they break glasses, throw cherry pits into the street, spill wine onto the floor, tear up banknotes. At first, these acts of littering take place within the confines of the bedroom they inhabit together, marking their affects' continued presence and accumulation in this small space. But even within this room, the affects they express only create shapeless piles of debris. The fragmentariness of this residue becomes even more precarious and vulnerable when Giovanni and David begin to fight with each other and take their quarrels out into the streets. Once these characters drift away from their shared bedroom, their affective expression and awareness lose consistency. David and Giovanni find that they can neither entirely eliminate these affects from their lives, nor take full stock of them moment by moment. There remains of these affects only a sense—as one of Giovanni's friends puts it—of being "dirty."[35] Giovanni ultimately expresses his despair over losing David by literally and metaphorically getting blood on his hands—enacting the kind of violence that Giovanni and David often feared from their surrounding communities. Waiting to hear the news of

Giovanni's execution, David tries to assuage his guilt by obsessively cleaning his new bedroom, which, it is worth adding, he does not share with anyone.

One could naturally read the various stains and spills David "scrub[s]" off "the tub, then . . . the floor" (71) as self-hating Freudian transpositions of ejaculation. Indeed, some of the ways in which Baldwin's characters dirty or stain their environments do involve intercourse, and Drowne interprets these images of sullied rooms as follows: "The internal struggle within both characters between the homophobe and the homosexual, the orderly and the disorderly, becomes overtly visible in the dirt and clutter that overwhelm the physical spaces they occupy."[36] But Baldwin is equally concerned with highlighting David's difficulty in articulating and holding on to the felt significance of such an intimate act. These images of dirt signify not only social stigma but also—just as insistently—the incoherence and fragmentation of David's sense of himself.

Many of Baldwin's other novels—*Go Tell It On the Mountain, Tell Me How Long the Train's Been Gone*, or *If Beale Street Could Talk*—center on a single, introspective protagonist whose relationship to small, private spaces often parallels David's. (For instance, throughout *Tell Me How Long the Train's Been Gone*, Leo Proudhammer narrates his life story while lying in bed.)[37] Much of *Another Country* could similarly be seen as an attempt to draw attention to such private forms of awareness and to efforts at dignifying them. In early parts of the novel, one of the main characters named Rufus only admits the depth of his resentment toward the oppressiveness of white society in the context of domestic life with his white girlfriend Leona. Rufus's friends also typically experience their major affective revelations when a small, confined space allows for unexpected intimacy between them and someone else to whom they had not realized they could be drawn or with whom they did not know they could be honest. For example, Rufus's friend Vivaldo realizes that he might be homosexual or bisexual—and, indirectly, that he may have been attracted to Rufus—when he and his gay friend Eric sleep together in Vivaldo's bedroom. Cass, the wife of Vivaldo's mentor Richard, discovers how little she still trusts in the continuation of her marriage when she and Eric spend time in her apartment and become lovers.

As in *Giovanni's Room*, these self-discoveries lead Baldwin's characters to express their affects in confident and generalized (or even overgeneralized) ways. "I want you to be with me," Vivaldo insists to Rufus's sister Ida. "I want that more than I've ever wanted anything in the world."[38] When they make love a second time, Ida exclaims: "It never happened to me before—not like this, never" (525). Eric and Yves, a gay couple, reiterate their love to each other in similar fashion: "There *are* no boys like you. Thank God," says Yves to Eric (526). "I'm crazy about you," Eric tells Yves a little later in the novel (564). "*Tell me you'll love me forever. Yes. Forever. Forever,*" Richard prays as he and Cass are having sex (697). "I want you to love me all my life," Vivaldo tells Eric after they spend the night together (721).

These episodes register as moments of affective revelation. A contingently restricted context lets these characters explore a different part of themselves, to which they might not otherwise have access. It also reinforces these characters' sense of the significance of the affect they finally manage to articulate on their own, or with the help of one other person. At the same time, these exchanges highlight the difficulty with which the characters hold on to such realizations and use them to meaningfully inflect the rest of their lives. Vivaldo and Eric's affair remains a one-night stand, and Cass and Richard soon become unfaithful to each other. Eric only loosens the initial hold that his communities' homophobia has on him by relocating to Paris. *Another Country* compounds the unmooring effects of *Giovanni's Room* through the cumulative experience of hearing similar affects expressed by many different couples, to similarly uncertain effect. All of these characters lose themselves in vague, conventional hopes for happiness. They are unable to describe their affects to themselves and to others in ways that will prepare them for the specific directions in which these affects develop or for the consequences that the expression of these affects may bring.[39]

Eric vividly reflects on this uncertainty and its interpersonal dimensions when reminiscing about Rufus in Paris:

> But had he ever loved Rufus? Or had it simply been rage and nostalgia and guilt? and shame? Was it the body of Rufus to which he had clung, or the bodies of dark men, seen briefly, somewhere, in a garden or a clearing, long ago, sweat running down their chocolate chests and shoulders . . . ? Certainly he had never succeeded in making Rufus believe he loved him. Perhaps Rufus had looked into his eyes and seen those dark men Eric saw, and hated him for it. (194)

When he and Rufus were alone together, Rufus seemed like the only person who mattered to Eric. This belief was hard to keep up, Eric recalls, whenever he found himself back out in the street, among other people whose bodies appeared to resemble Rufus's body. Amid the confusion he feels between the bedroom and the street, even the feeling he thought he had for Rufus becomes blurred: he can no longer tell if it was "love" or maybe "rage," "nostalgia," "guilt," or even "shame." He also fears that, when Rufus looked into his eyes, what he saw was this confusion and not the love of which Eric was, at the time, sincerely confident: even the thought of his lover's watchful presence, let alone the presence of third parties, suffices to shake the confidence of his affective introspection. Eric is lying in bed with his French lover Yves as these reflections unravel in his mind; and though he describes Yves as "trusting," he does not recount any of these thoughts to him, as if anticipating a series of similar misunderstandings.

To a far greater extent than *Giovanni's Room*, *Another Country* is also a study of what happens when a person cannot reach even one moment of actionable affective clarity: when the awareness for which this person yearns comes to her very belatedly or not at all.[40] In a way that echoes the fiction of F. Scott Fitzgerald, *Another Country* is replete with episodes during which someone's opportunity for a moment of affective awareness is squandered or lost. In one striking scene, Cass watches Ida dance with a man named Ellis in a way that becomes increasingly sexual. Ida has been involved with Vivaldo; her growing closeness to this new suitor gives Cass a premonition that their whole friend group might soon fall apart. Cass lists the details of the pair's growing excitement as she watches them: "Ida was suddenly dancing as she had probably not danced since her adolescence, and Ellis was attempting to match her. Ellis's forehead turned slick with sweat, his short, curly hair seemed to darken, Cass almost heard his breathing. Ida circled around him, in her orange dress, her legs flashing like knives, and her hips cruelly grinding." Finally, their intensity becomes apparent to everyone else in the barroom: "Others on the floor made way for them—for her: it must have seemed to Ellis that the music would never end" (688–689).

This description echoes the affective revelations staged in *Giovanni's Room*. Every detail of these characters' bodies and surroundings announces to Cass that her two friends desire each other. Her revelation is enabled by a physical space, small enough for Cass to grasp it entirely, which makes her awareness of this affect seem at once totalizing and manageable. In emphasizing the "cruel" movements of Ida's body, Cass also presages the violence this affair will do to Ida and her broader community. But unlike in *Giovanni's*

Room, this moment of revelation does not even temporarily reach its most appropriate audience. The character who comes to this awareness is not Ellis or Ida but Ida's friend, Cass. After the dance, Cass does not share her insight with any of her friends. It hovers in the novel as a piece of affective knowledge that never reaches the people who might have benefited from it most.

Ida's brother Rufus experiences this sense of dislocation perhaps most poignantly of all. Ngai's discussion of anxiety as a constant, failed attempt to discern the object of one's fears provides a useful model for the affects to which Rufus falls prone in the early sections of *Another Country*.[41] Rufus desperately tries to grasp the exact obstacles to which his affects are responding, but he can only picture these obstacles in very vague terms. His environment offers him fodder for fantasies about the difficulties he faces, but it does not furnish any definite means of responding to them.

The opening of the novel finds Rufus at what he believes to be a turning point in his life. In one of its first sections, he is about to prostitute himself to another man in exchange for food, and everything he sees seems to announce his imminent fall. He describes this episode as a moment when his whole life might collapse: "'I'd rather have a sandwich,' Rufus muttered, and thought *You've really hit the bottom now*" (402). But Rufus does not, in the end, let this other man have sex with him, and a few pages after this encounter he returns to his sister's apartment. With her help, he manages to sustain himself for several more months.

In the scenes that follow this sequence, Rufus constantly wonders when and how he will finally hit the bottom that, in these early pages, he believed himself to have already reached: "He was thrown out of bars. The eyes of his friends told him he was falling. His own heart told him so. Perhaps now, though, he had hit bottom. One thing about the bottom, he told himself, you can't fall any farther. He tried to take comfort from this thought" (412). Rufus believes that his immersive sadness corresponds to some palpable material reality. He acts as if his whole environment were physically closing in on him, confronting him on all sides with signs of doom. The pathos of Rufus's misapprehensions lies in the fact that his despair and claustrophobia *do* respond to a real set of social conditions that constrain his existence, even though he cannot translate these affective experiences into any consistent social or even personal self-understanding. In a way that is reminiscent of Woolf's Septimus Smith and Fitzgerald's Dick Diver, Rufus treats every momentary humiliation or difficulty as if it already comprised the sum total of his disempowerment and suffering. Meanwhile, none of the people and environments that surround him actually dispel Rufus's frustration or clarify it.

Susan Feldman argues that Baldwin's characters in *Another Country* are blinded by their refusal to face their social and cultural history: "Their unwillingness to explore the buried truths behind their experiences—the absence and loss which, left unexamined, renders them destined to repeat the past—makes them strangers to themselves and, consequently, to each other."[42] But the pathos of this novel paradoxically lies in the persistence with which characters such as Rufus do find themselves believing, time and again, that they have discovered deep social truths through their immediate affective experiences. Baldwin suggests that, if only these characters could find more manageable and responsive communities away from the constant flux of the industrialized, racially segregated city in which they have no lasting homes, they could take stock of their affects more precisely and to greater effect. The temporary, belated clarity that rooms give some of them only highlights their generally limited means of guarding against their near-constant affective confusion. It also highlights the risk these characters take whenever they entrust themselves to a momentary, circumscribed form of insight, which—right as it seems to them—often cannot be supported or sustained in any wider setting.

Baldwin makes this sense of urgency and helplessness perhaps most explicit in his representation of Rufus's death. We find out about it by hearsay, not even from the perspective of his sister or his best friend, Vivaldo, but in an exchange between two of Rufus's more distant friends, Richard and Cass. "He's dead," Richard says to Cass, "They found his body floating in the river" (458). There is a double irony to this narrative choice. Rufus does finally find himself in an inescapable situation. But even though, throughout the narrative, he describes the feeling of impending death as a sensation of "hitting bottom," his actual death leaves him floating on the surface of a river. The narrative itself also lets Rufus slip through the cracks—as if, after all, there were no forces in this plot to keep him firmly in its bounds, no "bottom" to his narrative that would provide his story with a clear and satisfying end. Even Baldwin's narrator apparently cannot represent the exact circumstances of Rufus's death or the affects that occasioned it.

These narrative choices and the affective experiences behind them bear comparison to the fragment of *Notes of a Native Son* in which Baldwin describes seeing an exhibit at the Louvre: "I was forced to recognize that I was a kind of bastard of the West. These were not really my creations, they did not contain my history; I might search in them in vain forever for any reflection of myself. I was an interloper; this was not my heritage. At the same time I had no other heritage which I could possibly hope to use—I had certainly been unfitted for the jungle or the tribe."[43] The plight Baldwin describes here does not quite match Rufus's plight. But the disconnectedness Rufus experiences involves a similar discovery—namely, that his communities do not make any effort to take stock of the experiences he might have within them, even though he urgently needs such outward support for his self-awareness. Cleaver accuses Baldwin of racial self-hatred in relation to passages such as this one.[44] For Porter and Feldman, by contrast, such moments exemplify Baldwin's productive double vision. They argue that Baldwin's incomplete sense of belonging to his society and his self-consciousness about his own place in its history allow him to critique this environment with greater force and insight.[45] I agree that this quotation and Baldwin's representation of Rufus do highlight how the history of slavery and racism disrupts and damages the lives of Baldwin's contemporaries. However, Baldwin makes this point in a paradoxical way: not by trusting either his own affects or those of his characters, but by suggesting that both the author *and* his characters struggle with these affects in environments that do not offer stable foundations or reflections for them. As in Proust, this attitude hinges on continually contesting the notion of affective introspection as something one can undertake easily and spontaneously. Instead, Baldwin depicts such inward self-scrutiny as a process that a person can accomplish and whose conclusions she can hold onto only within a precarious favorable context that shields her from distractions and especially from the potentially judgmental presence of hostile or uncomprehending others.

Through narrative strategies such as these, Proust and Baldwin draw attention to the vulnerable, inherently dependent conditions under which their characters become aware of their affects. This dependency exposes these characters' bodily and mental limitations and, especially in Baldwin, the socioeconomic pressures put on them. In both authors, the felt experience of social marginality and affective minorness leads one to discover the contingency of one's ability to act on one's affects, as well as the constrained contexts in which one can name and embrace these affects in the first place. Trying to understand an affect that is at odds with the conventions of one's community, Proust and Baldwin both show, forces one to confront not only this community's potential hostility, but also one's own highly constrained, context-dependent capacity to hold on to any form of affective awareness at all. The reasons why these novelists' characters cannot test out their affects in more expansive social settings could not be more different. Proust depicts his narrator as struggling with an easily overwhelmed, socially unacceptable hypersensitivity; Baldwin's characters face the constant potential of much more violent outward repression. But from these two divergent starting points, both novelists arrive at a strikingly similar notion of their characters as forced to associate their most original and potentially transformative affective insights with strict spatiotemporal limits beyond which they cannot readily transpose their sense of themselves. These characters and the novels that depict them can only invite into their enclosures an equally solitary reader.[46]

Ralph Ellison, whose *Invisible Man* I examine in the following chapter, approaches this question of affective awareness from an inverse perspective. Without returning to the somewhat greater expansiveness of Woolf's and Fitzgerald's social spaces, Ellison does reintroduce into his novel a concern with the lives and beliefs of other people that Baldwin's and Proust's characters frequently lack. In the process, *Invisible Man* flips around the question of affective awareness with which Proust's and Baldwin's protagonists struggle. Ellison's protagonist notices how dependent other people are on him to make sense of affects they otherwise claim to have already named and understood; he then begins to use this observation to increasingly subversive political ends. No longer mourning—as Baldwin and Proust still do—for the self-knowing, autonomous introspective subject, Ellison finds a paradoxical path toward resisting social ideologies and people who insist on them, precisely in his protagonist's apparent cognitive failures.

Chapter 4

Basement

Ralph Ellison

"What is your name?" a doctor writes on a piece of paper and hands it to Ralph Ellison's unnamed narrator in *Invisible Man*. Ellison's narrator has just undergone electroshock therapy. His head is spinning, but as soon as he sees this question, he springs to attention: "A tremor shook me; it was as though he had suddenly given a name to, had organized the vagueness that drifted through my head."[1] The narrator is then "overcome with swift shame" at not being able to answer. In early parts of *Invisible Man*, Ellison's narrator frequently feels humiliated and disempowered by his inability to make sense of his overstimulated mind and body. The novel reaches a turning point when the narrator realizes that such unwanted delays and gaps in the accounts of himself he gives to others frequently threaten these people's sense of themselves as powerfully as his own.

Ellison narrates *Invisible Man* from an enclosure that is at once tightly embedded within other social spaces and hidden from them. His narrator's retreat into a basement—which resonates with, and drains into itself, the sounds and energy of other buildings—helps model this narrator's absorptive affective responsiveness to his larger social world. This basement also represents the narrator's insistence that his responsiveness does not and should not be expected to readily contribute to other people's affective awareness. Indeed, it has its greatest impact on others precisely to the extent that he refuses to be their affects' interpreter.

In its acceptance and pragmatic redeployment of its protagonist's cognitive delays and dependencies, Ellison's fiction marks, at once, a break with and a significant development within the modernist engagements with limits to self-awareness that I follow in this book. If Baldwin's and Proust's fiction mourns for a certain form of subjectivity that has become unsustainable—and Fitzgerald's and Woolf's novels record intimations of this unsustainability—Ellison imagines an unexpected escape path out of this disempowered pessimism. Departing from a sense of overwhelmed affective confusion similar to that of Baldwin's protagonists, Ellison turns this confusion into a tool of political subversion. He does so, in great part, by rejecting the ideals of introspective self-knowledge that Baldwin's novels generally uphold. One can read *Invisible Man* as a narrative of the gradual renouncement of autonomous introspection not only as a goal, but even— the way Baldwin still sees it—as a distant ideal. Instead, Ellison's novel redefines its protagonist's understanding of himself and his society around experiences of cognitive constraint and slowness and of the interpersonal dependencies this slowness entails. The self Ellison's novel depicts is inherently relational in its awareness; it takes its agency from confronting others with confusions akin to its own, and with the way these confusions force them to look to surrounding people for help. Moments of affective inarticulacy allow Ellison's protagonist to catch a glimpse of an analogous belatedness in those around him. He finds that even people who seem confident about their views and values share the precariousness of his quest for a more comprehensible inner life. Ellison's protagonist further discovers that both he himself, and the people around him, have great trouble acknowledging the challenge that the cognitive help they constantly demand from others poses to their pretenses of knowing their own values and motivations. *Invisible Man* depicts its characters' inward sense of themselves as incoherent, and their relations to others as motivated by a desire to resolve this incoherence into expressions of more consistent (and often ideologically motivated) world views and values. The fact that they cannot actually align their sense of themselves with such values and world views before someone else has helped them do so constitutes, in the novel, a source first of great frustration, and then of considerable hope. Ellison's narrator reaches a kind of meta-awareness of his cognitive limitations that Fitzgerald's and Woolf's narrators have about their characters, but which characters such as Dick Diver or even Clarissa Dalloway never reach—and which Proust's and Baldwin's narrators only articulate in their resistance to it. Developing such meta-awareness in himself and encouraging it in others becomes, in Ellison's novel, a major aesthetic and political aim and the goal toward which his narrator's *Bildung* progresses. Ellison sees it as a means by which a society starkly divided by racist ideologies can be forced to appreciate its deep cognitive dependence on, and intertwinement with, its Black members—and thereby see the latter as agents and as people in their own right.

The overlapping networks of mutual awareness Ellison constructs in *Invisible Man* might immediately remind one—not incorrectly—of Frantz Fanon's *Black Skin, White Masks*, originally published in French in the same year (1952). Echoing Fanon, Ellison insists that his characters' sense of themselves has less to do with autonomous self-knowledge, and more with the opinions they gather about themselves from the outside. However, where Fanon suggests that nothing less than a collective psychoanalytic effort would be necessary for the communities he describes to be freed from their preconceptions, Ellison finds a measure of political agency in the very cognitive difficulties that might induce one to adopt someone else's notion of oneself. Sharing many of Fanon's concerns, but not his emphasis, Ellison highlights the precariousness with which even the makers of social ideologies are able to maintain the coherence of their sense of themselves. He represents the darkly comic urgency with which supposed social educators constantly need to have their self-awareness complemented and reinforced by the very people whom they claim to teach; he also highlights how rarely members of a society look to each other for anything beyond a means of shoring up their wobbly sense of themselves.

In this regard, Ellison's attitude toward affects bears further comparison with the work of Lauren Berlant and with her notion of affects as paths toward rebelling against one's social and political context.[2] Berlant stresses that affects can help us reject the unsatisfying conditions in which our environments place us. She describes these processes as forms of "counterabsorption" in a "surrealistic affectsphere" that replace one's surrounding world with real or imagined alternatives. For Berlant, this subversive quality of affects flows from their microscopic accuracy as means of diagnosing our environments: affects allow us to reimagine these environments because they help us discern them better in the first place. Describing affective experience as "a site of potential elucidation," Berlant argues that it "saturates the corporeal, intimate, and political performances of adjustment that make a shared atmosphere something palpable and, in its patterning, releases to view a poetics, a theory-in-practice of how a world works."[3]

Invisible Man occasionally stages moments of affective illumination analogous to the ones Berlant describes here—and it would overstate the alternative reading I offer to suggest that Ellison's novel does not find value in them. But much like Baldwin, Ellison also insists that most of our supposed affective self-knowledge comes from more frantically collected, relatively haphazard bits of outward sensation and discourse by which our confusions about what our minds and bodies register or demand are temporarily assuaged. *Invisible Man* suggests, moreover, that the urgent effort we put into elucidating our affects often prevents us from imagining the stakes that other people might have in their interactions with us. Ellison's narrator is eventually disappointed by the central place that clarifying one's own affects occupies in his relationships with others, as well as in their attitudes toward him. Developing interpersonal ties that do not center around such desires for affective clarification becomes a necessary goal of the alternative forms of community he wants to nurture. He sees it as a means of combating his society's prevalent, prejudiced beliefs more effectively than merely by replacing these beliefs with other ones.

One might see Ellison's use of affects as a first step toward Berlant's critical position: we must admit to the confusing nature of our affects in order to recognize their full complexity and critical potential. However, the divergence between these two positions does not reduce itself to such quasi-Hegelian dialectical progress: it also stems from Berlant's and Ellison's different emphases. Berlant presents her work as instructing a disempowered, ideologically manipulated subject to develop alternative means of understanding herself through affects. For Ellison, it is significant that each person's affective delays and confusions have interpersonal consequences. His protagonist struggles against other people's need to give their lives a more continuous sense of clarity and meaning than any of them can supply on their own, as well as against his own temptation to ask the same of others whenever the opportunity arises. Ellison thus uses affects to fragment what might otherwise seem like a binary political conflict between racism and antiracism, or like a power struggle between a Hegelian master and bondsman, into a more nominalist dynamic among various overstimulated human bodies whose incomplete self-cognizance these ideologies can hide only haphazardly and piecemeal. This fragmentation and the surprisingly parallel cognitive vulnerabilities it discloses both in the victims of racism and in its perpetrators crucially inflect Ellison's critiques of existing social norms. Ellison takes the ineradicability of these vulnerabilities as grounds for less introspectively driven notions of personhood and community that could prevent those around him from reducing each other to social types.

At the outset, Ellison's narrator feels disempowered by, and ashamed of, his easily ignited, blinding sensitivity. Throughout the first parts of *Invisible Man*, managing the overwhelming stimuli cast at him by other people remains the narrator's most pressing task. His surrounding communities continually force him to absorb the effects of their bodily and mental expression and to make sense of them as quickly as possible. As Ellison remarks in interviews, each section of *Invisible Man* opens a separate world onto itself, with its own set of conventions: "Each section begins with a sheet of paper; each piece of paper is exchanged for another and contains a definition of his identity, or the social role he is to play as defined for him by others."[4] His narrator stumbles into each such set of conventions dramatically and unwittingly. Every section throws him into confusion about where he has found himself and what will be expected of him. Throughout these rapid shifts of context, Ellison's narrator is disciplined and questioned by other characters who demand from him some strong assertion of his conformity to their standards. Amid these ongoing, aggressive misrecognitions, he discovers what in the first chapter of the novel he describes as his "invisibility": none of the people by whom he is surrounded want to know him, and even those who question him already have in mind ready-made answers (ones that, moreover, reflect their own sense of self much more than his).

This cognitive rush and confusion should inflect our understanding of Ellison's aesthetics to a greater extent than critics have tended to assume. The question of how Ellison relates immediate personal experiences such as affects to larger social structures and histories has long dominated the study of his novels. Several early critics—most famously, Irving Howe—accuse him of political quietism and solipsism. Howe claims that Ellison mistakes self-absorption in one's individual, immediate cares for a subversive rejection of his society's racial norms.[5] Turning this point around, later scholars frequently argue that Ellison sees hopes of political and social renewal in the individual's assertive irreducibility to social structures and ideologies.[6] I propose that Ellison's character construction commits itself much more than either interpretation suggests to representing interpersonal dimensions of affective experiences and of their rise to consciousness. As do the other authors *Spaces of Feeling* examines, Ellison depicts affective awareness as inherently distributed and dispersed in its origins. His focus on the individual indirectly always involves a recognition of the many others to whom this person looks, and who in turn look to this person, to help name their experiences and beliefs.

In early chapters of *Invisible Man*, Ellison highlights the effort with which his narrator strives, but fails, to become cognizant of the intense affective states into which he falls because of other people's words or actions. Ellison records the disparity or at times even the inverse relationship between the intensity of his narrator's bodily and mental responses and his ability to make sense of them. He finds that—even though he continually feels compelled to elucidate his affects, if only because of the pressures put on him by the surrounding world—he is unable to do so to anyone's satisfaction, not even his own. Here, for instance, the sheer flood of these stimuli, which he depicts, literally, as a current of electricity, prevents him from being able to hold on to the name he tries to give to their effect on him:[7] "And suddenly my bewilderment suspended and I wanted to be angry, murderously angry. But somehow the pulse of current smashing through my body prevented me. Something had been disconnected."[8]

This overwhelmedness and the narrator's desperate attempts to reduce it provide the early sections of *Invisible Man* with their broad structuring principles. At the beginning of the novel, a dream warns the narrator that the people around him are trying to "keep" him "running": "'To Whom It May Concern,' I intoned. 'Keep This Nigger-Boy Running'" (33). The narrator does spend most of his early life, as he recounts it, forced to flee from a series of environments that rapidly become insupportable. Such experiences of flight intensify the narrator's rebellion against his current conditions. They also deepen this narrator's awareness that his bodily and mental responsiveness cannot, in itself, prevent him from feeling lost and uprooted. Indeed, this responsiveness is one major reason why he cannot remain within any environment for very long.

Elaborating on this sense of loss and confusion, Ellison shows that his narrator's overwhelming responses to his environments frequently distort or divert his sense of them. When he looks to his mind and body for some insight into his condition, he often finds only a mockery of such insight. When the narrator undergoes electroshocks, the shocks order themselves into the opening chords of Beethoven's Fifth Symphony: "They were holding me firm and it was fiery and above it all I kept hearing the opening motif of Beethoven's *Fifth*—three short and one long buzz, repeated again and again in varying volume" (232). While considering these seemingly symphonic noises, the narrator temporarily forgets about the events that lead him to be subjected to electroshocks in the first place. The semblance of coherence he finds in his environment is dramatically disconnected from the causes and conditions of his anger and pain. In another, similarly tragicomic episode, when the narrator takes Mr. Norton to the farm of a man recently charged with incest, he starts to see all around him uncanny resonances between the pregnancy and other human bodies. "The children had stopped playing and now looked silently at the car, their arms behind their backs and their new oversized overalls pulled tight over their little pot bellies as though they too were pregnant" (48). The narrator's attempts to rein in his growing fear makes more present in his purview the fact he is afraid of disclosing. But they do not help him discern the reasons why this interaction might soon prove disastrous; nor do they illuminate the consequences it might have for his college career. It is striking both how intently, inquisitively alert this narrator becomes in this state of heightened affect and how unable he is to find, among the many details he fearfully notices, anything that might elucidate his fear or assuage it.

It is tempting to read *Invisible Man* as tracing a gradual path away from this affective confusion and toward a diagnostic clarity that Berlant sets up as a critical ideal. "Affect's saturation of form," Berlant argues, "can communicate the conditions under which a historical moment appears as a visceral moment."[9] Ellison's novel initially tends toward a similar goal: his narrator tries to make sense of his affects in ways that might make them coherent and actionable. He believes that his life might become easier if he could figure out, in real time, what social structures and networks create the stimuli that frustrate or move him. He also begins to assume that such forms of clarity are the best gift that he could offer others and best foundations for a society in which he could feel seen and understood.

In a way that bears comparison to the revelations Baldwin's characters have in their bedrooms, Ellison's narrator begins to find temporary, secluded spaces in which he becomes able to name his affects with unexpected precision. Here, he goes through this introspective process when confronted by an elderly man in the basement of a factory where he works for a few hours:

> He had said it again and something fell away from me, and I seemed to be telling myself in a rush: *You were trained to accept the foolishness of such old men as this, even when you thought them clowns and fools; you were trained to pretend that you respected them and acknowledged in them the same quality of authority and power in your world as the whites before whom they bowed and scraped and feared and loved and imitated, and you were even trained to accept it when, angered or spiteful, or drunk with power, they came at you with a stick or strap or cane and you made no effort to strike back, but only to escape unmarked.* But this was too much . . . he was not grandfather or uncle or father, nor preacher or teacher. Something uncoiled in my stomach and I was moving toward him, shouting, more at a black blur that irritated my eyes than at a clearly defined human face. (225)

In this passage, a mounting anger moves the narrator to reconsider the social norms that would normally prevent him from hitting his supervisor. Remembered phrases and injunctions come into his mind, and he suddenly discerns his response to this man as paradigmatic of the way he has been taught to respond to older men in general. His intense bodily reaction—a "something" that "uncoiled in [his] stomach"—leads him to put his anger at the inequality between them into practice. He and the supervisor get into a fight, after which the latter no longer bullies or threatens him. In this episode, his perception of this other man tellingly remains "blur[ry]" and the momentary success of his angry outburst is undone a few minutes later: an explosion in this factory's gas pipes, to which both men stopped attending, breaks up the fight and sends the narrator to the hospital. But passages such as these do begin to express a hope that this narrator might be able to give his affects a more articulate sense of origin and purpose. Elucidating these affects, Ellison's narrator optimistically expects, could help him gain some clarity about the contexts in which he feels oppressed and uprooted. It could allow him to better discern that the people who push him around are "foolish old men" whom he can challenge.

The second part of Ellison's novel (which begins after he meets the Brotherhood, a veiled representation of the Communist Party) records the narrator's eager and then dramatically shattered hope for such reliable affective awareness. Just as importantly, it also undoes his assumption that his developing a more coherent way of understanding himself could in itself consistently benefit a wider African American community. In the environments he enters in the second part of *Invisible Man*, the narrator frequently encounters objects that promise him new insights into himself and others. Each of these objects appears to hold within itself an alternative history from which the narrator's current affects and his very bodily presence arise. They include his suitcase and high school diploma, the chain link given to him by his fellow activist Tarp, as well as hot potatoes and chitterlings, familiar foods that remind him he remains a Southerner despite his new location and appearance. As he receives those things, the narrator eagerly reads larger social histories out of them. He describes the chain link as "a thick dark, oily piece of filed steel that had been twisted open and forced partly back into place, on which I saw marks that might have been made by the blade of a hatchet." These "marks," he continues, testify to Tarp's "haste and violence, looking as though it had been attacked and conquered before it stubbornly yielded" (389).

Many critics—including Sara Blair, Susan Blake, and Paul Allen Anderson—focus on these objects as anchors around which the narrator's affective responses to his environment gain depth and articulacy. Anderson calls them a "dialectical residue" that gives this narrator an alternative to the oppressive norms and conventions in which others try to make him believe.[10] Blair describes them as "a myriad of images and symbolic objects that variously challenge longstanding associations between vision, knowledge or self-knowledge, and social progress."[11] As I argue later in this chapter, the final sections of the novel place increasing emphasis on the difficulty with which such self-discoveries can be transposed onto one's ongoing social interactions—and on the dangers of making them seem too easily transposable. Still, as the narrator settles into New York, they come to the foreground as means by which his affective upheavals are temporarily clarified and affirmed. As he carries these objects on his person or (in the case of Southern food) quite simply eats them, he accepts them as pieces of evidence that make his responses to his environments more intelligible.

In parallel with these growing attachments to his possessions, the narrator begins to draw around himself the attention and awe of a wide human community. He discovers that, when he expresses himself in front of other African American inhabitants of New York, they act as if he were naming their own affects. In his clarified anger and frustration he might embody and give voice to a much larger community whose relationships to their environments he articulates. Just as he draws comfort from his own moments of affective clarity, so too—he hopes—he can bestow such clarity on others.

One of the novel's greatest turning points comes when in his spontaneous, surprisingly successful speech to a crowd protesting an eviction, Ellison's narrator moves this crowd to action by aligning their affects with his. "No, no," I heard myself yelling. "Black men! Brothers! Black Brothers! That's not the way. We're law-abiding. We're a law-abiding people and a slow-to-anger people." As he speaks to the people assembled before him, the narrator has the sensation of reaching into some deep, previously unknown part of himself. "Beneath it all," he says, "there boiled up all the shock-absorbing phrases that I had learned all my life. I seemed to totter on the edge of a great dark hole" (272).

Enjoining these people to act on their compassion for the evicted couple rather than on their anger toward the gathering policemen, the narrator presents himself as someone who already knows how they feel. He calls those who assemble around him "a slow-to-anger people," and they do start to act like people who are slow to anger. A member of the Brotherhood sees the effect Ellison's narrator has on this assembly and urges him to become a social activist. The success the narrator rapidly begins to enjoy as a spokesperson seems to confirm this initial impression that his words might serve as a catalyst and a revelation for many people whose affects are just as confusing to them as his own often are to him. He also seems to find proof that the self-discoveries he reaches in relative solitude can easily be made part of a broader communal understanding. *"Something strange and miraculous and transforming is taking place in me right now . . . as I stand here before you!"* he shouts to a similar crowd a few chapters later. "I feel the urge to affirm my feelings . . . I feel that here, after a long and desperate and uncommonly blind journey, I have come home" (245–246).

In this picture of personhood—into which he temporarily buys after he joins the Brotherhood—examining his easily triggered sensitivity seems to give him a profound understanding of the whole community in which he lives. He takes these other people's responses to him as indications that the names he gives to his affects and the causes he assigns to them are consistently accurate and illuminating. It appears not only that this narrator has finally become satisfyingly aware of his affects, but also that—in doing so—he has revealed something new and revolutionary about the affects of many other people.

The narrator retrospectively, with much irony, associates the perspective this leads him to adopt with the obsessive magical thinking of a gambler. "Thus for one lone stretch of time," he says, "I lived with the intensity displayed by those chronic numbers players who see clues to their fortune in the most minute and insignificant phenomena: in clouds, on passing trucks and subway cars, in dreams, comic strips, the shape of dog-luck fouled on the pavements" (381–382). As Baldwin's characters frequently do, Ellison's narrator begins to doubt how well his inward affective understanding can be translated into a broader social setting. The outward responsiveness of the people around him, which the narrator initially interprets as experiences of direct mutual communication, soon comes to seem much less deep and reliable than it did at first. His own desire to see his affects reflected in and reaffirmed by the people around him becomes similarly suspect.

Critics often read the swerve Ellison's narrative takes with these disappointments as a move away from naïve Marxism toward a more or less convincing individualism: away from seeing people primarily as parts of a larger social structure and toward trying to appreciate the uniqueness of each human being's affects and sensations. Although that is partly right, *Invisible Man* does not simply turn to singular minds and bodies in order to affirm them as ultimate sources of social knowledge. Ellison's novel also seeks to divert attention away from reliable affective self-awareness as a consistently attainable social and political goal. In response to a sequence of disenchantments, Ellison's narrator starts to appreciate his affects as reminders of how much other people's political and personal identities depend on accounts of their immediate experience provided by others. He also acknowledges and accepts the extent to which his own mind and body rely on, and yearn for, such outward clarifications, in a way that frequently prevents him from discerning other people's own, different stakes in the discourses and ideas that he takes from them. The narrator begins to speculate about forms of social interaction and agency in which a full understanding of one's affects loses its central significance. He begins to wonder whether the people around him might paradoxically relate to each other more successfully if they devoted less time and effort to trying to make their affects intelligible to themselves—and rechanneled this effort toward appreciating that the people around them exist beyond, and are irreducible to, the resolutions they occasionally help one find to one's inward turmoil.

This shift in the narrator's attitude toward his affects begins with his surprised realization that one can perceive oneself as a political agent without rushing to relate one's inward angers and frustrations to a broader social and historical condition. When he meets a rival group of African American activists in one of these late sections of the novel, the narrator marvels at their indifference to the long social histories of which the Brotherhood made him feel a part. "For," he says, "they were men outside of historical time, they were untouched, they didn't believe in Brotherhood, no doubt had never heard of it; or perhaps like Clifton would mysteriously have rejected its mysteries; men of transition whose faces were immobile" (440). "Untouched" and "immobile," and apparently unaware of their larger contexts, Raj (the leader of this group) and his supporters embody a state of ignorance whose very possibility the narrator finds illuminating. The narrator does not join Raj's cause; he does not believe in the mystical tones that Raj's movement gives to its disbelief in history. But in the final sections of the novel, Ellison's narrator starts to ponder what it would be like to not take for granted that his affects always can and should be tied back to a larger view of social structures and contexts.

His early doubts harden after a series of disenchantments that call into question the ties between the narrator's affects and his social and material environments. The narrator begins to suspect that many members of the Brotherhood follow more selfish impulses than his sense of affective affinity with them made him believe. He also begins to fear that, in his enthusiasm, he has served a similar role for them as he did for people like the racist philanthropist Mr. Norton: he has provided an embodied confirmation of a certain way they want to feel about themselves. In the following passage, the narrator accuses Brother Jack of treating him and Tod Clifton, as well as other African Americans who have joined the Brotherhood, as his slaves: "'But are you sure you aren't their great white father?' I said, watching him closely, aware of the hot silence and feeling tension race from my toes to my legs as I drew my feet quickly beneath me. 'Wouldn't it be better if they called you Marse Jack?'" (473).

Refusing to confirm the purity of his white collaborators' intentions, the narrator throws the question back at them. They have hitherto relied on his enthusiasm and friendship to resolve such doubts—as when, earlier in the novel, the narrator politely laughed off a racist stereotype someone invoked. Now that he asks them to answer a charged question themselves, they cannot do so either to his or—apparently—even to their own satisfaction. In a manner that echoes earlier depictions of his frustrated or confused affects, the narrator describes his growing anger as a rising muscular "tension" that confines itself only to his now withdrawn, suspicious mind and body. At the first party where he met these people, the narrator focused on the way in which the loudness of their laughter and their shared body heat united them. Here, he describes the space between him and his former comrades as a "hot silence." The silent heatedness of their angers highlights how little the many characters experiencing them might have in common with each other, in a way that the habits and memories they formed in this shared room cannot change. It also suggests how little they can articulate, with confidence, even about their own feelings, now that the narrator refuses to act as if these feelings were already clear to him. Earlier in the novel, the narrator often inadvertently caused authority figures similar tremors and confusions: as when he shocked Mr. Norton with news of a local case of incest or when, speaking on behalf of the Brotherhood, he dismayed them by animating a crowd with a message they had not previously approved. Now, he creates a similar discomfort consciously, reminding those around him how much their air of propriety and uprightness depends on his cooperation.

Furthermore, Ellison's narrator realizes that his own successes in forging affective ties to the communities these activists try to reach did not hold as much meaning as he thought. As he escapes from the Brotherhood into the streets of New York, he is struck by the inability of passersby to recognize him for what he is now—an angry, confused refugee. When he walks out onto the street in unfamiliar clothing, inhabitants of the very neighborhoods in which he felt deeply understood easily mistake him for a small-time criminal named Rinehart. As the narrator grows more confident in this role, he realizes what minimal adjustments—or no adjustments at all—it requires on his part. Steve Pinkerton describes Rinehart as a depiction of "the extreme *possibilities* of African American (non)identity."[12] Barry Shank similarly claims that this alter ego redeems the narrator's lack of a stable identity by transforming this instability into a source of creative potential.[13] To some extent, the many roles the narrator performs as Rinehart are indeed a more controlled, playful version of this narrator's prior rapid escapes from one social context to the next. Yet this late section of the novel highlights not only the narrator's adaptability but also its discomfiting effortlessness. Other people give him power over themselves without knowing who he is; indeed, these other people seem to respond to him only as a hastily drawn and re-drawn social type. These are some of the people whose awareness of themselves and other members of their community the narrator thought he was deepening; now, he is coming to realize how little they are willing to probe their environments at all.

Amid these disappointments, the narrator also changes his attitude toward the objects through which he sought to explicate his society and history. Destroyed or bent out of shape in the urgency of his new fears or angers, these objects are now reduced to temporary means of these affects' expression or enhancement. The narrator dents and loses Tarp's chain link in a scuffle with a former political ally. He then burns his many documents and letters in order to light up the basement from which he eventually begins to narrate his story. "I started with my high-school diploma, applying one precious match with a feeling of remote irony, even smiling as I saw the swift but feeble light push back the gloom" (567). These objects, none of which helped him discern the dead end into which he was walking in his involvement with the Brotherhood, turn out to be more useful to him in their immediate physical qualities—such as their weight or their flammability. The ease with which they can be taken out of their affectively charged historical or personal contexts, to be used merely as torches or weapons, reminds him of how separable from his subjective networks of connection the material world around him effectively is.

In the few public speeches he gives after these episodes, Ellison's narrator persistently refuses to treat himself or anyone else as a reliable source of insight into anybody's affects. As he points out, both he and those around him reach for such outward elucidations too eagerly and too quickly. This shift in attitude comes through during the speech the narrator gives at Tod Clifton's funeral. "There's nothing here to pity," he says, "no one to break down and shout. The story's too short and too simple. His name was Clifton, Tod Clifton, he was unarmed and his death was as senseless as his life was futile"

(457). David Messmer describes this funeral as the narrator's final attempt to transform his larger social sphere through his personal disillusionment and anger: "While Clifton's funeral march is a striking and potentially powerful event, the narrator soon learns that all of his efforts are for naught unless he has the agency to turn the physical energy of the Harlem community into rhetorical energy that is able to influence the racial discourse of American society."[14] On one level, the narrator does of course rally this crowd around him. But the way he achieves this end breaks away from his prior speeches. The narrator challenges not only social structures that overlook African American men and women's suffering but also certain means by which the people around him try to give meaning to their affects. Clifton's death, as he describes it, is "senseless" and "futile" in a way he refuses to recuperate. Rather than ask his community to recognize the wider significance of Clifton's fate, the narrator challenges this community to appreciate him as a person from whom it might be impossible to draw comfort or insight.

The narrator reaffirms and develops his comments about Clifton through his self-seclusion in the basement from which he tells his story. At the start of the novel, he famously describes how he has wired this basement with over thirteen hundred lights. "In my hole in the basement there are exactly 1,369 lights. I've wired the entire ceiling, every inch of it" (7). In its last sections Ellison finally discloses how the narrator found himself in this basement, and what he has abandoned on his way. Given how broadly he has traveled and how many people he has met and influenced, his final isolation is even starker than it might have appeared in the novel's opening pages. His anger now finds expression in a startling amount of light and energy instantly swallowed up in darkness. Lit up by the intense glare he turns on himself, the narrator highlights both how much voltage he draws from the surrounding buildings and how easily the room's absorption of these outer energies remains unnoticeable to others. Indeed, the narrator surmises, this loss of energy will remain an unresolvable mystery to the surrounding neighborhoods. The basement thus reinforces the surprisingly agential quality of what the narrator earlier describes as his "invisibility." It redefines the narrator's invisibility not only as the outward inaccessibility of his feelings, or as other people's capacity to reduce him to a non-entity or stereotype, but also—more counterintuitively—as his capacity to detach himself from other people's affective and cognitive needs, however much of their expression he might be able to absorb and notice. As a metaphor for *Invisible Man* as a whole, the basement also suggests that this narrative's final irresolution paradoxically constitutes one of its most idealistic political provocations. The novel metaphorically insists that it should be possible to make one's surroundings realize how little they know about where their bodily and mental energies escape to. It also suggests that such realizations are a necessary stepping stone toward making these other people appreciate the irreducibility of those around them to their own affective reflections.

These final self-descriptions echo "The Little Man at Chehaw Station," an essay in which Ellison notes that seemingly average and conventional environments often contain unaccountably acute forms of sensitivity. Behind the stove of a provincial train station, one might find an otherwise unremarkable man who proves to have an extremely refined appreciation of music. "These individuals," Ellison comments, "seem to have been sensitized by some obscure force that issues undetected from the chromatic scale of American social hierarchy: a force that throws off strange, ultrasonic ultrasemi-semitones that create within those attuned to its vibrations a mysterious enrichment of personality."[15] Such an accidentally revealed sensitivity makes one aware of the ways in which, day by day, the acuteness with which some people respond to their environments might remain unintegrated into their community's understanding of itself. There is something vulnerable and vaguely comic about this man's affective energies. They flow with such special refinement only toward one very particular and often barely noticeable kind of sensation: the man is preternaturally receptive to music alone. But both in this essay and in the last sections of *Invisible Man*, Ellison willfully embraces such acts of sensitivity. Their uncommon, unarticulated intensity in itself poses a challenge to the communities in which they occur. The man at Chehaw Station reveals something "obscure" about how people develop within and absorb their social conditions. His unaccountable and generally unnoticeable attunement to certain sensations suggests that the society in which he lives does not notice as much about itself as it pretends to. It highlights, within this society, nodes of care and sensitivity about which many of its members know little or nothing, and which persist without such broader knowledge of them.

Ellison's novel famously ends with an attempt at communication. "Who knows but that, on the lower frequencies, I speak for you," the narrator speculates in its last lines (581). Invoking radio broadcasts, this metaphor also echoes the "ultrasemi-semitones" of the man at Chehaw Station. These incompletely audible lower frequencies suggest possibilities for an interpersonal communion that does not reduce itself to the mutual shoring up of affective clarity. They affirm the value of ties between individuals who acknowledge themselves to be incompletely aware of their potential lines of connection to other people and do not seek immediately to assuage the uncertainties that this partial lack of awareness causes. One might describe these ties as a more knowing form of the one that binds Clarissa Dalloway to Septimus Smith toward the end of Woolf's novel: the people involved in them implicitly acknowledge both their cognitive interdependencies and the difference between these interdependencies and full mutual awareness. They thereby create the possibility for more generously open-ended interpersonal relationships to develop, even though this narrator is as yet only able to articulate this possibility in negative or speculative ways.

If contemporary affect theorists such as Berlant focus on the alternatives affects help us find to staid social ideologies,[16] Ellison's *Invisible Man* thus depicts our affective confusions as—paradoxically—both a source of temptation because of which we fall for such ideologies, and a possible means of escaping them.[17] Berlant values affects for their richness of responsiveness and association, which enhance the depths to which we can look into ourselves. In a way that could be seen as a critical complement to Berlant's view, Ellison additionally reminds us how much we can learn about ourselves and others from moments when our introspective efforts stall and fail to the point of tempting us to ask others to facilitate them—and another person turns out to have the capacity to refuse us. Ellison builds around this intersubjective dependence models of an ideal community in which mutual communication is not intended primarily to forestall such contingencies. His novel also shows how deeply our expectations both of ourselves and of others would need to be reshaped in order for us to consistently want such a community, let alone build it: even for this narrator, the basement serves as a prosthesis of sorts that makes these alternative interpersonal ties easier to imagine.

Ellison describes forms of intersubjective affective recognition as resonances or sound waves. John Ashbery's poems, which I examine in the following chapter, depict acts of affective awareness more visually, as the experience of being enveloped by imagined cities or landscapes. Ashbery's fragmented, never quite self-knowing, speakers want their attempts at introspection to become redundant in the face of their environments' apparently instantaneous capacity to divine how they feel. Analogously to Ellison's model of affects as illuminating precisely through their imperfections, Ashbery's poems invoke this affective vulnerability to contest conventional assumptions about what constitutes an ideal community or a satisfying relation to oneself.

Chapter 5

MIRROR

John Ashbery

"One would like to stick one's hand / Out of the globe," says John Ashbery's speaker in "Self-Portrait in a Convex Mirror." "But its dimension, / What carries it, will not allow it."[1] Who is the "one" described here? The pronoun refers, ambiguously, both to the poem's speaker and to Parmigianino, the author of the self-portrait with whom this speaker identifies. Standing before this painting, the speaker blends together his hope of liberating himself from the solipsistic bubble of his own consciousness and a concurrent hope of having a blueprint for this liberation come to him from the outside, in a way that requires no agency on his part. A hand reaches out to him from its confinement; Parmigianino depicts for him the affective struggle whose terms he could not articulate on his own. The painter invites this speaker—or so he believes—to join him in a shared awareness of this struggle, fusing their retrospective solitudes into a state of communion and collaboration. But the poem continually reminds us that this speaker is only daydreaming: the long-dead Parmigianino does not care about how he feels. As the speaker beholds this painting and is tempted to see himself in it, the painting reflects back to him both his dream of outward recognition and the leap of faith required to believe that the surrounding world is actively trying to explain his mind and body to him.

This passage from "Self-Portrait" crystalizes a recurrent spatial metaphor Ashbery uses to represent his speakers' attempts at affective awareness. Affects, as Ashbery depicts them, conjure up fantasies of being intimately understood and cared for by others. Such fantasies that the task of elucidating their affects has been outsourced to the surrounding world highlight his speakers' uncertainty about how well they can articulate their affects themselves. These fantasies also allow his poems to convey a fear of how dependent we are on our environments for such clarifying reflections of our inner states. Images of the mirror serve as reminders that one often approaches one's surroundings with a burning need for introspective clarity, even though the stakes of one's affects never loom as large in other people's view as they do in one's own. As in Ellison, affects thus paradoxically become means of appreciating both one's dependence on the surrounding world and this world's separateness from oneself.

I return to poetry in this final chapter to show that representations of intersubjective cognitive dependencies—which would conventionally seem like the province of the novel—do make their way into the lyric genre as more than Plath's and Stevens's open-ended questions. Ashbery's poems insist that their speakers' self-awareness is always contingent and distributed, derived from surrounding environments whose help these speakers need to stabilize their sense of themselves. Much like Ellison's narrator, Ashbery's speakers do not discern the people around them very reliably because of the urgency with which they look to them for subjective clarification. The mirror—by far the most constrained, two-dimensional of the spaces of feeling this book examines—provides Ashbery with an image of the dependent solipsism required to see one's self as fully cognized by attentive observers. His poems acknowledge and often revel in the pleasures of such supposedly complete, outwardly derived cognizance. But they also show such pleased solipsism to be unviable in the long run. These poems thereby pave the way for ones—like "Wave" or "Three Poems"—in which experiences of cognitive dependence are definitively and, for the most part, quietly accepted as sources of aesthetic and intellectual pleasure. I will not discuss these latter poems here because they fall outside the scope of my central thesis. I see them as also including *The Tennis Court Oath* and much of Ashbery's poetry written after the 1970s, whose importance for an overall understanding of Ashbery's aesthetics I do not want to understate. But alongside Ashbery's other work, the poems I examine here can help us see more clearly the motivations Ashbery represents himself as having for abandoning a more introspectively driven lyric—as well as the role that affects and, in particular, questions of affective awareness play in his aesthetic choices.

The critical bent of these poems of intersubjective dependence is clarified by comparison to Eve Sedgwick's notion of "reparative" affective recognition. Sedgwick values affects as inspirations for mining the outer world for reflections of our values and needs. They move us to seek such reflections even in environments that are overtly hostile to, or neglectful of, our presence. The critical and aesthetic approach Sedgwick develops toward these fantasies, which she calls "reparative reading . . . is additive and accretive. Its fear, a realistic one, is that the culture surrounding it is inadequate or inimical to its nurture; it wants to assemble and confer plenitude on an object that will then have resources to offer to an inchoate self."[2] Sedgwick further describes an affectively driven critical and aesthetic practice as an attempt to "learn . . . the many ways selves and communities succeed in extracting sustenance from the objects of a culture—even of a culture whose avowed desire has often been not to sustain them."[3]

Ashbery's poems often focus on qualities of affective experience that closely resemble those described by Sedgwick. Like Sedgwick, Ashbery depicts affects as sources of a fantasy life that nurtures and develops alternative notions of the self. But unlike Sedgwick, Ashbery makes the self's dependence on the outside world seem vulnerably needy.[4] Refusing to depict his speakers' affects as mostly introspective affairs, Ashbery suggests that nothing less than a completely attentive, accommodating world would suffice to elucidate them. His speakers dream of being known and accepted from the outside because, like the characters and speakers I examine in prior chapters, they cannot count on their own minds and bodies to make sense of how they feel. This sense of dependence and the blind spots it creates within experiences of potential interpersonal communication are at the center of Ashbery's aesthetic engagements with affects.

Ashbery structures his representations of affective awareness around mirrors or mirrorlike surfaces, such as lakes, puddles, shiny cobblestones, and—more metaphorically—canvas. The ways in which Ashbery uses such reflective surfaces involve forms of spatial transformation and trompe l'oeil analogous to the ones I examine in earlier chapters. Even though, unlike most of the enclosures examined in prior chapters, these surfaces are two-dimensional, they produce similar effects of suddenly intimate confinement. Ashbery's poems highlight how little incentive their speakers need to believe that the outer world is reaching out to them. They hope to find this world eager to help make sense of their affects, even though no one but these speakers themselves cares much for their elucidation. These speakers then realize, with mixtures of disappointment and fear, just how dependent and solipsistic is the kind of self-understanding they are trying to reach.

I focus on two of Ashbery's early poems, "Some Trees" (1956) and "These Lacustrine Cities" (1962); and two later ones, "Self-Portrait in a Convex Mirror" (1975) and "Wet Casements" (1987). The first two poems show how Ashbery's representations of affects stem and gradually differentiate themselves from Romantic notions of interiority and introspection. These poems' relationship to the forms and tropes of the Romantic lyric could be described as falsely earnest. Apparently embracing many of these older generic conventions, his poems make them seem vulnerably hopeful and narrow-minded. In these early works, Ashbery represents the experience of temporarily forgetting, in one's enthusiasm, that the mere fact of being confronted and apparently interpellated by an outward correlative for one's affects does not prove that the world beyond one is particularly interested in one's affective confusion or even that the correlative one has found is readily intelligible to others. One might liken his speakers to more reflexive versions of characters from Woolf's novels. These speakers are dependent on moments of apparent outward recognition similar to those that give joy to Peter or Clarissa, but they also appreciate these moments' contingency and the likelihood that they do not actually stem from deep empathic engagement. In "Some Trees," Ashbery describes this process of falling into, and then becoming aware of, one's affective solipsism through metaphors of an open landscape that shrinks to become a canvas the speaker has painted. In "These Lacustrine Cities," his speaker looks out onto the poem's titular lakes and cities, or lakelike cities, and watches them erode until they merely reflect back to him the disempowered loneliness he has been trying to escape. Ashbery's speakers draw back from these imagined, suddenly solipsistic worlds without being able to unsee them. Such experiences make them increasingly aware of the unquestioning credulity with which they believed their feelings to have been the object of their surroundings' caring scrutiny.

"Some Trees," the title poem from Ashbery's first collection, depicts the narrowness of its speaker's affective concerns and cognitions as a discovery that breaks open the familiar conventions it initially follows. The poem stages a Romantic moment of self-recognition in nature. Its speaker finds himself in front of intertwining trees and realizes that he is in love with the person beside him. His budding feeling unexpectedly finds an embodiment in the physical landscape that surrounds them. Yet it gives rise not only to a revelation but also to an experience of "reticence"—a "reticence" that this speaker attributes to the external world, or at least both to himself and to the person he loves at once, because nothing actually happens in response to the affects that he assumes have just been incontrovertibly, collectively articulated. Speaking as "we," this speaker describes his affective discovery as one in which he and his beloved were equally involved. For a moment he dares to assume that they have both read the speaker's affection from its outer embodiment with equal clarity—and indeed, that they both share in this revealed affection with equal measure. Rather than moving him to confess his love to this other person, these affects lead him to imagine a fantastical world in which his love has already found abundant evidence. This dreamworld anticlimactically becomes ever more removed from the physical conditions with which the poem began, as well as from the speaker's beloved.

Moved by these trees and by what they reveal to him, the speaker states:

> . . . you and I
> Are suddenly what the trees try
>
> To tell us we are:
> That their merely being there
> Means something; that soon
> We may touch, love, explain. (26)

These trees show Ashbery's speaker that he and this other person "soon . . . may touch, love, explain." They spark in him an affect for which he at once finds a multitude of metaphors. As this affect continues, the speaker imagines before him "a silence already filled with noises; / A canvas on which emerges / A chorus of smiles, a winter morning" (26). These metaphors represent his affects as something that can be seen and has the potential to be voiced—and not only by him, but by a whole surrounding world. Within what are as yet only "a silence" and an empty "canvas," he finds latent "noises," "smiles," and the qualities of a "chorus." Each such new metaphor asserts his closeness to confessing his love for this other person or to hearing it confessed. Indeed, these metaphors suggest that, given the overwhelming presence of love all around him, he and this other person might not need to articulate it more explicitly at all. It seems as if this revelation will not require any further agency on their part, and would not come as a surprise to anyone.

Yet as Ashbery's metaphors proliferate, they also grow separate from the scene in which his speaker's joyful revelation started. As Wayne Koestenbaum puts it, this poem cannot sustain its expressions of love not even because it might be ironic, but because it shows indiscriminate trust toward the many imagined forms this expression of love might take.[5] And although the poem hints at a hopeful future, none of its phrases describe a shared world in which the speaker and his companion might declare their love and revel in that declaration's aftermath. Each line ends with a promise of some definitive revelation that the speaker and the person beside him could experience together, but each line break then postpones this promised revelation. The framing of this poem as a form of self-recognition in nature only makes more explicit the rapidity with which Ashbery's speaker spirals away from the initial correspondence between his affects and their supposed outward extensions. These affects are ever more obviously confined to the speaker's singular body and mind that have yet to "touch" his lover and "explain" themselves to him. Rather than coinhabit a shared, attentive world, the speaker has been merely trying to imagine it into being. This disappointed eagerness undercuts even the poem's metrical structure. At first glance, the poem's lines seem tight and regular. Short and divided into even four-line stanzas, they follow the traditional rhyme scheme of a song or a ballad. But read more carefully, these lines turn out to be linked mostly by slant rhymes (performance/chance; morning/agreeing; reticence/defense). These rhymes become especially imperfect in the third stanza, at the moment of the speaker's apparent sense of revelation (are/there; soon/explain). The poem strains and fails to sonically justify its speaker's leap of faith.[6]

These communicative deferrals could, of course, be described—as they have often been before—as representations of this speaker's growing subjective fragmentation and of the instability of the language he uses. The affective self-absorption I highlight coexists with these instabilities and fragmentations, but does not reduce itself to them. Ashbery's poem does not simply represent a communicative difficulty this speaker encounters. It also highlights that this speaker elides the experience of being compelled by the presence of another person to recognize his previously hidden feelings, with a belief in being cared for and understood by this other. Indeed, he makes the overhasty assumption that this act of mutual comprehension has already taken place. For Sedgwick, embracing such fantasies of affective recognition is a task that one undertakes with effort and commitment. She sees herself and other reparative critics as "trying . . . to keep faith with vividly remembered promises made to ourselves in childhood: promises to make invisible possibilities and desires visible; to make the tacit things explicit; to smuggle queer representation in where it must be smuggled and, with the relative freedom of adulthood, to challenge queer-eradicating impulses frontally where they are to be so challenged."[7] By contrast, Ashbery's poetry represents such fantasies as, above all, dreams of having one's experiences of exposure to one's communities and environments reframed as less threatening and benevolent; of being able to lean into such outward forms of recognition without fearing that they might be complicated by other people's inattentiveness or indifference.

"These Lacustrine Cities" reflects on a similar dream of uncomplicated and welcoming outward affective recognition. It does so by returning to mimetic strategies that echo and develop those of Stevens and Plath: as its speaker tries to introspect into his grief in the absence of a departed loved one, he finds that he cannot articulate his feelings to himself in this new state of solitude. Instead, he begins to dream about ever more fantastical others who could take over this task of introspection from him. Published six years after "Some Trees," "These Lacustrine Cities" responds to an unspecified personal loss. The speaker does not represent the history of this loss, but focuses on the turmoil into which it pulls him. The poem is structured as a series of rapidly alternating images. Its speaker pictures a series of landscapes out of which emanate feelings of love, grief, and longing. These landscapes promise and then fail to articulate what has just happened to him. By imagining that he can read his affects out of a landscape, the speaker gradually conveys both his continued lack of reliable external referents and his fear that he does not know how to supply them on his own. As the speaker falls into his grief, its experience is measured by his decreasing ability to even fantasize about a person or environment who could echo his affects for him acutely and precisely.

The poem's title promises "These Lacustrine Cities," and the pronoun "these" from the outset announces the cities as something that is immediately present and familiar. But Ashbery's writing instantly starts to confuse this appearance of accessibility. As Michael Clune puts it, "To attend to Ashbery's description of things is to note how the poems provide these things with a definite relation to an unknown context."[8] The images that constitute this landscape taper away before binding to any specific referent and without prefiguring the ones that follow. These images often fade before the speaker even begins to describe the qualities he claims they have.

The poem tells us that its successive images stem from "loathing" and "love." These affects hover in the opening lines as the impersonal attributes of an imagined urban space:

> These lacustrine cities grew out of loathing
> Into something forgetful, although angry with history . . .
>
> They emerged until a tower
> Controlled the sky, and with artifice dipped back
> Into the past for swans and tapering branches,
> Burning, until all that hate was transformed into useless love. (125)

The cities the speaker says grew from loathing become a bubble in which the anger that gave rise to them gradually blurs into its very opposite. The fantastical megalopolis whose central tower "dip[s] back / Into the past," hovers before us as a quasi-Romantic reflection of the speaker's affects. Yet, as Marjorie Perloff also describes him, this speaker cannot stabilize this landscape to give his affects an easily sharable expression.[9] The chains of association out of which the poem is constructed move with such rapid self-evidence that their content and significance become hermetic. The arcane decorations that encircle his cities' imagined tower "burn" before he can even begin to describe them and the past they supposedly evoke. Before the speaker even mentions the lakes adjacent to these cities (or expands on how these cities might themselves be like lakes), the cities themselves are gone. With each line break, the poem's landscape is eroded or distorted, becoming smaller

and vaguer than it initially appeared to be. Even between the first line and
the second one, the specific, plural noun "cities" becomes an unspecified,
singular "something." This pronoun makes these cities, or whatever they
turn into, sound like a confused, minimally animate being—a being whose
forgetfulness and anger are vulnerable and unmanageable since it is "angry" with nothing less than "history" itself.

By continually invoking the Romantic trope of correspondences between
affects and landscapes, "These Lacustrine Cities" makes its speaker's affective inarticulacy and displacement even more striking than does "Some
Trees." The components of its successive images—deserts, bodies of water,
and crowded cities—represent some of the most conventional sites through
which Romantic forms of self-recognition might take place. The speaker describes these landscapes as "all-inclusive" and ready for habitation, as if they
were features of a picturesque resort property. As the poem progresses, it becomes increasingly clear that its represented worlds cannot, in fact, deliver
any such sustainable forms of clarity. In successive stanzas, these lakes and
cities cease to even be the subjects of its sentences. Instead the poem's lines
begin with insistently repeated prepositions or personal pronouns that it no
longer "places" anywhere in particular:

> We have all-inclusive plans for you.
> We had thought, for instance, of sending you to the middle of the desert,
>
> To a violent sea, or of having the closeness of others be air
> To you. (125)

Eventually, these uncorroborated professions of certitude create an increasing impression of solipsism. The forms of reassurance that erupt within the
poem grow ever more oblique. They do not sound like actual plans or exchanges, but like stereotypical, B-grade movie fantasies of a world in which
all aspects of one's tumultuous experience are carefully staged and managed
from the outside. The "we" that speak here offer an unspecified "you" three
travel itineraries. Two of them sound like allegories of affective isolation and
turmoil; the third embodies a hope of reconciliation. Their similar delivery
belies the almost comical disparities between the kinds of landscapes these
successive lines offer and the different scales of experience—from the oce-
anic to the intimate—on which these landscapes operate. The travel plans

mentioned in this fragment never materialize, and none of these scenarios is pursued further. The implied "you" for whose benefit these "all-inclusive" plans are made and who might or might not be continuous with the implied speaker himself starts to resemble a persona. Toward the end of the poem, descriptions of these imagined landscapes devolve into mere placeholders: "You will be happy here"; "You have built a mountain of something."[10] These ever-emptier statements highlight the need that continues to erupt within this poem, amid the "hate" and "useless love," for a sense of enveloping comfort. They also make the speaker's desire for such comfort seem ever more futile.

As Bonnie Costello has argued, these imagined landscapes question the subjective coherence of Ashbery's fragmented, many-voiced speakers. But just as importantly, they also highlight that these speakers' worlds do not brim with travel agents avidly searching for the best correlates of their affects, however much the speakers might need them to do so. For Costello, "Landscape is . . . a fundamental, generating trope of knowledge in Ashbery's poetry—attractive . . . because it insistently invokes an observer and his or her environment and draws out assumptions of knowledge within our everyday accounts of what we know."[11] Costello reads another one of Ashbery's 'landscape' poems as follows:

> In the mental landscape, "the outcropping of peace" is presumably a pastoral respite from cognition, a promise of "presence" (thus an outcropping of what is otherwise submerged)—in the "blurred" afternoon "slope" of vision's mountain. In short, this is Eden, the travelers Adam and Eve, and their story a compressed version of human history.[12]

I agree with Costello that Ashbery's metaphors often invoke a wealth of potential personal or cultural meanings. Yet Ashbery's poems also insist on showing that these landscapes arise from absorptive, potentially solipsistic affective experiences. Costello's reading glosses over the strangeness of representing peace as an "outcropping" and "vision" as a "mountain." It similarly does not address the comedy of suggesting that such a series of oblique statements could in itself represent "Eden" and "Adam and Eve" and indeed constitute "a compressed version of human history." Ashbery endows these abstractions with such surreal, unvisualizable physicality that his metaphors highlight how little distance the speaker can take from the experiences to which he gives such detached labels. He represents the possible wealth of such cultural associations, but also the myopia required to see them as intentional outward explications of one's mental states.

Ashbery's early poems represent these forms of affective absorption merely as experiences of confusion or misprision, which leave the poems' implied speakers ever more disjointed and inarticulate. As his poetry develops, he gradually redescribes such hopes of outward help as affordances for considering one's relationships to others. In these later poems, Ashbery continues to depict his speakers as beings who yearn for a self-knowledge that they lack the capacity to consistently attain and whose world cannot be cajoled into a sense of urgency on their behalf. But his poems also begin to speculate about what it takes, under those circumstances, to recognize another person as something more than a source of support for one's self-understanding. On the one hand, these poems emphasize that many of our moments of affective clarity come from responding to someone else's self-expression as a message intentionally delivered by them to us and about us. On the other hand, they emphatically resist the idea that such acts of expressive recycling amount to mutual empathy. Even though we need other people's presence and expression to understand ourselves, these poems suggest, these people rarely if ever match our own investment in our introspective efforts. The insights they help us attain reach us from a state of relative indifference to and independence of our inward confusions, of which—in our self-involvement—we only ever catch occasional, mortifying glimpses. Acknowledging and lingering with such disenchantments is, for Ashbery, a necessary step toward developing an understanding of these other people as beings separate from, and irreducible to, ourselves.

The affects represented in "Some Trees" and in "These Lacustrine Cities" stem from implied personal histories. "Self-Portrait in a Convex Mirror," as many critics have noted, is more self-consciously aestheticized.[13] Laurence Lieberman describes the experience of reading "Self-Portrait" as follows: "I have lived with ["Self-Portrait"] as with a favorite mistress. . . . Often, for whole days of inhabiting *the room* of its dream, I have felt that it is the only poem—and Ashbery the only author—in my life."[14]

Ashbery's speaker in "Self-Portrait" dreams of inciting this kind of involvement; but he consistently calls such experiences into doubt as forms of actual mutual care or understanding. Turning to the trope of a mirror quite explicitly—as I began to outline at the start of this chapter—Ashbery represents his speaker as enchanted by another artist's self-portrait, but uncertain about the mutual relation in which this enchantment places them. Turning the tables on his reader much as Ellison's protagonist does on his community, this speaker then imagines his poem as the object of readerly identifications as needy as his own identification with Parmigianino.

"Self-Portrait" opens by expressing the speaker's surprise at finding in Parmigianino's self-portrait a deeply sensitive mirror of himself. The poem then positions itself as an ostensible explication of this act of recognition. "Self-Portrait" compares its formal presence against the form of the painting. The speaker is in a museum; he is looking at Parmigianino's self-portrait painted onto a half-sphere of wood:

> As Parmigianino did it, the right hand
> Bigger than the head, thrust at the viewer
> And swerving easily away, as though to protect
> What it advertises. (474)

Parmigianino's right hand "protect[s]" the image on whose boundary it rests. It seems to "thrust" itself "at the viewer," but then "swerv[es] easily away." The speaker tries to shape his poem "as Parmigianino did it," imitating with abrupt line breaks the similar abruptness of the painting's shifts in proportion and scale. But even as he does so, he continues to wonder about the actual kind and degree of affinity between him and the author of this painting. Is this image beckoning him or withholding itself from him? the speaker asks himself. He represents it as a world into which he might, however tentatively, be invited. But he also doubts that this painting reciprocates his own urge to see himself in it, to the point of wanting to shake hands with the painter. The portrait seems, at once, to burst out toward him and to withdraw deep beneath the surface of the bulging sphere of wood onto which it is drawn.

Soon after this opening—as Lee Edelman has observed—Ashbery multiplies the aims and contexts of this immersive poem. The "self-portrait" the poem seeks to represent is, at once, the Parmigianino painting and the self-portrait of the poem's speaker, as well as the portrait of this particular encounter between them.[15] Ashbery's speaker describes the appearance of Parmigianino's painting, its historical context, its current setting, and his own past and present life as its viewer. These details amplify the implicit

historical gap—and the resultant potential gap in mutual comprehension—
that separate him and Parmigianino from each other. As Lieberman puts
it, "The keynote is entrapment, alienation, detention, as the prevailing condition of the artist. . . . His smile is a mere 'pinpoint,' a 'perverse light'—it
can never release pain in a catharsis of laughter."[16] Even as he insists on this
mutual isolation and distance, Ashbery's speaker also marvels at how much
Parmigianino's painting lays itself open to anybody's apperception and
appropriation. This double sense of enclosure entraps the painter's (and by
extension, the speaker's) self not because they are insufficiently knowable,
but because they are paradoxically too knowable and therefore easy for anyone to absorb and then turn away from:

> The glass chose to reflect only what he saw
> Which was enough for his purpose . . .
> The soul establishes itself.
> But how far can it swim out through the eyes
> and still return safely to its nest? . . .
> The soul has to stay where it is,
> Even though restless, hearing raindrops at the pane,
> The sighing of autumn leaves trashed by the wind,
> Longing to be free, outside, but it must stay
> Posing in this place. It must move
> As little as possible. That is what the portrait says. . . .
> The secret is too plain. The pity of it smarts,
> Makes hot tears spurt: that the soul is not a soul,
> Has no secret, is small, and it fits
> Its hollow perfectly: its room, our moment of attention. (474–475)

The "soul" depicted by the painter might not be able to discern its own narrow boundaries. But a view from beyond, which integrates it into a much
larger landscape, instantly clarifies them. Our seemingly inexplicable, unbounded selves may appear much less unbounded, and their shapes much
more obvious, to someone else. This other person might therefore not even
notice the turmoil into which our affective confusions throw us. Ashbery's
line breaks repeatedly cut short the pathetic momentum of the speaker's engagement with this portrait. "The soul," this painting shows, "has no secret,
is small and it fits / its hollow perfectly." This "plain" fact of life does not
oppress or occlude one's soul (if one still calls it that). The poem emphasizes

the plainness of this discovery by placing it at the start of the poem rather than at its end: the revelation fails to arrest the speaker's thought.

As "Self-Portrait" continues, it resides ever more firmly between these two pronouncements: about the potentially easy, unremarkable transparency of our self-expression to the surrounding world and about our inability to move the world to a greater investment in and a more durable attachment to us. We might believe others do not care about us because they do not know us. Parmigianino's painting leads Ashbery's speaker to realize that feeling someone else's impact on our self-understanding, or believing that we have contributed to another person's sense of themselves, does not necessarily translate into deepened mutual care.

As Vendler and Lieberman both describe it, lingering with this painting provokes Ashbery's speaker to a personal recognition and crisis.[17] Abruptly, the speaker turns away. As if hoping to prove himself wrong, he starts to test the aims and limits of his sensibilities:

> The balloon pops, the attention
> turns dully away. Clouds
> In the puddle stir up into sawtoothed fragments.
> I think of the friends
> Who came to see me, of what yesterday
> was like. (476)

The popping balloon metaphorically stands in for the wooden bulge of the painting we were just made to observe. This metaphor also stresses the ease with which the painting dissolves, in the speaker's mind, to less than nothing. While echoing the shape and qualities of this painting, they also suggest how partial and oblique the speaker's attachment to it has been.

Ashbery's speaker then notices a puddle and bits of clouds shakily reflected within it. Gazing into this puddle, he starts to think about his friends. The water fragments and flattens the sky above it, mirroring the fragmentariness and flatness of how he describes the day he spent with these people: "the friends / Who came to see me, . . . what yesterday / was like." In the course of this passage, Ashbery's lines change length unpredictably and generally become much shorter. His language shifts from the more florid terms of the earlier sections to plain one-syllable verbs and nouns whose stronger stresses make the speaker sound more forceful even as he becomes less vividly expressive. He moves from phrases such as "sawtoothed fragments" to the bland "what yesterday / was like." Not only the painting, but also his friends, can become as indistinct to his mind's eye as reflections of clouds in a pool of water, as soon as his brief enthusiasm for describing them wanes.

As "Self-Portrait" continues, it insists ever more forcefully that the affects it represents are potentially accessible to anyone—and maybe also more accessible from the outside than to the introspective self—but that no one besides their bearer would pay much sustained, empathic attention to them. This realization does not come easily to Ashbery's speaker. As he puts it shortly before the poem's ending, "The ache / Of this waking dream can never drown out / The diagram sketched on the wind, / Chosen, meant for me and materialized" (487). He will, he fears, hardly be able to prevent himself from hoping or assuming that some "diagram" of the "waking dream" he now experiences will remain somewhere out there, waiting for him. But the last lines' "cold pockets / Of remembrance, whispers out of time" represent the speaker's affective attachments as fragile, ephemeral entities, objects of recollection whose persistence the speaker—or the artist himself—cannot do much to control:

> The hand holds no chalk
> And each part of the whole falls off
> And cannot know it knew, except,
> Here and there, in cold pockets
> Of remembrance, whispers out of time. (487)

To the extent that Ashbery's speaker has recognized something about Parmigianino, the latter can no longer benefit from it. Nor will the speaker's own affective experiences persist in his surrounding world except as fragmented, "cold" reflections that are no longer united by a single mind's and body's acts of care. Ashbery sees Parmigianino as showing an awareness of this vulnerability precisely by—as he suggests in the opening lines of the poem—only pretending to protect himself from it with his powerlessly outstretched hand.

Christopher Nealon reads such subdued endings of Ashbery's poems as actively subversive gestures. He also describes "Self-Portrait" in particular as a turning point in Ashbery's aesthetic, in which the subversiveness of these gestures is fully developed. In poems leading up to it, "the poet describes scenes of spectacle, pageantry, and even apocalypse, which are made harmless by the poet's turning to face the other way, or drifting in a different direction." The speaker's capacity to divert each such impending "apocalypse" eventually starts to seem escapist and "wishful." In "Self-Portrait," Ashbery turns his speaker's constant urge to flee the crises erupting around him into a revelation about his—and perhaps any other person's—relative social insignificance. "He wants us to recognize his smallness, his minority—he wants us to know that he is in danger, like any of us, of being downsized."[18]

I argue that the kind of "recognition" Nealon describes here—which Ashbery's speakers do urgently desire—is also something that his poems deeply mistrust. As I see it, "Self-Portrait" expresses a more ambivalent and reflexive standpoint; it also places at least as much emphasis on intersubjective awareness as it does on introspection. Even though, Ashbery suggests, we often may discern much about each other—including one another's vulnerabilities—that, in itself, cannot guarantee anything like a shared attachment to these vulnerabilities or a shared commitment to clarifying them.

Ashbery's insistence on his lyric subjects' surprising combination of knowability and solitude comes through even more forcefully in "Wet Casements," written a decade later. In this poem, whose title refers to John Keats's "Ode to a Nightingale" and its "charm'd magic casements" (again invoking the Romantic context of "These Lacustrine Cities" and "Some Trees"), the speaker tries to combine somebody else's and his own perspective. He angrily finds himself unable to do so; and in his anger, he imagines a utopian state of intimacy between him and other people with whose viewpoints his own sense of himself could comfortably merge. The speaker is at first overjoyed and then frightened by this act of imagination; he cannot linger in it long without realizing how much his cares wilt and diminish under another person's gaze.

The speaker of "Wet Casements" fantasizes about a world filled with "falbalas," "shoes," "cosmetics," and "cocktail parties" that give expression to other people's hidden responsiveness to those around them (508). As he tries to fall in step with these people's inaccessible perception of him, he pictures himself as a "you" that someone else is costuming in the accoutrements of her perception. Speculating about the wealth of insight hidden beyond other people's eyes—and revealed only in flat, compressed reflections on these eyes' surface—makes this speaker feel isolated. Echoing the convex mirror of "Self-Portrait," Ashbery describes these impenetrable eyes as round "windowpanes" "streaming" with rain:

> The concept is interesting: to see, as though reflected
> In streaming windowpanes, the look of others through
> Their own eyes. A digest of their correct impressions of
> Their self-analytical attitudes overlaid by your
> Ghostly transparent face. (508)

Even in this initial speculation, the object of the speaker's scrutiny is vaguely ominous. Instead of enclosing "you" in a full environment of shared thoughts and relations, other people's eyes overlay onto each other, on one flat surface, "your / Ghostly transparent face" and a "digest" of their "attitudes" toward "you." One's own presence and the presence of the other person become flatter and more unreal in juxtaposition with each other. To gaze into another person's eyes, the speaker goes on to say, lets one see oneself as a "bottle-imp [rising] toward a surface which can never be / approached." Confronted with this imp, the "viewer," as Stephen Paul Miller puts it, "must also see her- or himself as a kind of apparition."[19]

The poem enacts this felt loss of material presence in its diminishing form. The first part of "Wet Casements" consists of a single stanza divided by a longer middle line; this extended middle line ends with the word "approached":

> The shoes perfectly pointed, drifting (how long you
> Have been drifting; how long I have too for that matter)
> Like a bottle-imp toward a surface which can never be approached,
> Never pierced through into the timeless energy of a present (508)

This word apparently pushes beyond, but cannot break, the limits of the poem (in most editions it is necessarily represented on its own separate line), mirroring the sense of confinement described by the speaker. The speaker imagines that masses of memories and sensations accumulate behind his interlocutor's eyes; yet they can only reach the speaker in a strained, instantly negated premonition. Following this stanza, "Wet Casements" slowly but inevitably contracts from long sentences and run-on lines to short phrases, down to a couplet made up of terse, abstract words. Having ascertained that the forms of communion it tries to approach are unattainable, the first section of the poem apparently loses its own physical footing.

As "Wet Casements" progresses, the speaker becomes angry at the distance between his sense of himself and other people's responses to it. This anger moves him to imagine a "bridge" that brings them together. This "bridge" connects them not as a narrow pathway between otherwise inaccessible worlds of experience, but as a shared dead end. The speaker describes it as a broken bridge like that of Avignon, an affordance not for crossing but for "dancing":

> I want that information very much today,
>
> Can't have it, and this makes me angry.
> I shall use my anger to build a bridge like that
> Of Avignon, on which people may dance for the feeling
> Of dancing on a bridge. I shall at last see my complete face
> Reflected not in the water but in the worn stone floor of my bridge. (508)

In the urgency of his anger, the detached "you" becomes an "I"; "a bridge" becomes "my bridge"; and the singular "I" is joined not only by the single person into whose eyes he imagined gazing, but by many "people" for whom this bridge might be as delightful as for the speaker himself. The speaker hopes that the "stone floor" of this bridge will reflect his face to him completely. He represents it as a site that is equally accessible and precious to himself and to others. In the real world, as he suggests in his opening reference to Franz Kafka, it never "rains" enough for one to be definitively sure that it is raining. In this imagined world, by contrast, our inner needs and outer conditions align into a sense of "complete" meaningfulness and certitude.

"Wet Casements" brings out the immersiveness with which the speaker falls into this fantasy, as well as its ever more obviously narrow limits. If this speaker and his interlocutor finally "blend" together in this passage, they do so, to use Stamelman's metaphor, "as light and fog."[20] Repeating the downward spiral of "These Lacustrine Cities," Ashbery's lines become ever simpler and more repetitive. As the speaker tries to hold on to his fantasy—but already starts to fall out of it—he retreats into short phrases and insistent reiterations of the word "bridge." In the last line of this stanza, he impossibly imagines this bridge as a mirror for his own affects, while all the other people mentioned in the poem disappear from view. His optimistic dream of community reduces to a fantasy of solipsistic (if deeply context-dependent) self-control and self-sufficiency.

Meanwhile, the very notion of aligning oneself with how others perceive one becomes increasingly unpleasant to the poem's speaker; the more completely this fantasy realizes itself, the more dramatically the speaker needs to pull away from it. The poem ends on a half-frightened, half-petulant note. "I shall keep to myself," the speaker says. "I shall not repeat others' comments about me" (508). This petulance reminds one that the affectively driven fantasy the speaker has just described is also a means of temporarily forgetting about how little other people might care even about the knowledge they do have about his mind and body. Beyond the challenge of knowing what these other people think about him, the speaker locates the second, apparently unforeseen challenge of accepting that, in these people's eyes, he might exist as nothing more than the subject of gossip.

After edging toward what Sedgwick might describe as a "reparative" attitude toward the speaker's feelings, "Wet Casements" thus pulls away from it. A more superficial reading of this poem might stress, in close accord with Sedgwick, that the moment of hopefulness preceding these lines constitutes an aesthetic and personal affordance. It allows Ashbery's speaker to conceive of—and perhaps even temporarily bring into being—a mode of relating to others that moves beyond the singular "you," which temporarily holds the indifference of the outer world in suspension. The impossible intimacy about which he initially just hypothesizes becomes an articulable object of desire. The imagined possibility of entrusting his self-knowledge to others makes this speaker acknowledge his eagerness to do so.

But—as I also argue in a briefer reading of this poem in the introduction—such an interpretation sells short the bitterness of the two lines with which "Wet Casements" ends. It also does not acknowledge the insistence with which Ashbery continues to show that a poem about this speaker's affective awareness inevitably becomes a poem about how these affects come across to others. Letting his speaker's sense of himself emerge from contexts and bodies that might not care about preserving and making sense of his affects allows Ashbery to dramatize his speaker's dependence on other people as well as the significant distinction between being able to count on another person for a fleeting reflection of one's affects and for sustained acts of concern about the mind and body that experiences them. It also lets the poem highlight the self-involvement of its speaker's desire for a communal form of awareness. Such sustained yearnings for clarity, Ashbery finally suggests, usually characterize only an affect's original bearer, little as he often knows about his feelings on his own. Moreover, their intensity stems less from these affects' intrinsic large-scale meaningfulness than from the puzzling bodily and mental confusions they provoke. Any affective self-awareness—hard-won as it may be—is, in Ashbery's poems, marked with the chill of this double realization. To the extent that these poems do, of course, present themselves as possible sites of analogous affective recognition or "mirroring" for their reader, they thereby also—as does Parmigianino in his self-portrait—hold this implied reader's experience at arm's length.

CONCLUSION

The works whose "spaces of feeling" this book examines frequently build toward moments of unexpected clarity that suggest the revelatory potential of affective experience. A character's or lyric speaker's body suddenly becomes, as Wallace Stevens puts it, quite "sure what it intends," and this represented person is affirmed and elated by it.[1] "It is Clarissa," Peter Walsh realizes as a figure on the staircase fills him with "extraordinary excitement."[2] "Daddy, Daddy, / you bastard, I'm through," Sylvia Plath's speaker exclaims once she finally comes to terms with the intensity of her anger.[3]

But *Spaces of Feeling* also seeks to undercut the impression that such moments of revelation always emerge from independent introspection or that the affects they elucidate are objects of great curiosity for anyone besides their bearer. As the novels and poems I examine here represent it, the experience of reflecting one our affects poses a radical challenge both to our introspective autonomy and to our capacity to gauge the outward significance of our supposed secrets. Such affective reflections thus also make us newly aware of the reality of people and environments that exist beyond ourselves and that our needs and cares do not immediately ignite.

Through their insistence on the intersubjectivity of affective awareness, the authors I examine subvert many assumptions with which critics usually approach the study of affect. These authors undermine our faith in our capacity to be independently cognizant of our affects and in the generalizability of what we might perceive as complicated, endlessly interesting affective conundrums. Their novels and poems also outline insights into our bodies and minds and their relations to the bodies and minds of others that can come from experiences of discarding these premises. They help us look toward new forms of community built around the paradoxical notion of ourselves as both more, and less, cognitively autonomous than we might think.

One might further clarify the conceptual shift to which *Spaces of Feeling* invites its readers by comparison to the conclusion of Rei Terada's *Looking Away*. In the last pages of this book, Terada discusses Sigmund Freud's *Civilization and Its Discontents* as a conceptual model whose lack of realism does not prevent it from being critically insightful. "What Freud produces, disturbingly and amusingly," Terada writes, "is a figure of the ideal analyst, the one whose theoretically infinite patience is literalized—an analyst who could wait out the acting out of world spirit." Terada qualifies this figure as an impossible and not even necessarily an optimistic idealization: "This is a utopian figure of plenitude, as well as a dystopian one that tries to take measure of the trouble civilization is in." While acknowledging the limitations of Freud's ideal in practice, Terada defends it as a model for the aspirations contemporary thinkers ought to bring to their attempts at understanding their own and other people's experiences. "Bringing this figure back to the critical debate about whether and how to think about impossible projects . . . may help to clarify why, for a reservation that seems both too small and too large to be spoken, an unconditional space is a better idea than the few seconds of tolerance we usually give ourselves." We ought to think about our affects and our lives in general—Terada suggests—by expanding the time and space we can afford to give their real or imagined examination, as much as possible.[4]

The aims of my project could not, in most respects, be more different from Terada's. Put in her terms, *Spaces of Feeling* remains firmly on the side of the "few seconds of tolerance" that Terada describes as our miserly gift to ourselves and that I treat as an inalienable aspect of our experience and awareness of affects. The literary representations of affect discussed in this book pointedly lack "an unconditional space" of "infinite patience" to take stock of one's bodily and mental states. Even less do these works suggest that any person could have an inexhaustible, satisfying capacity for affective reflection. Most importantly, they refuse to assume that we could ever be our own therapists—or that the kind of affective self-knowledge we should value comes from compelling another person to be our affects' endlessly patient amanuensis. David's sudden self-consciousness in a crowded gay bar, the overstimulated inarticulacy of Ellison's narrator, or the helpless eagerness Ashbery's lyric speakers express for being understood provide us with alternatives to the model of affective self-knowledge whose hyperbolic, hyperidealized extreme Terada articulates here. They also suggest reasons why aspects of affective experience that Terada's ideal elides—such as our affects' potential lack of interest to others or the belated, dependent difficulty with which we might make sense of even our most conventional feelings—are crucial to an understanding of our social worlds and of ourselves.

Notes

Introduction

1. James Baldwin, *Giovanni's Room* (New York: Random House, 1956; repr., New York: Doubleday, 2000), 38. Citations refer to the 2000 edition.

2. Massumi describes a famous experiment by Benjamin Libet as follows: "Brain waves of healthy volunteers were monitored by an encephalograph (EEG) machine. The subjects were asked to flex a finger at a moment of their choosing and to recall the time of their decision by noting the spatial clock position of a revolving dot. The flexes came 0.2 seconds after they clocked the decision, but the EEG machine registered significant brain activity 0.3 seconds *before* the decision." Brian Massumi, *Parables for the Virtual: Movement, Affect, Sensation* (Durham, NC: Duke University Press, 2002).

3. In this regard, my project attempts to speak back both to the relatively recent aesthetic turn in literary criticism and to the much more recent attempt—spearheaded by critics such as Michael Warner, Rita Felski, Sharon Marcus, and Stephen Best—to develop a model of reading that does not rest entirely on claims to detached aesthetic and social critique. See Stephen Best and Sharon Marcus, "Surface Reading: An Introduction," *Representations* 108, no. 1 (2009): 1–21; Rita Felski, *The Limits of Critique* (Chicago: University of Chicago Press, 2015); Felski, *Uses of Literature* (London: Wiley-Blackwell, 2008); Michael Warner, "Uncritical Reading," in *Polemic: Critical or Uncritical*, ed. Jane

Gallop (New York: Routledge, 2004) , 13–38; Heather Love, "Close But Not Deep: Literary Ethics and the Descriptive Turn," *New Literary History* no. 41 (2010): 371–391. For accounts of the earlier, aesthetic turn (also described as New Formalism) on which these critics partly build, see Marjorie Levinson, "What Is New Formalism?," *PMLA* 122, no. 2 (2007): 558–569; Jane Elliott and Derek Attridge, eds., *Theory after 'Theory'* (London: Routledge, 2011); Jacques Rancière, *The Politics of Aesthetics,* trans. Gabriel Rockhill (New York: Continuum, 2004).

4. In this context, it is, of course, important to remark that the word "affect" itself comes from psychoanalysis—it is the term applied by the analyst to the feelings she observes in the analysand. I would argue that the question of affect becomes much more critically interesting when—as is the case in contemporary theory—the theorist herself tries to play the double role of doctor and patient, attempting to both acknowledge and control the degree to which her affects take her by surprise.

5. Massumi, *Parables*, 1.

6. One recent theorist on whose work this project builds, in this regard, is Eugenie Brinkema. Brinkema's *Forms of the Affects* studies the forms taken by affective expression not only in human bodies but also in the works of art to which these bodies give rise. Like Brinkema, I shift our perspective away from readerly or writerly affects and toward the relationship between affect and the form of an artwork. At the same time, I do not assume that affects are present in poetry or fiction with any of the directness with which she claims they are present in cinema. Taking represented affects a little less seriously than she does, I treat them not as ends in themselves but as oblique paths toward understanding how affects structure first-person experience and the forms of expression or interaction that arise from it. Eugenie Brinkema, *The Forms of the Affects* (Durham, NC: Duke University Press, 2014), xvi.

7. Ruth Leys, "The Turn to Affect: A Critique." *Critical Inquiry* 37 (2011): 434.

8. In this sense, within the context of literary criticism, my argument returns to and generalizes from debates about reader response, authorial intention, and critical solipsism undertaken by critics such as Stanley Fish, Wayne Booth, W. K. Wimsatt, Monroe Beardsley, and many others. Unlike these critics, I see a way out of these debates neither in affirming the critic's affective responses to the text nor in removing the potential for this response, and for its influence on one's reading of a text, from consideration.

9. John Ashbery, *Collected Poems 1956–1987* (New York: Library of America, 2008), 475–476.

10. Charles Altieri, *The Particulars of Rapture: An Aesthetics of the Affects* (Ithaca, NY: Cornell University Press, 2003), 2.

11. In *The Particulars of Rapture*, Altieri argues that affects reveal parts of ourselves that trouble our conventional narratives of who we are. "An aesthetics of the affects," he shows, "becomes a means of elaborating how there may be profoundly incommensurable perspectives on values that are nonetheless all necessary if we are to realize various aspects of our human potential." Ngai's *Ugly Feelings* examines negative affects that she claims offer insights even though, and indeed precisely because, they distort one's sense of reality. She puts this point as follows, borrowing the lan-

guage of Paolo Virno: "Even an unattractive feeling like opportunism can provide the 'kernel' from which to shape 'transformative behavior.' For all its pettiness, the feeling calls attention to a real social experience and a certain kind of historical truth." Massumi's *Parables for the Virtual* insists that the experience of affect always challenges and exceeds our cognitive capacities. We can only barely and belatedly fall in step with it, in a way that is inevitably "disorienting." Altieri, *Particulars*, 5; Sianne Ngai, *Ugly Feelings* (Cambridge, MA: Harvard University Press, 2005), 5; Massumi, *Parables*, 35. Paolo Virno, "The Ambivalence of Disenchantment," in Paolo Virno and Michael Hardt, eds. *Radical Thought in Italy* (Minneapolis: University of Minnesota Press, 1996), 25.

12. These historical developments—and the sense of futurelessness they created—have been described by Paul Saint-Amour in *Tense Futures: Modernism, Total War, Encyclopedic Form* (New York: Oxford University Press, 2015).

13. Jonathan Flatley, *Affective Mapping: Melancholia and the Politics of Modernism* (Cambridge, MA: Harvard University Press, 2008).

14. Joseph Frank, "Spatial Form in Modern Literature: An Essay in Three Parts," *Sewanee Review* 53, no. 4 (1945): 643–653.

15. For extended theoretical accounts of rereading, see Matei Calinescu, *Rereading* (New Haven, CT: Yale University Press, 1993); or Namwali Serpell, *Seven Modes of Uncertainty* (Cambridge, MA: Harvard University Press, 2013).

16. In this regard, my account of rooms in these poems and novels goes against the conventional understanding of represented domestic spaces as metonymic representations of larger social norms and structures (see, e.g., Nancy Armstrong, *Desire and Domestic Fiction* [New York: Oxford University Press, 1987]; Gaston Bachelard, *The Poetics of Space*, trans. Maria Jolas [Boston: Beacon Press, 1994]).

17. Jonathan Crary describes this dimension of modernist aesthetics as an effort to turn literature and art into a near-scientific account of how acts of perception and attentiveness take place; Jonathan Crary, *Suspensions of Perception* (Cambridge, MA: MIT Press, 1999). See also Daniel Albright, *Quantum Poetics* (Cambridge: Cambridge University Press, 1997), 1–10; Peter Nicholls, *Modernisms: A Literary Guide* (New York: Macmillan, 1999), 76, 81; Elizabeth Abel, *Virginia Woolf and the Fictions of Psychoanalysis* (Chicago: Chicago University Press, 1989); Ann Banfield, *The Phantom Table* (New York: Cambridge, 2000), xiii; Philip Fisher, "Looking Around to See Who I Am: Dreiser's Territory of the Self," *ELH* 44, no. 4 (1977): 728–748; Bonnie Kime Scott, ed., *The Gender of Modernism* (Bloomington: Indiana University Press, 1990); Henry Louis Gates, *The Signifying Monkey* (New York: Oxford University Press, 1988).

18. T. J. Clark, *Farewell to an Idea* (New Haven, CT: Yale University Press, 1999), 160.

19. Douglas Mao, *Solid Objects: Modernism and the Test of Production* (Princeton, NJ: Princeton University Press, 1998); Georges Poulet, *Espace proustien* (Paris: Gallimard, 1982).

20. Marta Figlerowicz, *Flat Protagonists: A Theory of Novel Character* (New York: Oxford University Press, 2016).

1. Threshold

1. Wallace Stevens, *The Collected Poems of Wallace Stevens* (New York: Knopf, 1974), 130. Hereafter, citations to this work are given parenthetically in the text.

2. Put more facetiously, it is as if these poems' implied authors assumed that they were writing an introspective lyric of the kind theorized by Helen Vendler, belatedly to realize that their chosen genre follows rules that are more like those posited by Jonathan Culler: it makes room for a coherent and self-knowing sense of self as, at best, a temporary and contingent construct.

3. Altieri, *Particulars*, 136.

4. In *Wallace Stevens and the Demands of Modernity*, Altieri applies a version of his theory of affect to Stevens. "For Stevens," he says, "poetry manages most fully to engage in such philosophical questioning by putting imagination to work on what various affective registers within philosophy might entail or involve." In these explorations of affect, Stevens "fosters modes of pleasure that are themselves explorations of what powers we can still take as distinctively human even as he demonstrates for us the need to develop third-person distance from our fantasies that the world will honor or should honor these powers." This "distance" allows him, as Altieri puts it, to take "pleasure" in the process of feeling without tying himself down to any single object or aim on which his feelings temporarily settle. Charles Altieri, *Wallace Stevens and the Demands of Modernity* (Ithaca, NY: Cornell University Press, 2013), 6–7.

5. Altieri, *Particulars*, 230.

6. Altieri, *Demands*, 57.

7. Wallace Stevens, *Opus Posthumous: Poems, Plays, Prose* (New York: Vintage, 1990), 163.

8. Simon Critchley, *Things Merely Are: Philosophy in the Poetry of Wallace Stevens* (New York: Routledge, 2005), 73.

9. Charles Altieri, *The Art of Twentieth-Century American Poetry: Modernism and After* (New York: Blackwell, 2006), 131.

10. Marie Borroff, "An Always Incipient Cosmos," in *Wallace Stevens*, ed. Harold Bloom (New York: Chelsea, 1985), 106.

11. Vendler calls such transitions "a civilized passage from tone to tone, with a flicker of grossness, a tinge of humor, a touch of logic or illogic, as Stevens moves within the various discourses of his ample harmonium." Helen Vendler, *On Extended Wings: Wallace Stevens' Longer Poetry* (Cambridge, MA: Harvard University Press, 1969), 172.

12. Vendler, *On Extended Wings*, 189.

13. Critchley, *Things Merely Are*, 73–74.

14. Vendler, *On Extended Wings*, 196.

15. Altieri, *Demands*, 116.

16. Ibid., 35.

17. Helen Vendler, *Last Looks, Last Books* (Princeton, NJ: Princeton University Press, 2010), 31.

18. See, e.g., A. Alvarez, "Sylvia Plath," in *The Art of Sylvia Plath*, ed. Charles Newman (London: Faber and Faber, 1970), 67; Vivian Pollak, "Moore, Plath, Hughes, and 'The Literary Life,'" *American Literary History* 17, no. 1 (2005): 95; Deborah Nelson, "Plath, History, and Politics," *The Cambridge Companion to Sylvia Plath*, ed. Jo Gill (New

York: Cambridge University Press, 2006), 21; Robin Peel, *Writing Back: Sylvia Plath and Cold War Politics* (London: Associated University Presses, 2002), 108; Harold Fromm, "Sylvia Plath, Hunger Artist," *Hudson Review* 43, no. 2 (1990): 256; Susan Gubar, "Prosopopoeia and Holocaust Poetry in English: Sylvia Plath and Her Contemporaries," *Yale Journal of Criticism* 14, no. 1 (2001): 202.

19. Critics who read Plath through this lens include Steven Gould Axelrod, *Sylvia Plath: The Wound and the Cure of Words* (Baltimore: Johns Hopkins University Press, 1990), 143; Christina Britzolakis, "*Ariel* and Other Poems," in Gill, *The Cambridge Companion to Sylvia Plath*, 108; A. Alvarez, "Sylvia Plath," 67.

20. Ted Hughes, Introduction to *The Collected Poems of Sylvia Plath* (New York: Harper, 1981), 16. Hereafter, page references to Plath's *Collected Poems* are cited parenthetically in the text.

21. Robin Peel, "The Ideological Apprenticeship of Sylvia Plath," *JML* 27, no. 4 (2004): 61.

22. Plath states explicitly that miscarriage is the subject of the poem in a subsequent interview.

23. Helen Vendler, *Coming of Age* as a Poet (Cambridge, MA: Harvard University Press, 2003), 138.

24. Marjorie Perloff, "On the Road to 'Ariel': The 'Transitional' Poetry of Sylvia Plath," *Iowa Review* 4, no. 2 (1973): 97.

25. Altieri, *Particulars*, 230.

26. Jacqueline Rose, *The Haunting of Sylvia Plath* (Cambridge, MA: Harvard University Press, 1993), 5.

27. Christina Britzolakis, *Sylvia Plath and the Theater of Mourning* (New York: Oxford University Press, 2000), 184.

28. Heather Clark, "Tracking the Thought-Fox: Sylvia Plath's Revision of Ted Hughes," *JML* 28, no. 2 (2005): 106.

29. Vendler, *Last Looks*, 54.

30. Altieri, *Particulars*, 20.

2. Living Room

1. Virginia Woolf, *Mrs. Dalloway* (1925; repr., London: Harcourt, 1981), 118. Hereafter, page references to the 1981 edition are cited parenthetically in the text.

2. Massumi, *Parables*, 21.

3. The virtuality of affects, claims Massumi, is one reason why the consciously felt effects they produce—which he terms "emotion"—are so overwhelming: "Emotion is the most intense (most contracted) expression of that *capture*—and of the fact that something has always and again escaped. This is why all emotion is more or less disorienting, and why it is classically described as being outside of oneself, at the very point at which one is most intimately and unshareably in contact with oneself and one's vitality." Massumi, *Parables*, 35 and 103.

4. In my reading of *Mrs. Dalloway*, I follow many prior scholars—including Maria DiBattista, George Ella Lyon, and Tori Haring-Smith—who show that this novel is

narrated through the prism of intimate feelings. Woolf defends these felt experiences against the repressive social conventions of her time. She also treats her characters' affective states as keys to a better understanding of the sociopolitical conditions in which these characters find themselves. I agree with these other critics that Woolf depicts feelings as reminders of how deeply we are shaped by our particular personal and social histories. But *Mrs. Dalloway* also focuses on the immediate inarticulacy of the affective attachments these histories lead its characters to form and maintain. See George Ella Lyon, "Virginia Woolf and the Problem of the Body," in *Virginia Woolf: Centennial Essays*, ed. Elaine K. Ginsberg and Laura Moss Gottlieb (Troy, NY: Whitston, 1983), 118; Maria DiBattista, *Virginia Woolf's Major Novels: The Fables of Anon* (New Haven, CT: Yale University Press, 1980), 35; Tori Haring-Smith, "Private and Public Consciousness in *Mrs. Dalloway* and *To the Lighthouse*," in Ginsberg and Moss Gottlieb, *Virginia Woolf*, 143; Howard Harper, *Between Language and Silence: The Novels of Virginia Woolf* (Baton Rouge: Lousiana University Press, 1982), 3; Jean O. Love, *Worlds in Consciousness: Mythopoetic Thought in the Novels of Virginia Woolf* (Berkeley: University of California Press, 1970), 108; DiBattista, *Virginia Woolf's Major Novels*, 45; Wendy B. Faris, "The Squirrel's Heart Beat and the Death of the Moth," in Ginsberg and Moss Gottlieb, *Virginia Woolf*, 83; Abel, *Virginia Woolf and the Fictions of Psychoanalysis*. Some critics give this reading an explicitly feminist angle: see Brenda Silver, *Virginia Woolf: Icon* (Chicago: University of Chicago Press, 1999); Ellen Marcus, *Art and Anger: Reading like a Woman* (Columbus: Ohio State University Press, 1988); Michele Pridmore-Brown, "1939–40: Of Virginia Woolf, Gramophones, and Fascism," *PMLA* 113, no. 3 (1998): 408–421. For others, the import of such affective self-probing is primarily philosophical. See, e.g., Louise Westling, "Virginia Woolf and the Flesh of the World," *New Literary History* 30, no. 4 (1999): 855–875; Banfield, *Phantom Table*, 2007; Martha Nussbaum, "The Window: Knowledge of Other Minds in Virginia Woolf's *To the Lighthouse*," *New Literary History* 26, no. 4 (1995): 731–753; Tammy Clewell, "Consolation Refused: Virginia Woolf, The Great War, and Modernist Mourning," *MFS* 50, no. 1 (2004): 199.

5. Virginia Woolf, *Mr. Bennett and Mrs. Brown*, Hogarth Essays (London: Hogarth Press, 1924), 9.

6. Jane Duran, "Virginia Woolf, Time, and the Real," *Philosophy and Literature* 28, no. 2 (2004): 302. See also Karen Smythe, "Virginia Woolf's Elegiac Enterprise," *NOVEL: A Forum on Fiction*, 26, no. 1 (1992): 73.

7. Liesl M. Olson praises *Mrs. Dalloway* as a novel that succeeds in representing the "cotton wool of daily life." For Olson, Woolf excels at showing that our lives are not composed of grand singular events but of small habits we repeat unthinkingly. Passages such as this one do draw attention to such unsung forms of experience. Yet they also stage a sense of disenchantment with what one can convey even about one's most significant affective experiences. Liesl M. Olson, "Virginia Woolf and the 'Cotton Wool of Daily Life,'" *JML* 26, no. 2 (2003): 44.

8. Brian Phillips highlights Woolf's Dickensian fascination with the grotesque. Septimus's visions are, arguably, one major example of this fascination. Brian Phillips, "Reality and Virginia Woolf," *Hudson Review* 56, no. 3 (2003): 415–416.

9. Susan Bennett Smith, "Reinventing Grief Work," *Twentieth Century Literature* 41, no. 4 (1995): 315; David Neal Miller, "Authorial Point of View in Virginia Woolf's *Mrs. Dalloway*," *Journal of Narrative Technique* 2, no. 2 (1972): 126.

10. Nussbaum, "The Window," 752.

11. Massumi, *Parables*, 109.

12. Mitchell Breitwieser further describes Fitzgerald's novels as representations of his generation's failure to understand its faltering economy and social structures. Mitchell Breitwieser, "Jazz Fractures: F. Scott Fitzgerald and Epochal Representation," *American Literary History* 12, no. 3 (2000): 359–381. See also Richard D. Lehan, *F. Scott Fitzgerald and the Craft of Fiction* (London: Feffer and Simons, 1966), 73; Keath Fraser, "Another Reading of *The Great Gatsby*," in *Critical Essays on F. Scott Fitzgerald's* The Great Gatsby, ed. Scott Donaldson (Boston: G. K. Hall, 1984), 150; Kirk Curnutt, "'A Unity Less Conventional but Not Less Serviceable': A Narratological History of *Tender Is the Night*," in *Twenty-First Century Readings of* Tender Is the Night, ed. William Blazek and Laura Rattray (Liverpool: Liverpool University Press, 2007), 122.

13. See Lehan, *F. Scott Fitzgerald and the Craft of Fiction*, 73; Fraser, "Another Reading of *The Great Gatsby*," 150; Curnutt, "'A Unity Less Conventional,'" 122.

14. F. Scott Fitzgerald, *Tender Is the Night* (New York: Scribner, 2003), 19. Originally published in 1934; citations refer to the 2003 edition.

15. T. Austin Graham, "The Literary Soundtrack: Or, F. Scott Fitzgerald's Heard and Unheard Melodies," *American Literary History* 21, no. 3 (2009): 539.

16. W. T. Lhamon Jr., "The Essential Houses of *The Great Gatsby*," in Donaldson, *Critical Essays*, 172.

17. Ross Posnock, "'A New World, Material without Being Real': Fitzgerald's Critique of Capitalism in *The Great Gatsby*," in Donaldson, *Critical Essays*, 205.

18. Giles Gunn argues further that Gatsby's inability to realize that his dream has long expired puts him out of touch with his changing society: "Gatsby's dream belongs to a historical order which has long since ceased to exist, to a vision of possibility which had almost died on the eyes of those first Dutch sailors to these shores, who, paradoxically, were the last to look upon the American landscape with innocence." Giles Gunn, "F. Scott Fitzgerald's *Gatsby* and the Imagination of Wonder," in Donaldson, *Critical Essays*, 231.

19. In a way that further reinforces this point, critics have often noted that this novel is at once grounded in, and strikingly detached from, the growing social instability of the late twenties and early thirties. Milton Stern lists the almost comical multitude of current social issues and cultural themes the novel attempts to tackle: "The themes are many and complex. They include war . . . identity . . . wealth, the movies, acting, swimming, the New Woman, the fathers, Europe and America, priestliness, past and present, sun and moon, heat and coolness, black and white." At the same time, as Arthur Mizener puts it, the novel's principal actors are marginal to their country's current historical events and lead their lives in ways that are frequently oblivious of them. Milton R. Stern, "*Tender Is the Night* and American History," in *The Cambridge Companion to F. Scott Fitzgerald*, ed. Ruth Prigozy (Cambridge: Cambridge University Press, 2002), 99; Arthur Mizener, "*Tender Is the Night*," *Critical Essays on F. Scott Fitzgerald's* Tender

Is the Night, ed. Milton R. Stern (Boston: G. K. Hall, 1986), 163. See also Lehan, *F. Scott Fitzgerald and the Craft of Fiction*, 42; Linda De Roche, "Sanatorium Society: The 'Good' Place in *Tender Is the Night*," in Blazek and Rattray, *Twenty-First Century Readings*, 61; James F. Light, "Political Conscience in the Novels of F. Scott Fitzgerald," in Stern, *Critical Essays*, 137; Chris Messenger, " 'Out upon the Mongolian Plain': Fitzgerald's Racial and Ethnic Cross-Identifying in *Tender Is the Night*," in Blazek and Rattrey, *Twenty-First Century Readings*, 171.

20. Pamela A. Boker, "Beloved Illness: Transference Love as Romantic Pathology in F. Scott Fitzgerald's *Tender Is the Night*," *Literature and Medicine* 11, no. 2 (1992): 304.

21. Grenberg reads this episode as a form of dramatic political commentary: "Dick has been slowly but irresistibly crushed by the same force giving ascendance to Nicole: by the 'billions' and 'trillions' of the booming stock market, by the 'plentitude of money' which became 'an absorption in itself.' " John Callahan also treats this passage as Dick's assertion of how little he wants to depend on anyone but himself: "Time and time again, he blunts Nicole's critical perception of one or another of his failings by substituting detachment for spontaneous emotional response." Bruce Grenberg, "Fitzgerald's 'Figured Curtain': Personality and History in *Tender Is the Night*," in Stern, *Critical Essays*, 233. John Callahan, "The Way Home: But Here There Is No Light," in Stern, *Critical Essays*, 198.

3. Bedroom

1. "J'ai revu tantôt l'une, tantôt l'autre, des chambres que j'avais habitées dans ma vie.... chambres d'hiver,... chambres d'été ... parfois la chambre Louis XIV" (1:7). Marcel Proust, *A la recherche du temps perdu*, 7 volumes (Paris: Folio, 1992); Marcel Proust, *In Search of Lost Time*, trans. C. K. Scott Moncrieff and Terence Kilmartin, 6 volumes (New York: Modern Library, 2003). All passages from Proust are henceforth cited in the text, with the 2003 English edition quoted directly and the 1992 French edition appended in the notes.

2. "Stuplimity," as Ngai calls one of these affects, is "an indeterminate affective state that lacks the punctuating 'point' of an individuated emotion." Paranoia is a feeling whose need for clarity produces only superficial, "obvious" results. Of the experiences of cuteness, zaniness, and the interesting, Ngai similarly says, "Each of these aesthetic experiences revolves around a kind of inconsequentiality: the low, often hard-to-register flicker of affect accompanying our recognition of minor differences from a norm, in the case of the interesting; physical diminutiveness and vulnerability, in the case of the cute; and the flailing helplessness of excessively strenuous but unproductive exertion (and unfocused rage), in the case of the zany." Ngai, *Ugly Feelings*, 284, 308–309; Sianne Ngai, *Our Aesthetic Categories* (Cambridge, MA: Harvard University Press, 2012), 18.

3. Ngai, *Ugly Feelings*, 5. Indeed, Ngai argues, "it is arguably the stylistic triviality and verdictive equivocality of the zany, the cute, and the interesting that makes these categories particularly suited for the analysis of art and aesthetics in today's totally aestheticized present." Ngai, *Categories*, 19.

4. I follow a number of prior critics who, in more general terms, emphasize the importance Proust attaches to space. For Poulet, Proust's spaces are inscribed with truths

about our existential isolation. For Deleuze, they are made out of "hieroglyphs" that transmit to the narrator the pathos of his attempts to make sense of himself. Georges Poulet, *L'Espace proustien* (Paris: Gallimard, 1962), 61; Gilles Deleuze, *Proust and Signs*, trans. Richard Howard (1964; repr., Minneapolis: University of Minnesota Press, 2000), 102. Citations refer to the 2000 edition.

5. "Comme je les répétai, renouvelant le choc a plaisir, ces mots de hangar, de couloir, de salon, quand Saint-Loup fut parti! Dans un hangar, on peut se cacher avec une amie. Et dans ce salon, qui sait ce qu'Albertine faisait quand sa tante n'était pas là? Eh quoi?" (6:54).

6. The alternative translation of this title is *In The Shadow of Young Girls in Flower*.

7. "Clignant des yeux contre le soleil, il semblait presque sourire, je trouvai à sa figure vue ainsi au repos et comme au naturel quelque chose de si affectueux, de si désarmé, que je ne pus m'empêcher de penser combien M. de Charlus eût été fâché s'il avait pu se savoir regardé; car ce à quoi me faisait penser cet homme qui était si épris, qui se piquait si fort de virilité, à qui tout le monde semblait odieusement efféminé, ce à quoi il me faisait penser tout d'un coup, tant il en avait passagèrement les traits, l'expression, le sourire, c'était à une femme!" (4:6).

8. Eve Kosofsky Sedgwick, *The Weather in Proust* (Durham, NC: Duke University Press, 2012), 34.

9. "Il y avait bien une jeune fille assise, en robe de soie, nu-tête, mais de laquelle je ne connaissais pas la magnifique chevelure, ni le nez, ni ce teint et où je ne retrouvais pas l'entité que j'avais extraite d'une jeune cycliste se promenant coiffée d'un polo, le long de la mer. C'était pourtant Albertine. Mais même quand je le sus, je ne m'occupai pas d'elle.... Pour le plaisir je ne le connus naturellement qu'un peu plus tard, quand, rentré à l'hôtel, resté seul, je fus redevenu moi-même" (2:433–435).

10. "'Ne continue pas tes sorties pour rencontrer Mme de Guermantes, tu es la fable de la maison. D'ailleurs, vois comme ta grand-mère est souffrante, tu as vraiment des choses plus sérieuses que de te poster sur le chemin d'une femme qui se moque de toi,' d'un seul coup, comme un hypnotiseur, qui vous fait revenir du lointain pays où vous vous imaginiez être, et vous rouvre les yeux, ou comme le médecin qui, vous rappelant au sentiment du devoir et de la réalité, vous guérit d'un mal imaginaire dont vous vous complaisiez, ma mère m'avait réveillé d'un trop long songe" (3:360).

11. "What I find in *A la recherche*," says Katja Haustein, "is not only holistic emotionality, but its advancing displacement by the rapid increase in what I propose be called 'emotional cavities.' These are zones where there is no longer any interaction or closeness, no emotional contact or correspondence between the narrator and the world he perceives, but rather emotional distance and difference, zones where the narrator is left alone, standing before the frame." Still, passages such as this one do not simply depict the narrator's partial detachment from his material spaces. They also highlight his attempts to understand the limits to how many sensations he might be able to take in at once, or around how many of them he builds his sense of the persons he loves. Katja Haustein, "Proust's Emotional Cavities," *French Studies* 63, no. 2 (2009): 162.

12. Ngai, *Ugly Feelings*, 330.

13. "Disons du reste que le jardin de La Raspèlière était en quelque sorte un abrégé de toutes les promenades qu'on pouvait faire à bien des kilomètres alentour.... Et en

effet ils réunissaient autour du château les plus belles 'vues' des pays avoisinants, des plages ou des forêts, aperçus fort diminués par l'éloignement, comme Hadrien avait assemblé dans sa villa des réductions des monuments les plus célèbres des diverses contrées" (4:388).

14. "Nous le comprimes dès que la voiture, s'élançant, franchit d'un seul bond vingt pas d'un excellent cheval. Les distances ne sont que le rapport de l'espace au temps et varient avec lui. Nous exprimons la difficulté que nous avons a nous rendre à un endroit, dans un système de lieues, de kilomètres, qui devient faux dès que cette difficulté diminue. . . . il était facile d'aller dans un même après-midi à Saint-Jean et à La Raspelière, Douville et Quetteholme, Saint-Mars-Le-Vieux et Saint-Mars-Le-Vêtu, Gourville et Balbec-Le-Vieux, Tourville et Fêterne, prisonniers aussi hermétiquement enfermés jusque-là dans la cellule de jours distincts que jadis Méséglise et Guermantes, et sur lesquels les mêmes yeux ne pouvaient se poser dans un seul après-midi" (4:385–386).

15. "Le voyage idéal est, pour Proust, celui qui, abolissant d'un coup les distances, place côte à côte, comme s'ils étaient contigus et même communicants, deux de ces lieux dont l'originalité faisait pourtant qu'ils semblaient devoir exister pour toujours à part l'un de l'autre, sans possibilité de communication. Ainsi il est juste de dire que l'expérience du mouvement change les lois de l'univers." Poulet, *Espace proustien*, 95. My translation.

16. For an extended account of the historical context of Proust's interest in automobiles, see Sara Danius, "The Aesthetics of the Windshield: Proust and the Modernist Rhetoric of Speed," *Modernism/modernity* 8, no. 1 (2001): 99–126.

17. Diane R. Leonard, "Ruskin and the Cathedral of Lost Souls," *The Cambridge Companion to Proust*, ed. Richard Bales (London: Cambridge University Press, 2001), 45.

18. "Pour évaluer la perte que me faisait éprouver ma réclusion, c'est-a-dire la richesse que m'offrait la journée, il eut fallu intercepter dans le long déroulement de la frise animée quelque fillette portant son linge ou son lait, la faire passer un moment, comme une silhouette d'un décor mobile, entre les portants, dans le cadre de ma porte, et la retenir sous mes yeux" (5:129).

19. Ngai, *Categories*, 19.

20. Ibid., 18.

21. "Aussi immatériel que jadis Golo sur le bouton de porte de ma chambre de Combray, ainsi le nouveau et si méconnaissable Argencourt était là comme la révélation du Temps, qu'il rendait partiellement visible" (7:231).

22. Eve Kosofsky Sedgwick, *Epistemology of the Closet* (Berkeley, CA: University of California Press, 1990).

23. "Aussitôt la vieille maison grise sur la rue, où était sa chambre, vint comme un décor de théâtre s'appliquer au petit pavillon, donnant sur le jardin, . . . et avec la maison, la ville, . . . la Place où on m'envoyait avant déjeuner, les rues ou j'allais faire des courses, les chemins qu'on prenait si le temps était beau" (1:47).

24. "J'écarte tout obstacle, toute idée étrangère, j'abrite mes oreilles et mon attention contre les bruits de la chambre voisine" (1:44).

25. "L'être qui était rené en moi . . . cet être-là ne se nourrit que de l'essence des choses, en elle seulement il trouve sa subsistance, ses délices" (7:179).

26. See, e.g., Leo Bersani, *Marcel Proust: The Fictions of Life and Art* (New York: Oxford University Press, 1965); Martha Nussbaum, "Fictions of the Soul," *Philosophy and*

Literature 7, no. 2 (1983): 147; Samuel Beckett, *Proust and Three Dialogues* (London: Calder, 1965).

27. "Depuis le jour de l'escalier, rien du monde, aucun bonheur, qu'il vînt de l'amitié des gens, des progrès de mon œuvre, de l'espérance de la gloire, ne parvenait plus a moi que comme un si pâle grand soleil, qu'il n'avait plus la vertu de me réchauffer, de me faire vivre, de me donner un désir quelconque, et encore était-il trop brillant, si blême qu'il fût, pour mes yeux qui préféraient se fermer, et je me retournais du côté du mur" (7:347).

28. Henry Louis Gates, Jr., "The Fire Last Time," in *James Baldwin*, ed. Harold Bloom (New York: Chelsea, 2007), 15. Following Gates, the vast majority of Baldwin's recent critics have sought to locate and define in his fiction some vision of a new potential social order. See, e.g., Ryan Jay Friedman, "'Enough Force to Shatter the Tale to Fragments': Ethics and Textual Analysis in James Baldwin's Film Theory," *ELH* 77, no. 2 (2010): 385–412; Mikko Tuhkanen, "'Binding the Self: Baldwin, Freud, and the Narrative of Subjectivity," *GLQ* 7, no. 4 (2001): 555; Michael L. Cobb, "Pulpit Publicity: James Baldwin and the Queer Uses of Religious Words," *GLQ* 7, no. 2 (2001): 290.

29. Langston Hughes, "From Harlem to Paris," in *James Baldwin: A Collection of Critical Essays*, ed. Keneth Kinnamon (Englewood Cliffs, NJ: Prentice-Hall, 1974), 10.

30. Eldridge Cleaver, "Notes on a Native Son," in Kinnamon, *James Baldwin*, 68.

31. "Of course it is somewhere before me, locked in that reflection I am watching in the window as the night comes down outside. It is trapped in the room with me." Baldwin, *Giovanni's Room*, 10. Hereafter, all other excerpts from *Giovanni's Room* are cited parenthetically in the text. All citations in this chapter refer to the 2000 edition.

32. F. W. Dupee, "James Baldwin and the 'Man,'" in Kinnamon, *James Baldwin*, 12.

33. Kathleen N. Drowne, "'An Irrevocable Condition': Constructions of Home and the Writing of Place in *Giovanni's Room*," in *Re-Viewing James Baldwin: Things Not Seen*, ed. D. Quentin Miller (Philadelphia: Temple University Press, 2000), 73.

34. Ngai, *Ugly Feelings*, 10.

35. Baldwin, *Giovanni's Room*, 57.

36. Drowne, "'An Irrevocable Condition,'" 79–86.

37. Especially in these later novels, the language Baldwin uses to describe these events stems from communal experiences that include religious rituals, theater and jazz performances, as well as political rallies. For extended accounts of the influence of music and religion on Baldwin's imagery, see Sherley Anne Williams, "The Black Musician: The Black Hero as Light Bearer," in Kinnamon, *James Baldwin*, 147–154; Clarence E. Hardy III, "James Baldwin as Religious Writer: The Burdens and Gifts of Black Evangelicalism," in *A Historical Guide to James Baldwin*, ed. Douglas Field (Oxford: Oxford University Press, 2009), 61–82.

38. James Baldwin, *Another Country*, in *Early Novels and Stories*, ed. Toni Morrison (New York: Library of America, 1998), 398. Hereafter, page references to this edition are cited parenthetically in the text.

39. In a way that my point partly echoes, Amy Reddinger writes that *Another Country* "renders New York as a segregated, violent, passionate city in which love, sex, race, and gender all are constituted by the city while they at the same time demand a persistent retelling of the city as a space in which borders are crossed and sexual, racial, and class

boundaries are blurred." Amy Reddinger, "'Just Enough for the City': Limitations of Space in Baldwin's *Another Country*," *African American Review* 43, no. 1 (2009): 117.

40. By representing these failures, *Another Country* also asks how much historical awareness—and what awareness of oneself within it—his characters need in order to successfully act against, or even to expose, social oppression or prejudice. "To accept one's past—one's history—is not the same thing as drowning in it, it is learning how to use it," says Baldwin in the passage that Deak Nabers singles out as the central thesis of *The Fire Next Time*. James Baldwin, *The Fire Next Time*, in *Collected Essays*, ed. Toni Morrison (New York: Library of America, 1998), 333; Deak Nabers, "Past Using: James Baldwin and Civil Rights Law in the 1960s," *Yale Journal of Criticism* 18, no. 2 (2005): 221–242.

41. Ngai, *Ugly Feelings*, 209–211.

42. Susan Feldman, "Another Look at *Another Country*: Reconciling Baldwin's Sexual and Racial Politics," in Miller, *Re-Viewing James Baldwin*, 91.

43. James Baldwin, *Notes of a Native Son*, in *Collected Essays*, 7–8.

44. Cleaver, "Notes on a Native Son," 68.

45. Horace A. Porter, *Stealing the Fire: The Art and Protest of James Baldwin* (Middletown, CT: Wesleyan University Press, 1989), 169; Feldman, "Another Look at *Another Country*," 100.

46. The parallels and disjunctures between their insistence on self-enclosure and more negative conventional notions of being closeted can also be brought into conversation with recent research on earlier twentieth-century attitudes toward gay intimacy and secrecy. For critical engagements with Baldwin and Proust as queer authors, see, among others, Michael Lucey, "Proust's Queer Metalepses," *MLN* 116, no. 4 (2001): 795–815; Sedgwick, *Epistemology of the Closet*; Douglas A. Field, "Looking for Jimmy Baldwin: Sex, Privacy, and Black Nationalist Fervor," *Callaloo* 27, no. 2 (2004): 457–480; Mae G. Henderson, "James Baldwin: Expatriation, Homosexual Panic, and Man's Estate," *Callaloo* 23, no. 1 (2000): 313–327.

4. Basement

1. Ralph Ellison, *Invisible Man* (New York: Vintage, 1990), 239.

2. A similar comparison could be made, on this level, between Ellison's novel and the work of Sara Ahmed. Berlant's and Ahmed's writing differs in other ways—in terms both of their foci and their method—but both theorists share a commitment to finding alternatives to means of understanding and performing affect imposed on us by the social world. As Ahmed puts it in *The Promise of Happiness*, "Feelings do not . . . simply reside within subjects and then move outward toward objects. Feelings are how objects create impressions in shared spaces of dwelling" (14). To combat our current overemphasis on happiness as a source of such social and material meaning, she argues, "we will also need other kinds of critical and creative writing that offer thick descriptions of the kinds of worlds that might take shape when happiness does not provide a horizon for experience" (14). Sara Ahmed, *The Promise of Happiness* (Durham, NC: Duke University Press, 2010).

3. Following this insight in *Cruel Optimism*, Berlant shows how much our contemporary predilection for destructive, excessive enthusiasm reveals about the state of late capitalism. She also suggests other affective states—such as "impersonal" affection or melancholia—that offer possible alternatives to this condition. Lauren Berlant, *Cruel Optimism* (Durham, NC; Duke University Press, 2011), 263 and 16.

4. Ralph Ellison, *Shadow and Act* (New York: Vintage, 1995), 177.

5. "What astonishes one most about *Invisible Man*," Howe argues, "is the apparent freedom it displays from the ideological and emotional penalties suffered by Negroes in this country." Irving Howe, "Black Boys and Native Sons," *Dissent* (Autumn 1963), accessed April 30, 2014, www.writing.upenn.edu. Miele Steele provides a useful overview and bibliography of these debates in "Metatheory and the Subject of Democracy in the Work of Ralph Ellison," *New Literary History* 27, no. 3 (1996): 491–492.

6. See James M. Albrecht, "Saying Yes and Saying No: Individualist Ethics in Ellison, Burke, and Emerson," *PMLA* 114, no. 1 (1999): 47; Houston A. Baker, "To Move without Moving: An Analysis of Creativity and Commerce in Ralph Ellison's Trueblood Episode," *PMLA* 98, no. 5 (1983): 831; Lawrence Jackson, "Ralph Ellison's Invented Life: A Meeting with the Ancestors," in *The Cambridge Companion to Ralph Ellison*, ed. Ross Posnock (Cambridge: Cambridge University Press, 2005), 11–34; Anne Anlin Cheng, "Ralph Ellison and the Politics of Melancholia," in Posnock, *The Cambridge Companion to Ralph Ellison*, 123; Thomas F. Marvin, "Children of Legba: Musicians at the Crossroads in Ralph Ellison's *Invisible Man*," *American Literature* 68, no. 3 (1996): 587–608; Frederick T. Griffiths, "Copy Wright: What Is an (Invisible) Author?" *New Literary History* 33, no. 2 (2002): 337–338; Donald A. Pease, "Ralph Ellison and Kenneth Burke: The Nonsymbolizable (Trans)Action," *boundary 2* 30, no. 2 (2003): 80–81; Ross Posnock, "Ralph Ellison, Hannah Arendt, and the Meaning of Politics," in Posnock, *The Cambridge Companion to Ralph Ellison*, 214; Kenneth Warren, "Ralph Ellison and the Problem of Cultural Authority," *boundary 2* 30, no. 2 (2003): 170; Kevin Bell, "The Embrace of Entropy: Ralph Ellison and the Freedom Principle of Jazz Invisible," *boundary 2* 30, no. 2 (2003): 21–45.

7. The links between Ellison's depictions of his narrator's powerful affective experiences and of the physical electroshocks to which the narrator and others around him are often subjected are well known to criticism. For Johnnie Wilcox, these links are metaphors for hidden social forces reshaping and reestablishing American racial stereotypes, by which the narrator is ceaselessly altered and distressed. These parallels do highlight ways in which this narrator's intense affects are fueled and reignited by manifestly physical, outward sources and causes. But Ellison also uses such parallels to stress that the narrator is here being asked to carry the weight of affects that are not actually his own. Johnnie Wilcox, "Black Power: Minstrelsy and Electricity in Ralph Ellison's *Invisible Man*," *Callaloo* 30, no. 4 (2007): 1000.

8. Ralph Ellison, *Invisible Man*, 237. Hereafter, page references to this work are cited parenthetically in the text.

9. Berlant, *Cruel Optimism*, 16. Ahmed makes a similar point when she describes the process of "recogniz[ing]" our unhappiness and the many objects and contexts associated with it (159).

10. Paul Allen Anderson, "Ralph Ellison's Music Lessons," in Posnock, *The Cambridge Companion to Ralph Ellison*, 100; Susan L. Blake, "Ritual and Rationalization: Black Folklore in the Works of Ralph Ellison," *PMLA* 94, no. 1 (1979): 121–136.

11. Sara Blair, "Ellison, Photography, and the Origins of Invisibility," in Posnock, *The Cambridge Companion to Ralph Ellison*, 58.

12. Steve Pinkerton, "Ralph Ellison's Righteous Riffs: Jazz, Democracy, and the Sacred," *African American Review* 44, nos. 1–2 (2011): 199.

13. Barry Shank, "Bliss, or Blackface Sentiment," *boundary 2* 30, no. 2 (2003): 57–58.

14. David Messmer, "Trumpets, Horns, and Typewriters: A Call and Response between Ralph Ellison and Frederick Douglass," *African American Review* 44, no. 4 (2010): 601.

15. Ralph Ellison, *Going to the Territory* (New York: Vintage, 1986), 8.

16. In her interview for *Qui Parle*, Berlant thus argues that "while one can't intend an affect, one can become attentive to the nimbus of affects whose dynamics move along and make worlds, situations, and environments, and in attending to, representing, and standing for these alternative modes of being, provide new infrastructures for extending their potential to new planes of convergence. I hope!" Lauren Berlant and Jordan Greenwald, "Affect in the End Times: A Conversation with Lauren Berlant," *Qui Parle* 20, no. 2 (2012): 88. Ahmed echoes Berlant in the following passage: "We need to develop a language to describe qualitative differences in how we experience our activities and passivities. To do this, we must challenge the very separation of active and passive and how that separation works to secure different classes of being, from happy persons and crossing chickens to suffering souls and inert roads" (210).

17. Ellison's treatment of affect partly presages what, several decades later, becomes known as studies of alterity and the ethics of otherness. Where Ellison's novel differs from these more familiar models is in its paradoxical insistence that not even the bearer of a certain feeling can always elucidate it, even if he has at his disposal a very flexible ideological or discursive apparatus, and that noticing other people's relative indifference to us is at least as important to a proper understanding of their separate needs and experiences as the efforts we make to care more about these other people's feelings.

5. Mirror

1. John Ashbery, *Collected Poems 1956–1987* (New York: Library of America, 2008), 475.

2. Eve Kosofsky Sedgwick, *Touching Feeling* (Durham, NC: Duke University Press, 2003), 149. Sedgwick's reparative impulse has previously been applied to the literary period I examine by Samuel See. See applies the term "queer mythology" to the aesthetic practices of modernist writers such as Charles Henri Ford and Parker Tyler. He suggests that by fostering "mythologies" about their lives as gay men, these writers enact the kinds of reparative practices described by Sedgwick. Ford and Tyler represent the creation of queer communities within a hostile, heteronormative environment, as a process of nurturing local, idiosyncratic myths about one's feelings and sensations. Tyler and Ford's novel *The Young and Evil*, as See describes it, "enables the individual to overcome his or her 'feeling of separateness' by depicting a universally queer world—one that,

paradoxically, maintains a feeling of separateness as a criterion for inclusion in it." The impermanence and unreality of these utopian narratives, claims See, becomes an affordance for representing both the fragility of these communities and their aspirations. Samuel See, "Making Modernism New: Queer Mythology in 'The Young and Evil,'" *ELH* 76, no. 4 (2009): 1094.

3. Sedgwick, *Touching Feeling*, 150–151. "Sedgwick's mode of reading," as Berlant also explains it, "is to deshame fantasmatic attachment so as to encounter its operations as knowledge." Sedgwick seeks "to sustain the unfinished and perhaps unthought thoughts about desire that are otherwise defeated by the roar of conventionality." Berlant, *Cruel Optimism*, 122–123.

4. Catherine Imbriglio and John Shoptaw describe several of the poems I examine here as closeted, in the sense of trying to convey queer desires in an oblique, coded fashion. I would add that these poems are also explorations of the experience of the closet as a willful and ongoing narrowing of one's ranges of experience and expression. Catherine Imbriglio, "Our Days Put on Such Reticence: The Rhetoric of the Closet in John Ashbery's 'Some Trees,'" *Contemporary Literature* 36, no. 2 (1995): 249–288; John Shoptaw, *On the Outside Looking Out* (Cambridge, MA: Harvard University Press, 1998). See also John Vincent, "Reports of Looting and Insane Buggery behind Altars: John Ashbery's Queer Poetics," *Twentieth Century Literature* 44, no. 2 (1998): 155–175; Aidan Wasley, "The 'Gay Apprentice': Ashbery, Auden, and a Portrait of the Artist as a Young Critic," *Contemporary Literature* 43, no. 4 (2002): 667–708; Christopher Schmidt, *The Poetics of Waste: Queer Excess in Stein, Ashbery, Schuyler, and Goldsmith* (New York: Palgrave, 2014).

5. Wayne Koestenbaum, "John Ashbery's Lazy Susan," *Mississippi Review* 31, no. 3 (2003): 174.

6. I thank Ben Glaser for this observation.

7. Eve Kosofsky Sedgwick, *Tendencies* (Durham, NC: Duke University Press, 1993), 3.

8. Michael Clune, "'Whatever Charms Is Alien': John Ashbery's Everything," *Criticism* 50, no. 3 (2008): 449.

9. Marjorie Perloff, *The Poetics of Indeterminacy: Rimbaud to Cage* (1981; repr., Evanston, IL: Northwestern University Press, 1999), 270. Citations refer to the 1999 edition. Perloff also compares Ashbery's poems to dreams.

10. Ashbery, *Collected*, 125.

11. Bonnie Costello, "John Ashbery's Landscapes," in *The Tribe of John: Ashbery and Contemporary Poetry*, ed. Susan Schultz (Tuscaloosa: University of Alabama Press, 1995), 60.

12. Ibid., 76–77.

13. See Richard Stamelman, "Critical Reflections: Poetry and Art Criticism in Ashbery's 'Self-Portrait in a Convex Mirror,'" *New Literary History* 15, no. 3 (1984): 607–630; Helen Vendler, *Invisible Listeners* (Princeton, NJ: Princeton University Press, 2005); David Kalstone, *Five Temperaments: Elizabeth Bishop, Robert Lowell, James Merrill, Adrienne Rich, John Ashbery* (New York: Oxford University Press, 1977).

14. Laurence Lieberman, "Unassigned Frequencies: Whispers Out of Time; A Reading of John Ashbery's 'Self-Portrait in a Convex Mirror,'" *American Poetry Review* 6, no. 2 (1977): 4 (emphases in original).

15. Lee Edelman, "The Pose of Imposture: Ashbery's 'Self-Portrait in a Convex Mirror,'" *Twentieth-Century Literature* 32, no. 1 (1986): 79.

16. Lieberman, "Unassigned Frequencies," 5.

17. Helen Vendler, *Invisible Listeners*, 64–65; Lieberman, "Unassigned Frequencies," 5–6.

18. Christopher Nealon, *The Matter of Capital: Poetry and Crisis in the American Century* (Cambridge, MA: Harvard University Press, 2013), 78 and 101. Nealon's argument also echoes Andrew DuBois's earlier work about Ashbery's representations of attention. DuBois notes, with many other critics, that Ashbery "apes or maps the attention spans of the citizens of the age." DuBois shows that the apparent distractedness of Ashbery's speakers is not just a flaw Ashbery parodies, but a capacity in which he finds value. By letting themselves be distracted by new sensations constantly, these speakers draw attention to the wealth of persons and environments around them and to the claims many of these persons and environments could have on them. Just as, for Nealon, these speakers' passivity is paradoxically transformed into a form of political and aesthetic critique, for DuBois, the distractedness of these speakers becomes a tool of self-awareness about the richness and multiplicity of the world in which they live. Andrew DuBois, *Ashbery's Forms of Attention* (Tuscaloosa: Alabama University Press, 2006), xiv.

19. Stephen Paul Miller, "'Self-Portrait in a Convex Mirror,' the Watergate Affair, and Johns' Crosshatch Paintings: Surveillance and Reality-Testing in the Mid-Seventies," *boundary 2* 20, no. 2 (1993): 103.

20. Stamelman, *Critical Reflections,* 624.

Conclusion

1. Stevens, *Collected*, 390.

2. Woolf, *Mrs. Dalloway*, 194.

3. Plath, *Collected*, 183.

4. Rei Terada, *Looking Away: Phenomenality and Dissatisfaction, Kant to Adorno* (Cambridge, MA: Harvard University Press, 2009), 204.

Bibliography

Abel, Elizabeth. *Virginia Woolf and the Fictions of Psychoanalysis*. Chicago: Chicago University Press, 1989.

Ahmed, Sara. *The Promise of Happiness*. Durham, NC: Duke University Press, 2010.

Albrecht, James M. "Saying Yes and Saying No: Individualist Ethics in Ellison, Burke, and Emerson." *PMLA* 114, no. 1 (1999): 46–63.

Albright, Daniel. *Quantum Poetics*. Cambridge: Cambridge University Press, 1997.

Allen, Shirley S. "The Ironic Voice in Baldwin's *Go Tell it On the Mountain*." In Bloom, *James Baldwin*, 43–52.

Altieri, Charles. *The Art of Twentieth-Century American Poetry: Modernism and After*. New York: Blackwell, 2006.

———. "John Ashbery and the Challenge of Postmodernism in the Visual Arts." *Critical Inquiry* 14, no. 4 (1988): 805–830.

———. "John Ashbery as a Love Poet." In Schultz, *The Tribe of John*, 26–37.

———. *The Particulars of Rapture: An Aesthetics of the Affects*. Ithaca, NY: Cornell University Press, 2003.

———. *Wallace Stevens and the Demands of Modernity*. Ithaca, NY: Cornell University Press, 2013

Alvarez, A. "Sylvia Plath." In Newman, *The Art of Sylvia Plath*, 56–68.

Anderson, Paul Allen. "Ralph Ellison's Music Lessons." In Posnock, *Cambridge Companion to Ralph Ellison*, 82–103.

Anlen, Elad. "Reflections on SCT 2009." *Theory* (Fall 2009): 9.

Armstrong, Isobel. *The Radical Aesthetic*. Oxford, UK: Blackwell, 2000.

Armstrong, Nancy. *Desire and Domestic Fiction*. New York: Oxford University Press, 1987.

Ashbery, John. *Collected Poems 1956–1987*. New York: Library of America, 2008.

———. *Some Trees*. New Haven, CT: Yale University Press, 1956.

Auden, W. H. Foreword to *Some Trees*, by John Ashbery, 11–16. New Haven, CT: Yale University Press, 1956.

Axelrod, Steven Gould. *Sylvia Plath: The Wound and the Cure of Words*. Baltimore: Johns Hopkins University Press, 1990.

Bachelard, Gaston. *The Poetics of Space*. Translated by Maria Jolas. Boston: Beacon Press, 1994.

Baker, Houston A. "To Move without Moving: An Analysis of Creativity and Commerce in Ralph Ellison's Trueblood Episode." *PMLA* 98, no. 5 (1983): 828–845.

Baldwin, James. *Collected Essays*, ed. Toni Morrison.. New York: Library of America, 1998.

———. *Early Novels and Stories*, ed. Toni Morrison. New York: Library of America, 1998.

———. *Giovanni's Room*. New York: Random House, 1956.

Bales, Richard, ed. *The Cambridge Companion to Proust*. London: Cambridge University Press, 2001.

Banfield, Ann. *The Phantom Table*. New York: Cambridge, 2000.

Barthes, Roland. *The Rustle of Language*. Translated by Richard Howard. Berkeley: University of California Press, 1989.

Beckett, Samuel. *Proust and Three Dialogues*. London: Calder, 1965.

Bell, Kevin. "The Embrace of Entropy: Ralph Ellison and the Freedom Principle of Jazz Invisible." *boundary 2* 30, no. 2 (2003): 21–45.

Benjamin, Walter. *Illuminations*. Translated by Harry Zohn. New York: Schocken, 1968.

Bennett, Paula. *My Life a Loaded Gun: Female Creativity and Feminist Poetics*. Boston: Beacon Press, 1986.

Bennett Smith, Susan. "Reinventing Grief Work." *Twentieth Century Literature* 41, no. 4 (1995): 310–327.

Berlant, Lauren. *Cruel Optimism*. Durham, NC: Duke University Press, 2011.

Berlant, Lauren, and Jordan Greenwald. "Affect in the End Times: A Conversation with Lauren Berlant." *Qui Parle* 20, no. 2 (2012): 71–89.

Berman, Ronald. "*The Great Gatsby* and the Twenties." In Prigozy, *Cambridge Companion to F. Scott Fitzgerald*, 79–94.

Bersani, Leo. *Marcel Proust: The Fictions of Life and Art*. New York: Oxford University Press, 1965.

Best, Stephen and Sharon Marcus. "Surface Reading: An Introduction," *Representations* 108, no. 1 (2009): 1–21.

Blair, Sara. "Ellison, Photography, and the Origins of Invisibility." In Posnock, *Cambridge Companion to Ralph Ellison*, 56–81.

Blake, Susan L. "Ritual and Rationalization: Black Folklore in the Works of Ralph Ellison." *PMLA* 94, no. 1 (1979): 121–136.

Blazek, William, and Laura Rattray, eds. *Twenty-First Century Readings of* Tender Is the Night. Liverpool: Liverpool University Press, 2007.

Bloom, Harold. Introduction to *Wallace Stevens*. Edited by Harold Bloom, 1–14. New York: Chelsea, 1985.

———. *James Baldwin*. New York: Chelsea, 2007.

———. "John Ashbery: The Charity of Hard Moments." *Salmagundi* 22–23 (1973): 103–131.

———., ed. *Wallace Stevens*. New York: Chelsea, 1985.

———. *Wallace Stevens: The Poems of Our Climate*. Ithaca, NY: Cornell University Press, 1977.

Boker, Pamela A. "Beloved Illness: Transference Love as Romantic Pathology in F. Scott Fitzgerald's *Tender Is the Night*." *Literature and Medicine* 11, no. 2 (1992): 294–314.

Bone, Robert A. "James Baldwin." In Kinnamon, *James Baldwin*, 28–51.

Borroff, Marie. "An Always Incipient Cosmos." In Bloom, *Wallace Stevens*, 89–108.

Boym, Svetlana. *The Future of Nostalgia*. New York: Basic Books, 2001.

Breitwieser, Mitchell. "Jazz Fractures: F. Scott Fitzgerald and Epochal Representation." *American Literary History* 12, no. 3 (2000): 359–381.

Brinkema, Eugenie. *The Forms of the Affects*. Durham, NC: Duke University Press, 2014.

Britzolakis, Christina. "*Ariel* and Other poems." In Gill, *Cambridge Companion to Sylvia Plath*, 107–123.

———. *Sylvia Plath and the Theater of Mourning*. New York: Oxford University Press, 2000.

Brunner, Edward. *Cold War Poetry*. Chicago: University of Illinois Press, 2000.

Burt, Stephen. "Sestina! Or, the Fate of the Idea of Form." *Modern Philology* 105, no. 1 (2007): 218–241.

———. "Wallace Stevens: Where He Lived." *ELH* 77, no. 2 (2010): 325–352.

Calinescu, Matei. *Rereading*. New Haven, CT: Yale University Press, 1993.

Callahan, John. "F. Scott Fitzgerald's Evolving American Dream: The 'Pursuit of Happiness' in *Gatsby*, *Tender Is the Night*, and *The Last Tycoon*." *Twentieth Century Literature* 42, no. 3 (1996): 374–395.

———. *The Illusions of a Nation: Myth and History in the Novels of F. Scott Fitzgerald*. Urbana: University of Illinois Press, 1972.

———. "The Way Home: But Here There Is No Light." In Stern, *Critical Essays*, 187–211.

Caramagno, Thomas C. "Manic-Depressive Psychosis and Critical Approaches to Virginia Woolf's Life and Work." *PMLA* 103, no. 1 (1981): 10–23.

Carson, Luke. "'Render unto Caesura': Late Ashbery, Hölderlin, and the Tragic." *Contemporary Literature* 49, no. 2 (2008): 180–208.

Chakrabarty, Dipesh. "The Climate of History." *Critical Inquiry* 35 (2009): 197–222.

Cheng, Anne Anlin. "Ralph Ellison and the Politics of Melancholia." In Posnock, *Cambridge Companion to Ralph Ellison*, 121–136.

Clark, Heather. "Tracking the Thought-Fox: Sylvia Plath's Revision of Ted Hughes." *JML* 28, no. 2 (2005): 100–112.

Clark, T. J. *Farewell to an Idea*. New Haven, CT: Yale University Press, 1999.

Cleaver, Eldridge. "Notes on a Native Son." In Kinnamon, *James Baldwin*, 66–76.

Clewell, Tammy. "Consolation Refused: Virginia Woolf, The Great War, and Modernist Mourning." *MFS* 50, no. 1 (2004): 197–223.

Clune, Michael. "'Whatever Charms Is Alien': John Ashbery's Everything." *Criticism* 50, no. 3 (2008): 447–469.

Cobb, Michael L. "Pulpit Publicity: James Baldwin and the Queer Uses of Religious Words." *GLQ* 7, no. 2 (2001): 285–312.

Colum, Mary M. "The Psychopathic Novel." In Stern, *Critical Essays*, 59–62.

Comay, Rebecca. "Impressions: Proust, Photography, Trauma." *Discourse* 31, nos. 1–2 (2009): 86–105.

Costello, Bonnie. "John Ashbery and the Idea of the Reader." *Contemporary Literature* 23, no. 4 (1982): 493–514.

———. "John Ashbery's Landscapes." In Schultz, *The Tribe of John*, 60–80.

———. "Planets on Tables: Still Life and War in the Poetry of Wallace Stevens." *Modernism/modernity* 12, no. 3 (2005): 443–458.

Crary, Jonathan. *Suspensions of Perception*. Cambridge, MA: MIT Press, 1999.

Critchley, Simon. *Things Merely Are: Philosophy in the Poetry of Wallace Stevens*. New York: Routledge, 2005.

Curnutt, Kirk. "F. Scott Fitzgerald, Age Consciousness, and the Rise of American Youth Culture." In Prigozy, *Cambridge Companion to F. Scott Fitzgerald*, 28–47.

———. "'A Unity Less Conventional But Not Less Serviceable': A Narratological History of *Tender Is the Night*." In Blazek and Rattray, *Twenty-First Century Readings*, 121–142.

Danius, Sara. "The Aesthetics of the Windshield: Proust and the Modernist Rhetoric of Speed." *Modernism/modernity* 8, no. 1 (2001): 99–126.

Deleuze, Gilles. *Proust and Signs*. Translated by Richard Howard. Minneapolis: University of Minnesota Press, 2000. Originally published 1964.

De Roche, Linda. "Sanatorium Society: The 'Good' Place in *Tender Is the Night*." In Blazek and Rattray, *Twenty-First Century Readings*, 50–66.

DeShong, Scott. "Sylvia Plath, Emmanuel Levinas, and the Aesthetics of Pathos." *Postmodern Culture* 8, no. 3 (1998). Project Muse. Accessed August 2, 2012. http://muse.jhu.edu/journals/postmodern_culture/v008/8.3deshong.html.

DiBattista, Maria. *Virginia Woolf's Major Novels: The Fables of Anon*. New Haven, CT: Yale University Press, 1980.

Dimock, Wai Chee. *Through Other Continents*. Princeton, NJ: Princeton University Press, 2008.

Donaldson, Scott, ed. *Critical Essays on F. Scott Fitzgerald's* The Great Gatsby. Boston: G. K. Hall, 1984.

———. "The Trouble with Nick." In Donaldson, *Critical Essays*, 131–139.

Drowne, Kathleen N. "'An Irrevocable Condition': Constructions of Home and the Writing of Place in *Giovanni's Room*." In Miller, *Re-Viewing James Baldwin*, 72–87.

DuBois, Andrew Lee, Jr. *Ashbery's Forms of Attention*. Tuscaloosa: Alabama University Press, 2006.

Du Bois, W. E. B. *The Souls of Black Folk*. New York: Penguin, 1989.

Dupee, F. W. "James Baldwin and the 'Man.'" In Kinnamon, *James Baldwin*, 11–15.

Duran, Jane. "Virginia Woolf, Time, and the Real." *Philosophy and Literature* 28, no. 2 (2004): 300–308.

Eagle, Christopher. "On 'This' and 'That' in Proust." *MLN* 121, no. 4 (2006): 989–1008.

Edelman, Lee. *No Future: Queer Theory and the Death Drive.* Durham, NC: Duke University Press, 2004.

———. "The Pose of Imposture: Ashbery's 'Self-Portrait in a Convex Mirror.' " *Twentieth-Century Literature* 32, no. 1 (1986): 95–114.

Eeckhout, Bart. "Stevens and Philosophy." In *The Cambridge Companion to Wallace Stevens,* edited by John N. Serio, 103–117. Cambridge: Cambridge University Press, 2007.

Elliott, Jane and Derek Attridge, eds., *Theory after 'Theory'.* London: Routledge, 2011.

Ellison, Ralph. *Going to the Territory.* New York: Vintage, 1986.

———. *Invisible Man.* New York: Vintage, 1990.

———. *Shadow and Act.* New York: Vintage, 1995.

Ellison, Ralph, and Keneth Kinnamon. "Ellison in Urbana: Memories and an Interview." *Callaloo* 18, no. 2 (1995): 273–279.

Enfield, Jonathan. " 'As the Fashion in Books Shifted': *The Beautiful and Damned* as Arc-Light Fiction." *Modernism/modernity* 14, no. 4 (2007): 669–685.

Fabre, Michel. "Fathers and Sons in James Baldwin's *Go Tell It On the Mountain.*" In Kinnamon, *James Baldwin,* 120–138.

Fanon, Frantz. *Black Skin, White Masks,* translated by Richard Philcox. New York: Grove Press, 2008.

Faris, Wendy B. "The Squirrel's Heart Beat and the Death of the Moth." In Ginsberg and Moss Gottlieb, *Virginia Woolf,* 81–92.

Faust, Drew Gilpin. *This Republic of Suffering.* New York: Knopf, 2008.

Feldman, Susan. "Another Look at *Another Country*: Reconciling Baldwin's Sexual and Racial Politics." In Miller, *Re-Viewing James Baldwin,* 88–104.

Felski, Rita. *Uses of Literature.* London: Wiley-Blackwell, 2008.

———. *The Limits of Critique.* Chicago: University of Chicago Press, 2015.

Ferrier, Carole. "The Beekeeper's Apprentice." In Lane, *Sylvia Plath,* 203–217.

Ferry, Anne. " 'Thing' and 'Things' in Ashbery's Poems." *Harvard Review* 22 (2002): 113–119.

Field, Douglas, ed. *A Historical Guide to James Baldwin.* Oxford: Oxford University Press, 2009.

———. "Looking for Jimmy Baldwin: Sex, Privacy, and Black Nationalist Fervor." *Callaloo* 27, no. 2 (2004): 457–480.

Filreis, Alan. *Wallace Stevens and the Actual World.* Princeton, NJ: Princeton University Press, 1991.

Fink, Thomas A. "The Comic Thrust of Ashbery's Poetry." *Contemporary Literature* 30, no. 1 (1984): 1–14.

Fisher, Philip. "Looking Around to See Who I Am: Dreiser's Territory of the Self." *ELH* 44, no. 4 (1977): 728–748.

———. *The Vehement Passions.* Princeton, NJ: Princeton University Press, 2002.

Fitzgerald, F. Scott. *The Great Gatsby.* New York: Scribner, 2004. First published 1925.

———. *Tender Is the Night.* New York: Scribner, 2003. First published 1934.

——. *This Side of Paradise.* New York: Barnes and Noble, 2005.

Flatley, Jonathan. *Affective Mapping: Melancholia and the Politics of Modernism.* Cambridge, MA: Harvard University Press, 2008.

Ford, Charles Henri and Parker Tyler. *The Young and Evil.* New York: Ayer Co Pub, 1933.

Foster, John Bellamy. *Marx's Ecology.* New York: Monthly Review Press, 2000.

Francois, Anne-Lise. *Open Secrets: The Literature of Uncounted Experience.* Stanford, CA: Stanford University Press, 2008.

Frank, Joseph. "Spatial Form in Modern Literature: An Essay in Three Parts." *Sewanee Review* 53, no. 4 (1945): 643–653.

Fraser, Keath. "Another Reading of *The Great Gatsby.*" In Donaldson, *Critical Essays,* 140–152.

Freed-Thall, Hannah. " 'Prestige of a Momentary Diamond': Economies of Distinction in Proust." *New Literary History* 43, no. 1 (2012): 159–178.

Freud, Sigmund. *The Psychopathology of Everyday Life.* In *The Basic Writings of Sigmund Freud,* ed. A.A. Brill, New York: Modern Library, 1938.

Friedman, Ryan Jay. " 'Enough Force to Shatter the Tale to Fragments': Ethics and Textual Analysis in James Baldwin's Film Theory." *ELH* 77, no. 2 (2010): 385–412.

Fromm, Harold. "Sylvia Plath, Hunger Artist." *Hudson Review* 43, no. 2 (1990): 245–256.

Fussell, Paul. *The Great War and Modern Memory.* New York: Oxford University Press, 1975.

Galow, Timothy. "Literary Modernism in the Age of Celebrity." *Modernism/modernity* 17, no. 2 (2010): 313–325.

Gates, Henry Louis, Jr. "The Fire Last Time." In Bloom, *James Baldwin,* 11–22.

——. *The Signifying Monkey.* New York: Oxford University Press, 1988.

Gilbert, Roger. "Ludic Eloquence: On John Ashbery's Recent Poetry." *Contemporary Literature* 48, no. 2 (2007): 195–226.

Gill, Jo, ed. *The Cambridge Companion to Sylvia Plath.* New York: Cambridge University Press, 2006.

Ginsberg, Elaine K., and Laura Moss Gottlieb, eds. *Virginia Woolf: Centennial Essays.* Troy, NY: Whitston, 1983.

Glenday, Michael K. "American Riviera: Style and Expatriation in *Tender Is the Night.*" In Blazek and Rattray, *Twenty-First Century Readings,* 143–159.

Godden, Richard. "A Diamond Bigger than the Ritz: F. Scott Fitzgerald and the Gold Standard." *ELH* 77, no. 3 (2010): 589–613.

Graham, T. Austin. "The Literary Soundtrack: Or, F. Scott Fitzgerald's Heard and Unheard Melodies." *American Literary History* 21, no. 3 (2009): 518–549.

Grenberg, Bruce. "Fitzgerald's 'Figured Curtain': Personality and History in *Tender Is the Night.*" In Stern, *Critical Essays,* 211–238.

Griffiths, Frederick T. "Copy Wright: What Is an (Invisible) Author?" *New Literary History* 33, no. 2 (2002): 315–341.

Gubar, Susan. "Prosopopoeia and Holocaust Poetry in English: Sylvia Plath and Her Contemporaries." *Yale Journal of Criticism* 14, no. 1 (2001): 191–215.

Gunn, Giles. " F. Scott Fitzgerald's *Gatsby* and the Imagination of Wonder." In Donaldson, *Critical Essays,* 228–242.

Halberstam, Jack. *The Queer Art of Failure*. Durham, NC: Duke University Press, 2011.

Hardy, Clarence E., III. "James Baldwin as Religious Writer: The Burdens and Gifts of Black Evangelicalism." In Field, *Historical Guide to James Baldwin*, 61–82.

Haring-Smith, Tori. "Private and Public Consciousness in *Mrs. Dalloway* and *To the Lighthouse*." In Ginsberg and Moss Gottlieb, *Virginia Woolf*, 143–162.

Harper, Howard. *Between Language and Silence: The Novels of Virginia Woolf*. Baton Rouge: Louisiana University Press, 1982.

Harris, Trudier. "The Exorcising Medium: *Another Country*." In Bloom, *James Baldwin*, 97–128.

Haustein, Katja. "Proust's Emotional Cavities." *French Studies* 63, no. 2 (2009): 161–173.

Heaney, Seamus. *The Government of the Tongue: Selected Prose 1978–1987*. New York: Faber and Faber, 1988.

Henchman, Anna. *The Starry Sky Within*. New York: Oxford University Press, 2014.

Henderson, Mae G. "James Baldwin: Expatriation, Homosexual Panic, and Man's Estate." *Callaloo* 23, no. 1 (2000): 313–327.

Henke, Suzette A. " 'The Prime Minister': A Key to *Mrs. Dalloway*." In Ginsberg and Moss Gottlieb, *Virginia Woolf*, 127–142.

Holbrook, David. *Sylvia Plath: Poetry and Existence*. London: Athlone Press, 1976.

Howe, Irving. "Black Boys and Native Sons." *Dissent* (Autumn 1963). Accessed April 30, 2014. www.writing.upenn.edu.

Hughes, Langston. "From Harlem to Paris." In Kinnamon, *James Baldwin*, 9–10.

Hughes, Ted. Introduction to *The Collected Poems of Sylvia Plath*, 13–17. New York: Harper, 1981.

Imbriglio, Catherine. " 'Our Days Put on Such Reticence': The Rhetoric of the Closet in John Ashbery's *Some Trees*." *Contemporary Literature* 36, no. 2 (1995): 249–288.

Jackson, Lawrence. "Ralph Ellison's Invented Life: A Meeting with the Ancestors." In Posnock, *Cambridge Companion to Ralph Ellison*, 11–34.

Jackson, Mahalia. *In the Upper Room*. Apollo, 1957. Compact Disc.

James, William. *The Principles of Psychology*. New York: Dover, 1950.

Johnson-Roullier, Cyraina E. *Reading on the Edge: Exiles, Modernities, and Cultural Transformations in Proust, Joyce, and Baldwin*. New York: State University of New York Press, 2000.

Joyce, Justin A., and Dwight A. McBride, "James Baldwin and Sexuality: *Lieux de Mémoire* and a Usable Past." In Field, *Historical Guide to James Baldwin*, 111–140.

Kalstone, David. *Five Temperaments: Elizabeth Bishop, Robert Lowell, James Merrill, Adrienne Rich, John Ashbery*. New York: Oxford University Press, 1977.

Kendall, Tim. *Sylvia Plath: A Critical Study*. London: Faber and Faber, 2001.

Kenner, Hugh. "Sincerity Kills." In Lane, *Sylvia Plath*, 33–44.

Kent, George A. "Baldwin and the Problem of Being." In Kinnamon, *James Baldwin*, 16–27.

Kevorkian, Martin. "John Ashbery's Flow Chart." *New Literary History* 25, no. 2 (1994): 459–476.

Kime Scott, Bonnie, ed. *The Gender of Modernism*. Bloomington: Indiana University Press, 1990.

Kinnamon, Keneth. *James Baldwin: A Collection of Critical Essays.* Englewood Cliffs, NJ: Prentice-Hall, 1974.

Koestenbaum, Wayne. "John Ashbery's Lazy Susan." *Mississippi Review* 31, no. 3 (2003): 173–175.

Lane, Gary, ed. *Sylvia Plath: New Views on the Poetry.* Baltimore: Johns Hopkins University Press, 1979.

Lant, Kathleen Margaret. "The Big Strip Tease: Female Bodies and Male Power in the Poetry of Sylvia Plath." *Contemporary Literature* 34, no. 4 (1993): 620–669.

Lehan, Richard D. "F. Scott Fitzgerald and Romantic Destiny." *Twentieth-Century Literature* 26, no. 2 (1980): 137–156.

——. *F. Scott Fitzgerald and the Craft of Fiction.* London: Feffer and Simons, 1966.

——. "*The Great Gatsby* and Its Sources." In Donaldson, *Critical Essays*, 66–74.

Leonard, Diane R. "Ruskin and the Cathedral of Lost Souls." In Bales, *Cambridge Companion to Proust*, 42–57.

Levenson, Michael. *The Genealogy of Modernism.* Cambridge: Cambridge University Press, 1984.

Levinson, Marjorie. "What Is New Formalism?" *PMLA* 122, no. 2 (2007): 558–569.

Leys, Ruth. "The Turn to Affect: A Critique." *Critical Inquiry* 37 (2011): 434–473.

Lhamon, W. T., Jr. "The Essential Houses of *The Great Gatsby*." In Donaldson, *Critical Essays*, 166–174.

Lieberman, Laurence. "Unassigned Frequencies: Whispers Out of Time; A Reading of John Ashbery's 'Self-Portrait in a Convex Mirror.'" *American Poetry Review* 6, no. 2 (1977): 4–18.

Light, James F. "Political Conscience in the Novels of F. Scott Fitzgerald." In Stern, *Critical Essays*, 132–138.

Longenbach, James. *Wallace Stevens: The Plain Sense of Things.* New York: Oxford University Press, 1991.

Love, Heather. *Feeling Backward: Loss and the Politics of Queer History.* Cambridge, MA: Harvard University Press, 2007.

——. "Close But Not Deep: Literary Ethics and the Descriptive Turn," *New Literary History* no. 41 (2010): 371–391.

Love, Jean O. *Worlds in Consciousness: Mythopoetic Thought in the Novels of Virginia Woolf.* Berkeley: University of California Press, 1970.

Lucey, Michael. "Proust's Queer Metalepses." *MLN* 116, no. 4 (2001): 795–815.

Luck, Jessica Lewis. "Exploring the 'Mind of the Hive': Embodied Cognition in Sylvia Plath's Bee Poems." *Tulsa Studies in Women's Literature* 26, no. 2 (2007): 287–308.

Lyon, George Ella. "Virginia Woolf and the Problem of the Body." In Ginsberg and Moss Gottlieb, *Virginia Woolf*, 111–126.

Manning, Erin, and Brian Massumi. *Thought in the Act: Passages in the Ecology of Experience.* Minneapolis: University of Minnesota Press, 2014.

Mao, Douglas. *Solid Objects: Modernism and the Test of Production.* Princeton, NJ: Princeton University Press, 1998.

Marcus, Ellen. *Art and Anger: Reading like a Woman.* Columbus: Ohio State University Press, 1988.

Marcus, Sharon. *Apartment Stories.* Berkeley: University of California Press, 1999.

Marvin, Thomas F. "Children of Legba: Musicians at the Crossroads in Ralph Ellison's *Invisible Man.*" *American Literature* 68, no. 3 (1996): 587–608.

Marx, Karl. *The German Ideology.* In *The Marx-Engels Reader*, edited by Robert C. Tucker. New York: Norton, 1978.

Massumi, Brian. *Parables for the Virtual: Movement, Affect, Sensation.* Durham, NC: Duke University Press, 2002.

———. *Semblance and Event: Activist Philosophy and the Occurent Arts.* Cambridge, MA: MIT Press, 2011.

McGurl, Mark. "The Posthuman Comedy." *Critical Inquiry* 38 (2012): 533–553.

McHale, Brian. "How (Not) To Read Postmodernist Long Poems: The Case of Ashbery's 'The Skaters.'" *Poetics Today* 21, no. 3 (2000): 561–590.

Messenger, Chris. "'Out upon the Mongolian Plain': Fitzgerald's Racial and Ethnic Cross-Identifying in *Tender Is the Night.*" In Blazek and Rattray, *Twenty-First Century Readings*, 160–176.

Messmer, David. "Trumpets, Horns, and Typewriters: A Call and Response between Ralph Ellison and Frederick Douglass." *African American Review* 44, no. 4 (2010): 589–604.

Miller, D. A. *The Novel and the Police.* Berkeley: University of California Press, 1989.

Miller, David Neal. "Authorial Point of View in Virginia Woolf's *Mrs. Dalloway.*" *Journal of Narrative Technique* 2, no. 2 (1972): 125–132.

Miller, D. Quentin. *Re-Viewing James Baldwin: Things Not Seen.* Philadelphia: Temple University Press, 2000.

———. "Using the Blues: James Baldwin and Music." In Field, *Historical Guide to James Baldwin*, 83–110.

Miller, J. Hillis. *Poets of Reality.* Cambridge, MA: Harvard University Press, 1965.

Miller, Stephen Paul. "'Self-Portrait in a Convex Mirror,' the Watergate Affair, and Johns' Crosshatch Paintings: Surveillance and Reality-Testing in the Mid-Seventies," *boundary 2* 20, no. 2 (1993): 84–115.

Mizener, Arthur. "*Tender Is the Night.*" In Stern, *Critical Essays*, 159–170.

Moore, G. E. *Principia Ethica.* New York: Dover, 2004.

Morse, Jonathan. "Typical Ashbery." In Schultz, *The Tribe of John*, 15–25.

Moyer, Kermit W. "*The Great Gatsby*: Fitzgerald's Meditation on American History." In Donaldson, *Critical Essays*, 215–228.

Nabers, Deak. "Past Using: James Baldwin and Civil Rights Law in the 1960s." *Yale Journal of Criticism* 18, no. 2 (2005): 221–242.

Narbeshuber, Lisa. "The Poetics of Torture: The Spectacle of Sylvia Plath's Poetry." *Canadian Review of American Studies* 34, no. 2 (2004): 185–203.

Nealon, Christopher. *The Matter of Capital: Poetry and Crisis in the American Century.* Cambridge, MA: Harvard University Press, 2013.

Nelson, Deborah. "Plath, History, and Politics." In Gill, *Cambridge Companion to Sylvia Plath*, 21–35.

Newman, Charles, ed. *The Art of Sylvia Plath: A Symposium.* London: Faber and Faber, 1970.

———. "Candor Is the Only Wile—The Art of Sylvia Plath." In Newman, *The Art of Sylvia Plath*, 21–55.

Ngai, Sianne. *Our Aesthetic Categories.* Cambridge, MA: Harvard University Press, 2012.

———. *Ugly Feelings.* Cambridge, MA: Harvard University Press, 2004.

Nicholls, Peter. *Modernisms: A Literary Guide.* New York: Macmillan, 1999.

Novak, Jane. *The Razor Edge of Balance: A Study of Virginia Woolf.* Coral Gables, FL: University of Miami Press, 1975.

Nussbaum, Martha. "Fictions of the Soul." *Philosophy and Literature* 7, no. 2 (1983): 145–161.

———. "The Window: Knowledge of Other Minds in Virginia Woolf's *To the Lighthouse.*" *New Literary History* 26, no. 4 (1995): 731–753.

Oliver, Elisabeth. "Aestheticism's Afterlife: Wallace Stevens as Interior Decorator and Disruptor." *Modernism/modernity* 15, no. 3 (2008): 527–545.

Olson, Liesl M. "Virginia Woolf and the 'Cotton Wool of Daily Life.'" *JML* 26, no. 2 (2003): 42–65.

Pater, Walter. *The Renaissance: Studies in Art and Poetry.* New York: Macmillan, 1903.

Pease, Donald A. "Ralph Ellison and Kenneth Burke: The Nonsymbolizable (Trans) Action." *boundary 2* 30, no. 2 (2003): 65–96.

Peel, Robin. "The Ideological Apprenticeship of Sylvia Plath." *JML* 27, no. 4 (2004): 59–72.

———. *Writing Back: Sylvia Plath and Cold War Politics.* London: Associated University Presses, 2002.

Perloff, Marjorie. "'Angst' and Animism in the Poetry of Sylvia Plath." *JML* 1, no. 1 (1970): 57–74.

———. "On the Road to 'Ariel': The 'Transitional' Poetry of Sylvia Plath." *Iowa Review* 4, no. 2 (1973): 94–110.

———. *The Poetics of Indeterminacy: Rimbaud to Cage.* Princeton, NJ: Princeton University Press, 1999. Originally published 1981.

———. "'A Ritual for Being Born Twice': Sylvia Plath's *The Bell Jar.*" *Contemporary Literature* 13, no. 4 (1972): 507–522.

Phillips, Brian. "Reality and Virginia Woolf." *Hudson Review* 56, no. 3 (2003): 415–430.

Pinkerton, Steve. "Ralph Ellison's Righteous Riffs: Jazz, Democracy, and the Sacred." *African American Review* 44, nos. 1–2 (2011): 185–206.

Plath, Sylvia. *The Bell Jar.* New York: Knopf, 1998.

———. *The Collected Poems of Sylvia Plath.* New York: Harper, 1981.

Pollak, Vivian. "Moore, Plath, Hughes, and 'The Literary Life.'" *American Literary History* 17, no. 1 (2005): 95–117.

Porter, Horace A. "The South in *Go Tell It on the Mountain*: Baldwin's Personal Confrontation." In Bloom, *James Baldwin*, 53–68.

———. *Stealing the Fire: The Art and Protest of James Baldwin.* Middletown, CT: Wesleyan University Press, 1989.

Posnock, Ross, ed. *The Cambridge Companion to Ralph Ellison.* Cambridge: Cambridge University Press, 2005.

———. "'A New World, Material without Being Real': Fitzgerald's Critique of Capitalism in *The Great Gatsby.*" In Donaldson, *Critical Essays*, 201–214.

———. "Ralph Ellison, Hannah Arendt, and the Meaning of Politics." In Posnock, *Cambridge Companion to Ralph Ellison*, 201–216.

Poulet, Georges. *L'Espace proustien.* Paris: Gallimard, 1962.

———. *Etudes sur le temps humain.* Edinburgh: Edinburgh University Press, 1949.

Pridmore-Brown, Michele. "1939–40: Of Virginia Woolf, Gramophones, and Fascism." *PMLA* 113, no. 3 (1998): 408–421.

Prigozy, Ruth, ed. *The Cambridge Companion to F. Scott Fitzgerald.* Cambridge: Cambridge University Press, 2002.

Proust, Marcel. *In Search of Lost Time.* Translated by C. K. Scott Moncrieff and Terence Kilmartin. New York: Modern Library, 2003. Six volumes.

———. *A la recherche du temps perdu.* Paris: Folio, 1992. Seven volumes.

Ramazani, Jahan. "'Daddy, I have had to kill you': Plath, Rage, and the Modern Elegy." *PMLA* 108, no. 5 (1993): 1142–1156.

Rancière, Jacques. *The Politics of Aesthetics,* trans. Gabriel Rockhill. New York: Continuum, 2004.

Rattray, Laura. "An 'Unblinding of the Eyes': The Narrative Vision of *Tender Is the Night.*" In Blazek and Rattray, *Twenty-First Century Readings,* 85–102.

Reddinger, Amy. "'Just Enough for the City': Limitations of Space in Baldwin's *Another Country.*" *African American Review* 43, no. 1 (2009): 117–130.

Revell, Donald. "Some Meditations on Influence." In Schultz, *The Tribe of John,* 91–100.

Rose, Jacqueline. *The Haunting of Sylvia Plath.* Cambridge, MA: Harvard University Press, 1993.

Saint-Amour, Paul. *Tense Futures: Modernism, Total War, Encyclopedic Form.* New York: Oxford University Press, 2015.

Serpell, Namwali. *Seven Modes of Uncertainty.* Cambridge, MA: Harvard University Press, 2013.

Scarry, Elaine. *The Body in Pain.* New York: Oxford University Press, 1987.

Schmidt, Christopher. "The Queer Nature of Waste in John Ashbery's Vermont Notebook." *Arizona Quarterly* 68, no. 3 (2012): 71–102.

———. *The Poetics of Waste: Queer Excess in Stein, Ashbery, Schuyler, and Goldsmith* (New York: Palgrave, 2014).

Schultz, Susan, ed. *The Tribe of John: Ashbery and Contemporary Poetry.* Tuscaloosa: University of Alabama Press, 1995.

Scott, Lynn Orilla. "Challenging the American Conscience, Re-Imagining American Identity: James Baldwin and the Civil Rights Movement." In Field, *Historical Guide to James Baldwin,* 141–176.

———. *James Baldwin's Later Fiction.* East Lansing: Michigan State University Press, 2002.

Sedgwick, Eve Kosofsky. *Epistemology of the Closet.* Berkeley: University of California Press, 1990.

———. *Tendencies.* Durham, NC: Duke University Press, 1993.

———. *Touching Feeling.* Durham, NC: Duke University Press, 2003.

———. *The Weather in Proust.* Durham, NC: Duke University Press, 2012.

See, Samuel. "Making Modernism New: Queer Mythology in 'The Young and Evil.'" *ELH* 76, no. 4 (2009): 1073–1105.

Seguin, Robert. "Ressentiment and the Social Poetics of *The Great Gatsby*: Fitzgerald Reads Cather." *Modern Fiction Studies* 46, no. 4 (2000): 917–940.

Shank, Barry. "Bliss, or Blackface Sentiment." *boundary 2* 30, no. 2 (2003): 47F–64.

Sherry, Vincent. *The Great War and the Language of Modernism*. New York: Oxford University Press, 2003.

Shoptaw, John. *On the Outside Looking Out*. Cambridge, MA: Harvard University Press, 1998.

Showalter, Elaine. *The Female Malady: Women, Madness, and English Culture, 1830–1980*. London: Virago, 1987.

Silver, Brenda. *Virginia Woolf: Icon*. Chicago: University of Chicago Press, 1999.

Silverberg, Mark. "Laughter and Uncertainty: John Ashbery's Low-Key Camp." *Contemporary Literature* 43, no. 2 (2002): 285–316.

Siraganian, Lisa. "Wallace Steven's Fascist Dilemmas and Free Market Resolutions." *American Literary History* 32, no. 2 (2011): 337–361.

Smythe, Karen. "Virginia Woolf's Elegiac Enterprise." *NOVEL: A Forum on Fiction* 26, no. 1 (1992): 64–79.

Sprinker, Michael. *History and Ideology in Proust*. New York: Verso, 1998.

Stamelman, Richard. "Critical Reflections: Poetry and Art Criticism in Ashbery's 'Self-Portrait in a Convex Mirror,'" *New Literary History* 15, no. 3 (1984): 607–630.

Steele, Miele. "Metatheory and the Subject of Democracy in the Work of Ralph Ellison." *New Literary History* 27, no. 3 (1996): 473–502.

Stern, Milton R., ed. *Critical Essays on F. Scott Fitzgerald's* Tender Is the Night. Boston: G. K. Hall, 1986.

——. *The Golden Moment: The Novels of F. Scott Fitzgerald*. Urbana: University of Illinois Press, 1970.

——. "*Tender Is the Night* and American History." In Prigozy, *Cambridge Companion to F. Scott Fitzgerald*, 95–117.

Stevens, Wallace. *The Collected Poems of Wallace Stevens*. New York: Knopf, 1974.

——. *Collected Poetry and Prose*. Edited by Frank Kermode and Joan Richardson. New York: Library of America, 1997.

——. *The Necessary Angel: Essays on Reality and the Imagination*. London: Faber and Faber, 1951.

——. *Opus Posthumous: Poems, Plays, Prose*. New York: Vintage, 1990.

Stewart, Susan. *On Longing*. Durham, NC: Duke University Press, 1993.

Terada, Rei. *Feeling in Theory: Emotion after the "Death of the Subject."* Cambridge, MA: Harvard University Press, 2001.

——. *Looking Away: Phenomenality and Dissatisfaction, Kant to Adorno*. Cambridge, MA: Harvard University Press, 2009.

Trachtenberg, Alan. "The Journey Back: Myth and History in *Tender Is the Night*." In Stern, *Critical Essays*, 170–186.

Trilling, Lionel. "F. Scott Fitzgerald." In Donaldson, *Critical Essays*, 13–21.

Tuhkanen, Mikko. "'Binding the Self': Baldwin, Freud, and the Narrative of Subjectivity." *GLQ* 7, no. 4 (2001): 553–591.

Veblen, Thorstein. *Conspicuous Consumption*. New York: Penguin, 2006.

Vendler, Helen. "Ashbery's Aesthetic." *Harvard Review* 22 (2002): 81–96.

——. *Coming of Age as a Poet*. Cambridge, MA: Harvard University Press, 2003.

——. *Invisible Listeners*. Princeton, NJ: Princeton University Press, 2005.

———. *Last Looks, Last Books*. Princeton, NJ: Princeton University Press, 2010.

———. *On Extended Wings: Wallace Stevens' Longer Poetry*. Cambridge, MA: Harvard University Press, 1969.

———. *Part of Nature, Part of Us: Modern American Poets*. Cambridge, MA: Harvard University Press, 1980.

Vincent, John. "Reports of Looting and Insane Buggery behind Altars: John Ashbery's Queer Poetics," *Twentieth Century Literature* 44, no. 2 (1998): 155–175

Virno, Paolo. "The Ambivalence of Disenchantment," in Paolo Virno and Michael Hardt, eds. *Radical Thought in Italy*. Minneapolis: University of Minnesota Press, 1996, 13–36.

Warner, Michael. "Uncritical Reading," in *Polemic: Critical or Uncritical*, ed. Jane Gallop. New York: Routledge, 2004, 13–38.

Warren, Kenneth. "Ralph Ellison and the Problem of Cultural Authority." *boundary 2* 30, no. 2 (2003): 157–174.

Wasley, Aidan. "The 'Gay Apprentice': Ashbery, Auden, and a Portrait of the Artist as a Young Critic," *Contemporary Literature* 43, no. 4 (2002): 667–708.

Watkins, Mel. "The Fire Next Time This Time." In Bloom, *James Baldwin*, 177–182.

Westling, Louise. "Virginia Woolf and the Flesh of the World." *New Literary History* 30, no. 4 (1999): 855–875.

White, Eugene. "The 'Intricate Destiny' of Dick Diver." In Stern, *Critical Essays*, 125–132.

Wilcox, Johnnie. "Black Power: Minstrelsy and Electricity in Ralph Ellison's *Invisible Man*." *Callaloo* 30, no. 4 (2007): 987–1009.

Williams, Sherley Anne. "The Black Musician: The Black Hero as Light Bearer." In Kinnamon, *James Baldwin*, 147–154.

Woolf, Virginia. *Mr. Bennett and Mrs. Brown*. Hogarth Essays Series. London: Hogarth Press, 1924.

———. *Mrs. Dalloway*. London: Harcourt, 1981. Originally published 1925.

Yacobi, Tamar. "Ashbery's 'Description of a Masque': Radical Interart Transfer Across History." *Poetics Today* 20, no. 4 (1999): 673–707.

Zaborowska, Magdalena J. *James Baldwin's Turkish Decade: Erotics of Exile*. Durham, NC: Duke University Press, 2009.

Ziarek, Krzysztof. *Inflected Language*. New York: State University of New York Press, 1994.

INDEX